ANTI-LAWYERS

'A work of enormous significance and stunning originality – beautifully written'

Peter Fitzpatrick, University of Kent at Canterbury

After the carnage of religious civil war, in early modern Europe law emerged as one of the few non-religious orderings of social life. Yet the separation of law from religion has never been complete. Religious fundamentalists and critical intellectuals alike persist in seeking to realign the conduct of government and the legal apparatus in accordance with moral principle – whether individual autonomy or communal self-determination.

Tracing the still unresolved contest of religion and law from the times of Hobbes's *Leviathan* to American law texts of the 1990s, in *Anti-lawyers: religion and the critics of law and state* David Saunders asks how we might regard today's critics of government and law in the light of the early modern effort to separate secular government from spiritual salvation and to disengage law from conscience.

David Saunders is Associate Professor and Dean in the Faculty of Arts at Griffith University, Australia.

ANTI-LAWYERS

Religion and the critics of law and state

David Saunders

ROUTLEDGE

London and New York

First published 1997
by Routledge
11 New Fetter Lane, London EC4P 4EE

Simultaneously published in the USA and Canada
by Routledge
29 West 35th Street, New York, NY 10001

Typeset in Garamond by M Rules
Printed and bound in Great Britain by
T. J. International Ltd.

British Library Cataloguing in Publication Data
A catalogue record for this book is available from the British Library

Library of Congress Cataloguing in Publication Data
Saunders, David
Anti-lawyers : religion and the critics of law and state /
David Saunders.
p. cm.
Includes bibliographical references and index.
1. Church and state. 2. Religion and law.
3. Freedom of religion. I. Title.
K3280.S28 1997
342' .0852–dc21 97–18759
CIP

ISBN 0–415–10304–5

In memoriam GWS

CONTENTS

Foreword viii
Acknowledgements xi

1 RELIGION BY OTHER MEANS 1

2 INVISIBLE AND SPIRITUAL: VISIBLE AND EXTERNAL 15

3 CONSCIENCE AND LAW 21

4 THE COMMON LAW'S CRITICS 30

5 THE COMMON LAW'S DEFENDERS 41

6 RELIGION, LAW AND CIVIL MANNERS 55

7 SEPARATION OF POWERS 73

8 THE CONFESSIONAL STATE 79

9 CONFLICT OF CONFESSIONS; CONFLICT OF FACULTIES 89

10 SECTS, LAWS AND RIGHTS 112

11 THE LAW TRANSFORMED; THE LAWYER LOST 124

12 NOW THAT THE SAINTS ARE MARCHING IN 142

Notes 154
Bibliography 170
Index 177

FOREWORD

> One day the moment arrived at which mankind said to God, like the son to the father in the Gospel: Come on, share with us, let us have the inheritance that belongs to us.
>
> (Sören Kierkegaard: journal entry, 18 July 1840)

> This delay (whose importance the reader will appreciate later) was due to a desire on the part of the authorities to act slowly and impersonally, in the manner of planets or vegetables.
>
> (Jorge Luis Borges: 'The Secret Miracle')

> Ours is a society that promises to liberate itself from the very laws that have made it possible.
>
> (Michel Foucault: *History of Sexuality*, vol. 1)

In early modern Europe a sphere of civil life was created, governed by a law that was secular in purpose rather than Christian in its end. This sphere was then – and perhaps is now – one of our few non-religious orderings of life. Three centuries later, we all too easily take a non-sectarian civil life for granted, forgetting that in a proselytising religious culture it stands as an exceptional accomplishment. In fact the separation of spiritual discipline from secular government and conscience from law was never complete. It remains our own unfinished business, a contest unresolved since early modern times.

This continuing contest is carried through today's attack by religious fundamentalists on existing government and law. It is carried also by the more refined yet no less incessant claims of critical intellectuals to reshape governmental institutions and the legal apparatus in accordance with a moral principle, typically some vision of individual autonomy or communitarian self-determination. What follows in these pages is a historical essay. It discusses how we might regard today's moral critics of government and law – for instance the critical legal studies movement – in the light of the early modern effort to disengage religion from government and law.

To amplify the field of discussion I introduce one or two new names. The German social historians of the early modern State, Heinz Schilling and Reinhart Koselleck, bring issues of religious observance and Church–State relations centre stage. Some of my other sources – Max Weber and Michel

Foucault – are familiar to English-language readers of the literature on liberalism, governmentality, social history, law and society, jurisprudence and critical theory. From Schilling I draw an account of 'confessionalisation'. He coins this term to identify the process whereby post-Reformation Christian Churches competed to 'confessionalise' whole populations into their own universalising world-view, be it Lutheran, Calvinist or Roman Catholic. As traditional political relations fragmented in the mid-sixteenth century, confessionalisation overlapped with a second but quite different process: the emergence of the centralising territorial State. Despite their different objectives – the one spiritual and redemptive, the other worldly and productive – Church and State worked together, finding common cause in disciplining what would become national populations. They worked together until unbridled religious enthusiasms loosed uncontrollable civil war between perfect enemies: uncompromising rival confessions driven by purity of principle and communal hatred.

In *Critique and Crisis*, Reinhart Koselleck (1988) considers two subsequent developments in early modern Europe. The first was the rise of the Absolutist State. This he depicts as a political, legal and administrative response to the carnage of unstoppable religious civil war between confessional rivals. In the face of this intolerable conflict that no existing legal jurisdiction or political instrument could end, enough was enough. Helped by its jurists, the Absolutist State imposed peace on the warring confessional factions by creating a sphere of civil life that was grounded not in the promise of salvation but in this very act of State. To 'de-theologise' this sphere the State would deny a political role to the churches whose spiritual zeal had so inflamed the religious belligerents.

Koselleck accords Thomas Hobbes a leading role in furnishing a theory for Absolutist politics – *raison d'état* – that justified this separation of spiritual concerns from the exercise of civil power as ultimate power. In practice, however, the English circumstances were somewhat particular: the national territory was relatively unified and the common law was largely in place. Dissenters aside, the Anglican constitution allowed for one nation with a dual polity that harmonised the religious assembly of the Church and the political assembly of Parliament under the tutelage of the Crown. In effect the Anglican was a State-controlled Church.

The second early modern development addressed by Koselleck was the revenge of post-Enlightenment critics on the State that had sidelined them. Turning on the 'amoral' politics of the State and the 'formal' neutrality of law, they propounded a prophetic vision of future moral community that took sufficient hold on the imagination of the educated to provoke a crisis of legitimation for the existing State. In Revolutionary France, the crisis saw the fall of the Old Regime. Koselleck depicts the Revolution as another civil war of religion, not a fundamental moral advance for humanity. The critics' further success has been to obscure the actual history of how the peace-making State had responded to the circumstance of uncontrollable war by de-theologising the civil as its own sphere of action. The State not only defined its own limits. It also instituted the right to freedom of religion as a freedom to be practised privately, outside the civil sphere. The point was to protect territory and population from conflicts generated by religious difference.

Inverting the history, the critics wanted government rejoined to morality and State to society. They recast the State that had freed conscience as the threat to a free conscience. And so it remains, at least in the mind of those critical intellectuals who, with this extraordinary reversal of the actual history, made a new religion of morality. Koselleck's contribution is a genealogy that recognises post-Enlightenment moral critics of the State as the heirs of religion. Critique is religion by other means.

The trajectory of the present essay is straightforward. I first introduce the essay's central argument, Koselleck's religious genealogy of critique. The bedrock reference is the historical separation of religion from law, the Absolutist State's political response to the circumstance of religious civil war. Attention then focuses successively on historical demarcations of religion and law in early modern England, France, Germany and America. Finally, against this historical backdrop, I bring the argument to bear on the contemporary critical legal scene in American and British academic debate. If critique is religion by other means, how might we regard today's critics? How do their claims to realign law with moral principle look when set against the historical separation of religion from law? In seeking to reground State in community and positive law in moral principle, are today's critical programmes successors to the campaigns of confessionalisation?

These questions have their resonance beyond the particular legal history considered here. Wherever normative critical theory confronts a positive knowledge – in reflexive sociology, politics, jurisprudence, literary and cultural studies, theology – we observe the unrelenting attempt to rejoin existing institutions to morality.

There is a final opening point. To recognise the separation of religion from law is a first step to recognising the achievement of what Karl Llewellyn called the 'great institution of Law-Government'. Separated from the problem of spiritual salvation, the conduct of political government required legal officers and administrative personnel capable of a non-sectarian comportment. This was an ethical achievement in its own right. When set against the historical reality of religious conflict, the 'de-theologised' conduct of these professional men and women might register positively. From the critical perspective, however, their neutrality registers as immorality. It is habitually represented as the bland mask of relations of domination, a mask that the critic will strip away. As well as a historical contextualisation of criticism, then, the point is to recover a certain dignity for the mundane routines of institutional life in law, government and administration.

ACKNOWLEDGEMENTS

This essay aims to recover historical and ethical dignity for persons and institutions that, more usually, are the target of critical comment. It has benefited, as I have, from the generous support of my colleagues: WH, SM, DM, JM, BS, CS and DW. A special appreciation is for Ian Hunter. His longstanding friendship and acute advice have contributed to the essay in a way that cannot be recompensed in a few words, however well chosen.

My thanks go also to the historians, legal and political, social and cultural, on whose publications I have depended. I have drawn them into the ongoing contest of religion and law, something these scholars might not themselves have sought but with which, I hope, they will not be entirely unpleased.

1

RELIGION BY OTHER MEANS

To judge from Anthony Kronman's *The Lost Lawyer: Failing Ideals of the Legal Profession*, gloom is the order of the day. A brief initial reference to its author's disposition will help build the context of the present essay. *The Lost Lawyer* laments the passing of the 'lawyer-statesman' and a prudential practical wisdom revered in common law tradition. The following is a representative sketch of this persona:

> [H]owever deep a lawyer's devotion to the public good, one who possesses the traits [of prudential practical wisdom] also accepts, to a degree no moral zealot can, the irreconcilable diversity of human goods, and therefore tends to see in every controversial alteration of his society's arrangements some loss as well as an opportunity for gain. As a result, such a lawyer is unlikely to be moved by that passion for purity which motivates the adherents of every great political simplification and to be more comfortable with strategies of compromise and delay. Recognising the moral imperative for change, the lawyer who embraces this ideal will nevertheless prefer to move slowly and by small degrees. He or she will be repelled by all programs of utopian ambition, whether Platonic or Kantian or Benthamite in inspiration, and in the quirks and absurdities of the *status quo* will be likely to see what no utopian can: a whole series of unthought-out local compromises and adjustments that reflect the plurality of human goods and soften the consequences of their inevitable conflicts.
>
> (Kronman 1993: 161)

Now this persona and its prudence are in crisis, victims of critical programmes that, in various guises, have taken hold in the American law school. Outside the scholarly academy and the more intransigent sectors of the human rights community, lawyers no doubt continue lawyering according to the norms and routines of a professional second nature. But critique can hold sway when in the academy lawyers engage in forms of moral, political and theoretical reflection on law and on themselves. Kronman is forthright against 'an ever more theoretical style of teaching that encourages a simplifying view of law'

(Kronman 1993: 376). Little wonder if, at the very outset, he confesses that his reflections on the current state of the legal academy have led him to a lonely life and a 'gloomy conclusion'.

Is there a history to this gloom? The present essay undertakes an answer with reference to law's historical relations with 'programs of utopian ambition' whereby one or other 'moral zealot' has pursued a 'passion for purity'. Kronman's suggestion that a prudential lawyer is unlikely to be moved by such a passion can be translated into historical terms. It is a matter of tracing a boundary drawn between the sphere of religion and the sphere of law.

In 1676, in *Cook v. Fountain*, the English Chancellor, Lord Nottingham, drew a jurisdictional line:

> With such a conscience as is only *naturalis et interna* this court has nothing to do; the conscience by which I am to proceed is merely *civilis et politica*, and tied to certain measures.
>
> (*Cook* v. *Fountain*, 3 Swanston 600)

If Lord Nottingham drew so smart a distinction between a conscience that was legal and within his judicial scope and a conscience that was religious or, as he went on to say, 'as is only between a man and his confessor', this was to confirm that his adjudication was 'tied to certain measures'. These procedural measures defined the independent 'course' of his court. This routine confirmation of a legal distinction well established in Court of Chancery procedure was not an assertion of temporal sovereignty against the Pope, nor a repudiation of contemporary Puritans' elevation of the role of private conscience. But a definite boundary was being set between Church and State, a boundary that separated the religious and private from the legal and political 'departments of existence'.

Exactly one hundred years before Nottingham, in Book 3 of *De republica*, Jean Bodin had offered the following proposition:

> But it may be that the consent and agreement of the nobility and people in a new religion or sect, may be so puissant & strong, as that to repress or alter the same, should be a thing impossible, or at leastwise marvelous difficult, without the extreme peril and danger of the whole state . . . Wherefore that religion or sect is to be suffered, which without the hazard and destruction of the state cannot be taken away: The health and welfare of the Commonweal being the chief thing the law respecteth.
>
> (Bodin 1962: 382)

Here a leading figure of the French *Politiques* – the middle force of Catholics for peace – was responding to the circumstance of uncontrollable religious civil war in late sixteenth-century France. Four years earlier Bodin had witnessed the slaughter of Protestants on St Bartholomew's Day. Now he specified as the political imperative a certain relation between the sphere of religion and the sphere of law and State, a relation that no matter how expedient would preserve life and civil peace.

To complete this opening scene, in mid-eighteenth-century Germany we find another prescription for the relations of State reason and Christian faith:

> The ruler must not allow his own religious opinions to be the sole criterion of the goodness or badness of his subjects; but he must always treat that religion as true which has been introduced by the fundamental principles and constitutions of the state or by the treaties of his predecessors. The regent must nevertheless attempt to establish unity of faith among his subjects. On the other hand the welfare of the state must be preferred to unity of faith.
>
> (von Justi, in Small 1909: 336)

Here it was a German public administrator who, a century after *Cook v. Fountain* and of course completely unmindful of that case, differentiated between religious opinion and the State interest. For Johann von Justi, whichever confession the State's 'constitutions' recognised was the true one. As the highest end for civil life, the practical 'welfare of the state' took precedence over the 'unity of faith'. According to this *raison d'état*, the State must tolerate religion in all its confessional forms, provided these do not endanger civil peace and welfare. This proposition on religious freedom appeared along with many other detailed guidelines in von Justi's 1755 manual on *Staatswirthschaft* or State management, guidelines that – as the title page indicates – are 'requisite for the government of a country'.

In their different ways, Lord Nottingham's jurisdiction, Bodin's model for a peaceful realm and von Justi's manual of social policing drew an analogous boundary. All can be associated with a crucial development in Western Christian culture: the emergence of a sphere of civil life independent of the empire of religion. The practical importance of this cultural mutation no doubt outstrips an antiquarian interest in the legal doctrines of Chancery and, perhaps, a theoretical speculation on the nature of the modern State. This mutation forms the historical bedrock of the present essay.

Central to the argument is a thesis advanced by Reinhart Koselleck: that where the Absolutist State had detached religious rule from civil government, Enlightenment critics of that State subsequently sought to rejoin government and law to morality. Moral critique was and is religion pursued by other means. Koselleck expounded his thesis in *Kritik und Krise. Eine Studie zur Pathogenese der bürgerlichen Welt*, the English edition of which was published only in 1988, nineteen years later, as *Critique and Crisis: Enlightenment and the Pathogenesis of Modern Society*. His openness to the German tradition of State reason locates Koselleck in the intellectual lineage of Max Weber's historical sociology of the State and Carl Schmitt's politics of State action and legality. The latter links him back to Thomas Hobbes.

Critique and Crisis has a dual historical focus on 'two major themes of the early modern period' (Koselleck 1988: 1): the success of the Absolutist State in de-theologising politics in order to impose peace on warring confessions, and the subsequent emergence of Enlightenment as a compensatory intellectual movement of critique. Koselleck relates this thesis to his autobiographical circumstance. In the Cold War, two mutually exclusive world visions confronted one another, each holding religiously to the conviction that it alone knew the ultimate moral destiny and political future for all humanity. The thesis, he hoped, might illuminate how this principled impasse blocked all political compromise and thus endangered life itself. Koselleck (1988: 1) prefaces the English edition by two more specifically German references. First, *Critique and Crisis* 'represented an attempt to examine the historical preconditions of German National Socialism, whose loss of reality and Utopian self-exaltation had resulted in hitherto unprecedented crimes'. The second reference is to a certain intellectual habit: 'My original intention was to test my arguments [on the Enlightenment origins of claims to moral exclusiveness] by reference to Kant's critiques whose political function during the age of Absolutism I was planning to investigate. But as tends to happen to German scholars, I never got beyond the preliminaries'.

The starting point is thus the early modern separation of religion from civil government as a means of ending religious slaughter. Koselleck talks of a historical 'schism' of morals and politics. Faced with the high-minded butchery that went with inter-communal Christian strife, the Absolutist State represented the calculated response of government to the horrors of religious civil war. Its jurists and men of State fashioned a 'supra-sectarian legal order' (Koselleck 1988: 41) to protect the lives of citizens in this world from the killing inspired by salvation images of the next. The aim was to save the State from this salvation and to shield its citizens from the ravages that had followed when the diktat of Christian conscience was pursued without limit in a holy war of all against all. A State emerged that set itself above the theological doctrines and moral absolutes that had bonded the warring confessions into communities of mutual hatred. To impose peace on such perfect enemies required a different political order, one that disconnected spiritual redemption from the worldly politics of government. To remove the Church from the sphere of civil government was to de-theologise government and de-politicise religion, in short what Koselleck (1988: 39) terms the 'neutralisation of conscience by politics'.

Koselleck identifies his first theme – Absolutism as a calculated response to religious slaughter – with Thomas Hobbes, theorist of the Absolutist State. For Hobbes what mattered was the citizen and his survival in this world, not the man and his redemption in the next. Hobbes, like Bodin, had witnessed confessional bloodletting and recognised the political imperative to face up to the realities under which a State must operate in a warring Christian culture. It was not a matter of debating endlessly on good and evil but of deciding urgently between spiritual civil war and worldly civil peace. Indeed, 'for

Hobbes there could be no other goal than to prevent the civil war he saw impending in England, or, once it had broken out, to bring it to an end. In his old age he still maintained that concerning loyalty and justice nothing was more instructive than the memory of the late civil war' (Koselleck 1988: 23). One of Hobbes's steps to this unblinking end was to 'do without the customary employment of the word "conscience"' (Koselleck 1988: 26). *Leviathan* (1: 7) signals Hobbes's serial undermining of conscience as an ultimate ground of action: 'it was, and ever will be reputed a very Evill act, for any man to speak against his Conscience, or to corrupt or force another to do so . . . Afterwards, men made use of the same word metaphorically, for the knowledge of their secret facts, and secret thoughts . . . And last of all, men, vehemently in love with their own new opinions (though never so absurd), and obstinately bent to maintain them, gave those opinions that reverenced name of Conscience, as if they would have made it seem unlawful, to charge or to speak against them'. Worst of all, when private conscience 'mounts the throne', the threat of civil warfare is enhanced. To generate spiritual belligerence has been one function of the appeal to conscience.

To counter this threat of endless war, the Absolutist State moved to 'neutralise' moral conscience by statist politics:

> Hobbes introduces the State as a structure in which private mentalities are deprived of their political effect. In his constitutional law, private states of mind do not apply to the laws, and the laws do not apply to the sovereign. The public interest, about which the sovereign alone has the right to decide, no longer lies in the jurisdiction of conscience. Conscience, which becomes alienated from the State, turns into private morality.
>
> (Koselleck 1988: 31)

Disengaged from 'religious hopes', a 'supra-sectarian' positive law 'designates a formal domain of political decisions beyond any Church, estate or party'.

In *Leviathan* (2: 29) Hobbes draws a boundary similar to Lord Nottingham's: 'The Law is the publique Conscience . . . private Consciences . . . are but private opinions'. What we do as citizens and legal subjects is independent of what we do as moral men and women. In fact moral norms are contingent on the establishment of a legal order that is itself contingent on an act of State that establishes political order:

> For man as citizen . . . the prime cause of moral laws is no longer to be sought in God, but in the temporal power that puts an end to civil war. These laws are not moral because they correspond to an eternal legality of morals, although they may do this; they are moral because they have originated in a commandment derived directly from the political situation. They are laws of political ethics, on the basis of which decisions are made by the sovereign alone. It is not a frame of mind or a correct

> measure that makes a virtue out of virtue, but its political foundation. However, for man as a human being it is his frame of mind, his individual conscience, that remains the ultimate criterion of morality.
>
> (Koselleck 1988: 37)

Yet, as Koselleck adds, '[t]hat this, too, will take its bearings from political necessity is also just a hope'. The target – and limit – of Absolutist government was man as citizen, as subject of the sovereign law. Thus, '[m]oral neutrality was the distinguishing mark of the sovereign decision' (Koselleck 1988: 38–9). To have coerced citizens into any one particular religious belief would constitute a sectarian favour that enhanced the likelihood of civil war, the very thing the State existed to avoid.

If the State withdrew itself from a concern with the religious morality of its citizens, the aim was to oust the confessions from a role in civil government by deeming religion a private matter to which the State was indifferent. Religious privacy – and therefore freedom – was a privilege granted by the State to its citizens. It was 'toleration with a purpose' (Koselleck 1988: 16), the purpose being civil peace. Toleration of a private conscience was not the act of a self-limiting State at last recognising a supreme moral right inhering in the individual conscience. On the contrary, it was an instrumental action by an administrative State whose overriding ethical responsibility was pacification of belligerent confessional communities. Once pacification became the social finality pursued and imposed by reason of State, religious difference would no longer find expression in public disturbance.[1]

In suppressing religious civil strife, the State made its own reason absolute over religious principles or moral absolutes for the purpose of governing civil life. In circumstances where the faithful were slaughtered by and for the faithful, only this non-sectarian reason provided 'a fundament on which to build a State that would assure peace and security' (Koselleck 1988: 23). By contrast, even when it raised a moral hope that war would cease, religious conscience could not order peace. Given the 'changing righteousnesses of the civil war parties', conscience was the cause of an always just war between rival confessions:

> A man cannot escape this civil war even if he acknowledges his longing for peace to be a generally valid moral principle. For as the sole purveyor of a legal title to action, his subjectively pure will to peace is precisely what leads to claims of more stringent totality on the part of those who cite their conscience. In other words, since it is in fact a matter of several parties, the pure will leads not to peace but to its opposite, the *bellum omnium contra omnes.* Whoever refers to his conscience wants something, says Hobbes.
>
> (Koselleck 1988: 28)

This Hobbes remains unpalatable to anyone who seeks to save us – or law and government – by subordinating the achieved neutrality of legal rule and governmental order to moral 'conscience' and spiritual discipline.[2]

Koselleck cites Hobbes's positivist prescription for peace: an Absolutist State that would act and legislate to remove private conscience from any jurisdictional role in the public sphere. In this way those conflicts of doctrine and regiment that so divided the early modern Christian confessions would be quarantined aside as matters to which the State had declared its complete indifference. The discrepancy between inner disposition and outward action was radicalised. Private mentalities – conscience as mere opinion – lost the possibility of political effect.[3] But positive law gained independence as the instrument of pacification:

> Deliberately disregarding the content of religious or political party programmes, Hobbes did not ask about the structure of a particular state; he asked about what makes a State a State, about its statehood. He did not ask for legal detail, 'legibus speciatim'; he asked: 'Quid sint leges?' What are laws? What interested him was not the substance of laws but their function as warrants of peace.
>
> (Koselleck 1988: 35)

The lesson of *Leviathan* is that for civil peace a single jurisdiction must be sovereign and absolute, whatever its substantive content. Sovereign reason of state proposed a de-theologised neutral zone – that of political government – where the power of the prince was final law.

So generic a prescription must be qualified. The political circumstances of different national histories meant, for instance, that in the English case 'reason' had its historical specificity:

> Just as on the Continent the State had overcome the religious wars and acquired its Absolutist form, so in England it was reason which performed this constitutional and moral-philosophical task – the *ratio* which Hobbes knew to be as remote from the confused squabbles or irrational, superstitious, instinct-driven humans as the absolute ruler was from his subjects.
>
> (Koselleck 1988: 33)

Yet in England as on the Continent, reason had another trick to play, one quite unforeseen by Hobbes. If reason ended one civil war, the end (or purpose) of a subsequent civil war was 'reason':

> What manifests itself here is the juncture, still situational, of Absolutism and Rationalist philosophy. Reason, rising from the turmoil of religious warfare, at first remains under the spell of that warfare and founds the State. This is how we are to understand Hobbes's failure to see that the spirit of the Enlightenment enables reason to emancipate itself.
>
> (Koselleck 1988: 34–5)

Hobbes, it seems, 'did not know that reason has a gravitation of its own'. The privatisation of conscience might protect civil peace from the zealots of that conscience, but it had an unpredicted consequence: it provided an intellectual sanctuary for moral critics of the State. Thus, '[t]o the extent to which the initial situation, the religious civil war to which [the] State owed its existence and its form, was forgotten, *raison d'état* looked like downright immorality' (Koselleck 1988: 39). Enlightened critics of State and law successfully forgot their own historical dependence on that same State and law.

Before Koselleck, Carl Schmitt (in Reventlow 1985: 197, 202) had recognised in 'the freedom of thought and conscience conceded by Hobbes . . . a "flaw" in the system, a mark of death on the great Leviathan'. By creating a free space for private conscience, the Absolutist system left open 'a door to transcendence'. Critical claims to reshape the State and the legal apparatus in accordance with a moral society perpetuate this early modern contest as our own unfinished business. The Absolutist State had closed off moral community, spiritual discipline and divine law from government, civil order and positive law. Yet in making this separation, the State had opened that 'door to transcendence' through which the critical troops have since been pouring. For all its ultimate power over a civil sphere that it had cleared of confessional interference, the Absolutist State had its blind spot. The space of conscience had been instituted as a zone of private freedom that lay beyond the reach of State and law. From here, driven by the new clergy of Enlightened critics, a 'religion' of Reason emerged with a huge expansion of 'the mind's inner space' (Koselleck 1988: 38). If, as citizens, men and women were absolutely under the law, as humans they were absolutely free in this moral 'inner space'. To cite Hobbes's formulation from *Leviathan* (2: 31): 'Private, is in secret free'.

In this 'enclave' the 'authority of conscience remained an unconquered remnant of the state of nature, protruding into the formally perfected State' (Koselleck 1988: 39). Ejected from a role in civil government by the State's prioritising of technical imperatives for peace over spiritual questing for salvation, the new guardians of conscience entered as never before into their own 'moral interior'. The political and administrative State 'became the victim of its own restrictions' when, although in an 'enclave' on its margins, the moral critics outflanked it by claiming to operate in 'the one, infinite world' (Koselleck 1988: 183). These new spiritual spokesmen for universal morality defined themselves by opposition to the State. They translated its neutralisation of religious commands as immorality and they reinterpreted its historical grant of religious freedom as political oppression. In this way they elaborated a critique that, as Koselleck argues, brought Absolutism into crisis.

Central to this process was a 'pathogenesis' or generation of a moral 'society', counterposed to the political State and projected in utopian images of future moral community and transformed humanity. These critics and their 'moral doctrines' were and are 'the real heirs of religion' (Koselleck 1988: 39). They reimplanted the spiritual seed of confessional Christianity into the field of civic life. They represented themselves as the disinterested voice of universal morality, not as one moral faction among others. Predictably, they worked not on the citizen, that great invention of the jurists, but on the 'man as a human being [who] had intentionally been omitted from the State structure' (Koselleck 1988: 39). Although speaking for the rights of 'humanity' at large, the critics were in practice a 'new stratum' drawn from 'highly diverse groups' that were 'socially accepted but politically powerless like the nobility, or economically powerful but socially branded as upstarts like the financiers and rich urban tradesmen, or socially without a proper place but of the utmost intellectual importance like the philosophers' (Koselleck 1988: 65-6). Yet what held the stratum together was less moral community than the fact that these diverse interests 'shared the fate of being unable to find an adequate place within the Absolutist State's existing institutions'. The critics were in fact the creatures of a particular cultural milieu:

> Eliminated from politics as a whole, the members of society [the 'new stratum'] would meet in wholly 'non-political' localities: at the exchanges, in coffee-houses or at the academies, where the new sciences were studied without succumbing to the State-religious authority of a Sorbonne; or in the clubs, where one could not pronounce judgement but where one could discuss the contemporary judiciary; in the salons, in which *l'esprit* could rule without commitment and did not carry the official stamp it bore in pulpits and chancelleries, or in the libraries and literary societies where one talked about arts and letters, not about the policies of the State.
>
> (Koselleck 1988: 66)

In these safe and elegant settings was cultivated that habit of mind that criticises the State that supports it, a habit generalised through the humanities academy in our own fair-weather times. Without the civil peace made possible by the State which they deplored, the Enlightened ones would have had no secure social platform from which to project their vision of a new society and to preach their faith in a redemptive moral politics.

The exemplary denizen of this stratum was the member of the Masonic lodge. As leading lights of Enlightenment, the Masons' principal instrument was their mystery. The content of the mystery might vary from group to group, but its anti-Statist function was constant: to promote a new moral 'society' that would be fully expressive of the critics' own moral interior. As Koselleck (1988: 73) puts it: 'Freedom from the State was the real political appeal of the bourgeois lodges, more than their social equality . . . Protection by the State was replaced by protection from the State.' This reversal of the actual history reorchestrated the Absolutist disarticulation of religion and theology from government and law. Against the existing State and its institutions the Masonic and other critics set the image of a moral society beyond the reach of the State because of its grounding in inalienable rights and fundamental freedoms. Stripped of its historical role as the grantor and protector of religious freedom, the State was recast as the great threat to freedom.

At the same time, the critics reoriented themselves to a future society where morality would again govern and where men, escaping the confines of coercive legal citizenry, would at last be freely themselves. In reality no little external discipline was involved. Koselleck (1988: 78) records the 'sealed monthly reports' that the Masonic brethren filed on each other and the strictly hierarchical '"directorate of tolerance", which on the strength of the secret was already terrorising brethren in the name of morality' (Koselleck 1988: 79). On such a practice was built the 'new society' on whose behalf the excluded critics would comfortably adjudicate as the 'conscience of the world':

> What the secret made possible was one's seclusion from the outside world, which in turn led to a form of social existence which included the moral qualification to sit in judgement on that outside world. The medium of the secret widened the private conscience into a society; the society came to be a large conscience, a conscience of the world from which the society voluntarily excluded itself by way of the secret.
>
> (Koselleck 1988: 83)

Religious belief and personal morality had been de-politicised by the Absolutist State. The revenge of the new 'heirs of religion' was to promote the individual moral conscience in which they were so expert as the ultimate site of an uncompromising universal adjudication.

Because their incapacity for compromise made them a danger to peace, confessional intellectuals had been sidelined by the Absolutist State. However, their marginalised moral heirs could be as uncompromising as they desired, safe within their cultural enclave – a vacuum chamber for law and government, but as things turned out a pressure cooker for morality and critique. Koselleck (1988: 53) traces the 'triumphal march' of critical Enlightenment from within the enclave to the point where 'its private interior expanded into the public domain'. This expansion redrew the boundary of public and private, blurring the line between private conscience and public action that the State had drawn to protect against inter-confessional civil strife. As Koselleck (1988: 56) observes: 'The self-assurance of the moral inner space lies in its ability to "go public"'. The expansion is still under way, observable in the routine spectacle of critical intellectuals offering up their own moral interior to endless publication.

The new stratum of Enlightened critics pursued their vision of a moral society to supersede the administrative State that in fact protected them. They cultivated a constant moral dissatisfaction with existing institutions, a disposition that went along with being the 'world's better conscience' and its moral shepherd. In recognising the peculiar mode of intellectual conduct that resists the State that protects it, Koselleck (1988: 158) identifies a technique of 'antithetical thought' that operates by polarising the institutions of the present

State against images of a future moral society. In 'The historical-political semantics of asymmetric counterconcepts', Koselleck (1985) explores how such polarising has functioned as a moral and political device for generating dissatisfaction with the present and raising great expectations of quite different futures. The recasting of circumstances into polarities that construct polemical comparisons out of non-comparable terms remains a particular 'technique of negation'.

Exploring paired concepts that have been used to embrace all humanity, Koselleck selects the pairs Christian/Heathen and Human/Subhuman. The Christian antithesis of temporal and spiritual sustained a habit of mind that specialised in negation of the present and expectation of the future. When he distinguished between the totality of humans and the spiritual elect who had been saved by Christ, Paul showed how to 'negatively confront the totality of previous humanity with the (potential) generality of Christian humanity'. The semantic antithesis of Christian and Heathen was thus 'temporalised' into the eschatological future time of the 'new man': 'The Christian or, more precisely, he who lives in Christ, is the new man who has done away with the old' (Koselleck 1985: 175). This projection allowed one to be inwardly Christian and cosmic while bearing outwardly the actual role of Roman or Frank, the rank of king or peasant, the status of freeman or slave, the civic existence of citizen. In each case the existing worldly status was subordinated to a future spiritual completion. Earthly judgments thus asymmetrically anticipate those of the divine tribunal as human history unfolds towards the Last Judgement and the final transfiguration of the old life into new.[4] Exploiting this asymmetry, Augustine demanded of princes that their policy conform to Christian prescription. But the notion of a spiritual 'renovation' of the existing order always carried an extirpatory threat whereby 'those who are of the world are no longer allowed their own space' (Koselleck 1985: 185). A later instance of how Christians annihilate their adversaries is the English Puritans' capacity to 'breed high terms of separation' between themselves and 'the rest of the world':

> [T]he one sort are named The brethren, The godly, and so forth; the other, worldlings, time-servers, pleasers of men not of God, with such like . . . But be they women or be they men, if once they have tasted of that cup, let any man of contrary opinion open his mouth to persuade them, they close up their ears, his reasons they weigh not, all is answered with rehearsal of the words of John, 'We are of God; he that knoweth God heareth us': as for the rest, ye are of the world.
>
> (Hooker, in Koselleck 1985: 185)

For the Anglican Hooker, says Koselleck, the target was 'those who employ biblical texts to deduce a sense of rectitude transcendent of this world, but which at once obliges and enables them to act in this world'. This antithetical habit of thought 'testifies to an experiential framework, shot through with Christianity, simultaneously negating and laying claim to this world'.

The opposition of Human and Subhuman is also 'deeply polemical in form' (Koselleck 1985: 186). 'Human' began to cease to denote all humans, becoming instead one pole of a fundamental yet asymmetrical opposition. For Enlighteners, the appeal to humanity had a 'critical, even negating function with respect to the counterposition' (Koselleck 1985: 189). As Koselleck (1988: 36n) remarks in *Critique and Crisis*, Rousseau and Marx took over 'Hobbes's concept of absolute sovereignty, but put it in the service of "man". With this the boundary line to Utopianism was crossed; sovereignty itself became revolutionary'. *Critique and Crisis* shows 'humanity' coming into use as the future moral subject deployed against the existing 'amoral' institutions of the State. By speaking for humanity, the Enlighteners made an offer no one could refuse, 'for who wished to deny being human?' Citing Rousseau's formulation that a king can 'rise to the status of a *Mensch* [man]' only by renouncing his throne, Koselleck (1985: 191) records that to speak in the name of 'humanity' now became the mark of having risen to a level of moral freedom superior to all worldly constitutions.[5] This precisely reverses von Justi's proposition that, for the sake of civil peace, true religion was to be contingent on State constitution.

When Rousseau confronted king with man, the one continuum of moral judgment was imposed on both these statuses. Government was drawn back into the moral community of all humanity (which was not all humans). The positive law of kings was resubordinated to a higher law of moral nature inscribed in every individual. As in the confessional State, government and law lost their independence and were returned to being at best mere instruments for a superior power that was no longer the divine will envisioned by early modern theology but the moral community envisioned by post-Enlightenment criticism. Most chilling, however, is the appeal to humanity in the utopian discourse of National Socialism where '[t]he totalising concept of *Menschheit*, once applied politically, gave rise to totalitarian consequences' (Koselleck 1985: 193).

The critics' capacity to claim the moral future sustained a 'perpetual process of critique'.[6] The Enlighteners undertook a 'constant performance of censure' of institutions, persons and practices outside the moral enclave (Koselleck 1988: 57). There is potential for fanaticism here:

> Everything that was historically given, indeed history itself, was transformed into a process – the outcome of which, of course, remained open as long as the categories of private judgement could never catch up with the events they had helped to bring about.
>
> (Koselleck 1988: 10)

The divine plan was revised into the imagery of a moral future. But this was no less potent. Enlightened intellectual partisans of this 'future-oriented world-view' sought to reorient lives according to 'historico-philosophical images which caused the day's events to pale' (Koselleck 1988: 9). Dedicated to future transformation, they were completely dismissive of the given circumstances, whatever these might be: 'Criticism transformed the future into a maelstrom that sucked out the present from under the feet of the critic' (Koselleck 1988: 109). It was a remorseless exercise of suspicion and undermining, an exercise that prepared critical practitioners to be forever out of touch with actual circumstances.

In seeing historical factuality so negated and institutional arrangements so derided, Carl Schmitt expressed outrage at this mode of intellectual conduct. He termed it 'political romanticism':

> Every moment is transformed into a point in a structure. And just as romantic emotion moves between the compressed ego and expansion into the cosmos, so every point is a circle and every circle a point. The community is an extended individual, the individual a concentrated community. Every historical moment is an elastic point in the vast fantasy of the philosophy of history with which we dispose over the peoples and the eons. That is the way to guarantee the romantic supremacy over reality.
>
> (Schmitt 1986: 74–5)

Schmitt tagged this escalatory capacity for transforming any given reality into an occasion for unbounded self-analysis 'subjectivised occasionalism'. Its historical relation is to a Christian metaphysics in which God is forever transforming earthly events into occasions for the exercise of his spontaneous creation.

Koselleck's lexicon – inner space, moral interior, moral inner space, the extra-political intellectual interior, internal moral realm – points to an intense 'work on the self' that, by pathogenesis, produced today's critical persona. Canonised in Romantic aesthetics, this persona has been generalised through the humanities academy. Critics, the heirs of religion, have been enthroned as the 'moral judiciary' (Koselleck 1988: 82). Their claim was and is to reunify that which the early modern Absolutist State had set apart as separate spheres of life: 'The universality of an enlightened ethic crossed all the boundaries so painstakingly drawn by [Absolutist] politicians' (Koselleck 1988: 41). Then and now they adjudicate on everything in the name of humanity and its rights:

> The king as ruler by divine right appears almost modest alongside the judge of mankind who replaced him, the critic who believed that, like God on Judgement Day, he had the right to subject the universe to his verdict . . . Criticism goes far beyond that which had occasioned it and is transformed into the motor of self-righteousness.
>
> (Koselleck 1988: 118, 119)

Moral critique brought the State into crisis in two ways. First, by subjecting its political 'acts and attitudes . . . to a moral test they cannot pass' (Koselleck 1988: 152). Second, by spreading the notion that ethical conduct 'remained confined to the corridors outside the chambers of actual political decision-making' (Koselleck 1988: 2).

These are important history lessons for today's moral critics of government and law. Yet a question remains: does Koselleck's figure of 'crisis' (and its implied resolution) perpetuate the vision of a potential harmony of political State with moral society, a future reconciliation of law with morality and of government with religion? No doubt Koselleck disparages the particular version of this healing reconciliation preached by the post-Masonic moral critics. But his thesis leaves open the possibility that the historical separation of State and society remains an intellectual and moral problem to be resolved, not a historical accomplishment to be applauded.

It will be interesting to seek analogues among today's critics of law and government to those Enlighteners of whom Koselleck (1988: 95) writes, 'So great was the Illuminati's moral sense of self . . . that they believed they could eliminate the State not only here and now, but altogether.' But will this relieve Kronman's gloom, evoked at the start of this chapter? Two possibilities arise. First, there is Koselleck's suggestion that the future-oriented philosophy of history is just a 'compensation' for moral critics seeking to elude facticity. It is the device of those who can be so moral only by remaining aloof from 'actual political decision-making'.

Second, there is a question of approach. Koselleck historicises critique by recording the provenance of the moral-political culture that now looms large in the critical humanities and reflexive social sciences. His genealogy brings the critic into view as one who does not so much reject religious responses to this world as furnish a new vehicle for them. We might be relatively familiar, through Hobbes, with the politics of *raison d'état* and the Absolutist State. Much less familiar is Koselleck's identification of the Enlightenment critique of the State with the intransigent religiosity of a new *raison de conscience*. *Critique and Crisis* is a genealogy 'made for cutting' (Foucault 1977b: 154). But the cut in this case is the continuity that Koselleck discerns between post-Enlightenment reason and Christian religiosity where, previously, we saw a flattering rupture that set modern critical thinking free from traditional religion and theology.[7]

We might become less gloomy if, with Koselleck, we redescribe the relations of law and critique as a continuing contest between a form of spiritual discipline belonging to the religious realm and a lawyerly conduct formed partly in response to uncontrollable religious civil war. The ethical commitment of this essay surfaces here. It is a matter of men and women making themselves equal to the demands of given circumstances and mundane realities. It is not a matter of testing legal and administrative forms of conduct against other-worldly visions, religious or moral. The challenge is to throw a better ethical light on practices – the professional routines of law, government and administration – that are themselves routinely criticised as falling short on the scale of moral values. That is, if they are considered ethical forms of conduct at all.

2

INVISIBLE AND SPIRITUAL; VISIBLE AND EXTERNAL

In a statement that he references to Koselleck, Heinz Schilling (1988: 265) characterises 'confessionalisation' as a 'movement [that] so intensified the interpenetration of religion and society, confession and politics, that there arose irreconcilable, total confrontations that endangered social life as such'. Schilling is describing two separate conducts of life that emerged in the 1500s, one organised by the post-Reformation confessions and the other organised by the emerging territorial State. Having emerged separately, they then merged into the 'confessional State'. However, by the 1600s, the continuing process of 'confessionalisation' led to catastrophic civil wars between rival confessional communities that held each other in total scorn.

Two points are made here. First, far from any general relation of opposition between spiritual and temporal orders of living, confessionalisation rested on an 'alliance of ecclesiastical and state interests', exemplified for Schilling (1986: 27) in the 'cooperation of pastor and bailiff, pulpit and administration (*Kanzel und Amtshaus*)'. This alliance 'guided the transformation of the dispersed, fragmentary medieval society of separate groups graded by privilege into the early modern society of the territorial state, a body of subjects, all uniformly equal before the state, well controlled and well regulated through the state's ever growing activity'. Second, however, when government became so tightly bound to the confession that security lost out to salvation, the confessional State was engulfed in religious civil war between mutually exclusive confessions each claiming to be the one universal faith. Administration was conscripted to the pulpit. The population of citizens was overwhelmed by the community of souls.

Nevertheless, the reference to an 'interpenetration' of Church and State requires us to modulate any simple dualism of religion and law that Koselleck's thesis might encourage. In Germany, Church and State, the spiritual and the political had found common cause for a time. Then, most terribly in the Thirty Years War (1618–48), there followed the carnage to which the Absolutist State responded by disarticulating religion from government and law in the de-theologising manner described by Koselleck. This process does not entirely apply to the English settlement of Church and State. Limiting the geographical and historical applications of his thesis, Koselleck views English political history as differing chronologically but not thematically in respect of the rise of the State and the subsequent reaction of critical intellectuals.[1] In England these events had coincided. Koselleck does not explore specifics of English institutional history, such as an Anglican Church which continued both to occupy a particular worldly estate and, in the name of universal faith, to suppress the minority Catholics and dissenting Puritans. Nor does he explore the place of theological intellectuals in the dual polity of an Anglican establishment.[2] This is not to deny convergences between different national histories. Subsequently, prestigious models of intellectual conduct have crossed territorial borders. Morally driven anti-Statism is not the sole preserve of German intellectuals. In England and America, the critical humanities academy has thoroughly 'received' an originally German ethos of self-marginalisation from government and law.

In fact Koselleck builds his intellectual history on English political philosophy. Hobbes and Locke are principal sources. It was 'the English spirit' and the 'English Constitution' that some 400,000 refugees from continental Absolutism transmitted as the driving force of an Enlightenment critique of Absolutist rule (Koselleck 1988: 64). But Hobbes had seen the rise of States that denied religion any place in the government of civil life as the means of bringing peace to territories torn by religious war. Given its established territorial, legal and administrative unity, England avoided such total confrontations, helped also by the exceptional dual polity of Anglican Church and State as parallel aspects of the one nation.

Let us listen to John Whitgift, Anglican Archbishop of Canterbury from 1583, on the authority of the Church and, specifically, on the relationship of inner conscience to the outer ordering of life:

> There are two kinds of government in the church, the one invisible, the other visible; the one spiritual, the other external. The invisible and spiritual government of the church is when God by his spirit, gifts, and ministry of the world, doth govern it, by ruling in the hearts and consciences of men, and directing them in all things necessary to everlasting life, and it is in the church of the elect only. The visible and external government is that which is executed by man, and consisteth of external discipline, and visible ceremonies practised in that church, and over that church, that containeth in it both good and evil, which is usually called the visible church of Christ.
>
> (Whitgift 1968: 183)

No fundamental conflict is posited between the invisible and the visible Church. On the contrary, the two realms accommodate one another in such a way that the existing institutions of the visible order are not other than in keeping with God's all-embracing plan. This accommodation allows for two different modes of Christian life which, at their most divergent, represent an other-worldly mysticism and a worldly observance of the Church's forms and ceremonies of government.

In the Third Book of his immense *Of the Laws of Ecclesiastical Polity* (1593) Richard Hooker distinguished discipline from faith, worldly regiment from spiritual domain.[3] Particular forms of a 'Church-politie' were one thing; principles of scripture were another. Against his Reformed opponents the Anglican apologist argued:

> that matters of fayth, and in generall matters necessarie unto salvation are of a different nature from Ceremonies, order, and the kinde of Church-government; that the ones are necessarie to bee expresslie conteyned in the worde of God, or else manifestly collected out of the same, the other not so; that it is necessarie not to receive the one, unlesse there be some thing in scripture for them, the other free, if nothing against them may thence be alleaged.
>
> (Hooker 1977: 208)

Unswayed by the charge of 'misdistinguishing', Hooker (1977: 209–10) insisted: 'Touching matters belonging unto the Church of Christ this wee conceive, that they are not of one sute'. Yet it was hard 'to speak to the contentation of mindes exulcerated in themselves, but that somewhat there will be always which displeaseth'. Anglican management of visible and invisible displeased the Reformed intransigents, 'because matters of discipline and Church-government are (as they say) matters necessarie to salvation and of faith, whereas we put a difference betweene the one and the other'.

We can again draw a comparison with German circumstances, and anticipate our discussion of the Prussian civic jurist, Christian Thomasius, a post-Thirty Years War intellectual of the Absolutist State. Unlike Whitgift and Hooker, Thomasius sought to relegate the visible Church in favour of the invisible one. To this end he used the whole repertoire of Pietist arguments against ceremonies, sacraments and images. However, Thomasius's aim was not to perfect this world by spiritual discipline, as wanted by the radical Pietists. Rather it was to eradicate the Church as an institution of civil government. By making religion so purely a spiritual and inward matter, the Churches were rendered inapt for any worldly role. Religion was to be granted no space between this socially invisible and thus harmless spiritual commitment and a civil life that was solely an object of secular government. With the latter came a need to fashion appropriately 'a-moral' secular persons for the offices of this de-theologised civil sphere.[4]

English circumstances were more blurred. For instance, at the Inner Temple, one of the Inns of Court, as Master from 1585 Hooker preached the Sunday morning sermon in the Temple Church. His predecessor, Walter Travers—a radical Protestant and 'lieutenant' of Thomas Cartwright, the leader of the Presbyterians—continued to preach on Sunday afternoon. As Prest (1972: 194) records, 'so began a famous theological disputation, which attracted wide attention at the time and was still remembered seventy years later. For a year, "the forenoon sermon spoke Canterbury and the afternoon Geneva", until Whitgift intervened with a prohibition ordering Travers to cease preaching'.

Anglican thinking bound the Church into the institutions of an English State that it accepted as supreme. Church and State were part and parcel of an indigenous culture embodied in the 'laws and customs' of the realm. Legitimating doctrines were constructed from this background of settled laws, customs and institutions. This is the picture of an 'Ancient Constitution' that John Pocock has drawn, central to which is the 'common law mind' as exemplified in Sir Edward Coke's approach to 'history'. When Coke evoked an immemorial past of English law and life, he was deploying 'latent assumptions governing historical thinking, which had been planted deep in the English mind by centuries of practice of a particular form of law' (Pocock 1957: 46). Coke was, of course, using the Ancient Constitution in the struggle against the king.

Anglicanism was the preferred ideology of the common lawyers. But it is worth pausing on this apparent fit between a theological doctrine and a professional disposition. Was there something about the Anglican ideology – a certain externality? – that rendered it more sympathetic to the public and professional functions of the lawyer than an inwardly focused Puritanism? At first sight this looks attractive. Yet, returning to the case of Thomasius in Prussia, there an intensely inward Pietism aligned successfully with a vigorous administrative State. Something less profound and more political than theological doctrine is at issue. Historical and political circumstances meant that it was in the interest of a Prussian State to join with an anti-Lutheran confession – Pietism – in order to expel the Lutheran clerical and noble estate from their traditional grasp on civil authority.

It was not against the king but against the Non-conformist challenge that Whitgift and Hooker defended Anglican organisation as an immemorially right and constitutional way of living. Citing Hooker's proposition that the 'laws made concerning religion, do eventually take their essence from the power of the whole realm and Church of England', Kelley (1993: 71) emphasises the cultural integrity of this indigenous mode of thinking: 'Like English government more generally, the Anglican Church had accumulated its own usages and institutional arrangements in accordance with nature – but in the sense of common sense and the development of English national character within a Christian framework.'

Despite or because of its claim to such integrity, Anglicanism was challenged by dissident opinion. To describe the challenge as the confrontation of an old and a new Christian order has become more difficult in the light of current historians' reluctance to see English Puritanism in clear and unified opposition to the Anglican Church.[5] These were times of struggle waged by multiple groups, some bent on 'almost Manichean warfare against Satan and his worldly allies' in the cause of a future 'Holy Commonwealth' (Walzer

1963–4: 63–5) that would strip away every sedimented Anglican habit and legal establishment. This challenge rested on the promise of a 'sphere of relations that is consciously set over against the civil order, one whose internal order is regulated by a polity *intentionally different from*, and, so the Calvinists believed, *superior to civil polity*' (Little 1970: 141–2). These transformed relations were to be 'the model for all social life', a theological ground for what the godly State should be.

The old Anglican order was denounced as coercive. The new Puritan order was freely chosen, a conduct of life grounded in a self-directing private conscience. As Little (1970: 103–4) puts it, for the more radical Cartwright, the aim was 'to give the inward consciences and heart-felt commitments of men no respite until they rest in voluntary obedience to God's new order'. For Puritans, the 'fundamental objective called into question the very *nature* of the State and the law as agencies capable of determining and producing ultimate order'. In other words, the only ultimate order was the will of God. Thus William Perkins, the Cambridge lecturer and a moderate among Tudor Puritan theologians, set 'the courts of men and their authorities . . . under conscience':

> For God in the heart of every man hath erected a tribunal seat, and in his stead hee hath placed neither saint nor angel, nor any other creature whatsoever, but conscience itselfe, who therefore is the highest Judge that is or can be under God; by whose direction also courts are kept, and laws made.
>
> (in Little 1970: 123)

Positive law is subordinated to Christian conscience as a coercive command is subordinated to a freely chosen law of God. For Perkins, enacted law 'must be according to the rules of Christianitie'. The common law art of improvising positive remedies as need arose is dismissed as the imperfect way of the 'olde lawes'. By contrast, the proleptic 'rules of Christianitie' transcend all 'point and circumstance' since – for the new man – all doubt falls away before 'the infallible certainty of faith' (in Little 1970: 116).

In the Catholic tradition, of course, conscience was not so equated with a purely private moral sense and responsibility. In fact, just as Koselleck's Masons needed external discipline, so too the Puritans still needed direction of consciences. Self-direction was not yet a universal capacity. The existence of a Protestant casuistry, with its elaborate pedagogical literature of 'cases of conscience', calls into question any general identification of conscience with an innate moral sense. Whatever the doctrine might say, Calvinist practice did not rely on some natural dividing line between inner moral self and outer government. Given the existing flock's spiritual incompetence and the evidence that as yet 'wills are partially redeemed', the 'Word of God' relied on 'ministers and elders with *partial* force'. Around these prestigious 'officers' of the new order, a zone of spiritual privilege was claimed for the whole Puritan congregation, conceived as equals in a self-governing community whose members take themselves to be the 'wave of the future, the new elite' (Little 1970: 72–4).[6] The reference to the 'new elite' cuts against the assumption that Dissenters were the socially oppressed and therefore potentially democratic or simple humanity and thus the true moral community.

In principle, the ability to act well without external coercion was what set the Puritan 'above the law'. Uncoerced moral conduct – achieved by longing to put yourself in total obedience to God – disgraces any action performed under external authority, be it custom or legislation. The disciplines of a Puritan lifestyle produced remarkable men and women, able to abstract themselves from the existing order of things and set themselves above the worldly sphere. Yet the notion that the Puritan has 'become a law unto himself' (Little 1970: 125) sounds an alarm: it disqualifies existing law from having an authentic ethical value of its own.[7]

3

CONSCIENCE AND LAW

Lord Nottingham's life, from 1621 to 1682, embraced the years of religious and political strife leading to and following from the English Civil War. For a sense of the anguish of those years, including the middle 1650s when the country was ruled by a Christian millenarian army, let us listen to him speaking as Lord High Steward in the House of Lords on 7 December 1680. Lord Stafford had been impeached for high treason following the so-called Popish Plot. Nottingham found his part 'a very sad one'. It was the first time he had pronounced sentence of death. Invoking a 'general and desperate conspiracy of the papists', he outlined Stafford's role in the 'demonstration of zeal . . . against the person of the King' and directed to 'the ruin of the state', actions that were not those of one 'interested in the preservation of government [and] so much obliged to the moderation of it'. The sentence closes with the judgment: 'that you go to the place from whence you came; from thence you must be drawn upon a hurdle to the place of execution; when you come there, you must be hanged by the neck but not till you are dead; for you must be cut down alive, your privy members must be cut off and your bowels ript up before your face and thrown into the fire; then your head must be severed from your body and your body divided into four quarters and these must be at the disposal of the King. And God almighty be merciful to your soul.'

So spoke a moderate in 1680 in what were still times of acrimonious religious zealotry.[1] Not immune to the anti-Catholic ferment, Nottingham accepts that Papists caused the Great Fire that burned London in 1666.[2] The present plotting threatens renewed civil war, intensified by foreign interventions. Just five years after Stafford's conviction, in 1685, Louis XIV would revoke the Edict of Nantes, sending a shock wave through European Protestantism. In such circumstances, with mass expressions of confessional zeal, it was one thing for a judge to draw a technical distinction between a conscience that was legal and a conscience that was confessional, but quite another to stand entirely to one side of the times.

Those times have been called the 'Age of Conscience': 'For much of the century it was generally believed that conscience, not force of habit or self-interest, was what held together the social and political order . . . Every attempt by the State to prescribe the forms of religious doctrine and worship tested the consciences of those who believed it was their duty to obey the laws of the land but were also persuaded of the truth of a rival creed' (Thomas 1993: 29–30). The notion of a conscience that was strictly 'civil and political', namely pacific and prudent, nonetheless marked off a sphere of life regulated by the 'laws of the land' from a sphere regulated by the 'truth of a creed'.

In fact a legal mode of conscience already had a history. In 'The conscience of the court', Max Radin explored the question of a judge's obligations in conscience, starting from a 'case' reproduced in collections of Cases of Conscience that served as ethics manuals for early modern readers (Radin 1932: 508). A judge who witnesses a killing then has other witnesses testify in his court that the act was committed by another man, one whom the judge privately knows to be innocent. The case is referred to in a Year Book report from the time of Henry IV, but Radin's principal source is the Dominican Joannes Baptista Corradus's *Responsa Casuum Conscientiae* of 1596:

> [O]ur answer is that the judge ought not to decide according to his own free will, but according to the statutes and the laws (*leges et iura*). For since he is a public personage, he is obliged to proceed not in accordance with private knowledge, but in accordance with public knowledge, which depends on witnesses.
>
> (in Radin 1932: 509)

Because in his private conscience the judge knows the man is innocent, he must do everything legal to protect him. However, 'if this can in no way be done, [the judge] should leave him to be judged by his superior and should appear for him as witness and swear publicly that he knows him to be innocent. But if, under pressure of the other party, this cannot be done, then must he do what in the course of law should be done'. Corradus then stresses that the judge, condemning the innocent man to death 'in the course of the law', is himself guiltless, resting this conclusion on the authority of Aquinas.

The personal discipline required by those who take on the office of judge involves, finally, not following one's own inner conscience. Radin (1932: 511) cites the view of Peter of Aragon – expressed in the down-to-earth manner of casuistical guides – that the judge should assist the accused 'by hindering the accuser from coming to the court, or, if he can do so without scandal, by permitting the prisoner to escape, or by frightening the witnesses to prevent their testifying falsely'. As Radin puts it: 'This is certainly as far as one could expect the judge to go, and it is only if these extreme measures fail that Peter will let the judge condemn.'

Powerful authorities appear on either side. In late sixteenth-century France, the Protestant jurist François Hotman took the side of personal conscience. His compatriot Cujas accepted the case argued by Corradus. Radin (1932: 515) notes that '[t]he reason assigned is one of public policy, and [Cujas] calls particular attention to the fact that if a judge can acquit on the basis of his private knowledge, he can also condemn a man in this way, which would produce an intolerable situation'. In the English context, disagreement was equally intense. The late fourteenth-century reformer, John Wycliffe, noted the 'public policy' argument:

> They say that a civil judge knowing that the witnesses are giving false testimony ought, even against their conscience, give sentence according to what has been alleged and proven and thus grant the property of the true owner to some non-owner, because, otherwise as they say, the law would fail, although the law ought to take its course.
>
> (in Radin 1932: 517)

But this was merely the prelude to Wycliffe 'thundering' his contrary opinion that 'a false witness proves nothing at all and that a judge in basing his decision on a false statement himself takes part in the falsehood, commits murder, if the condemnation is capital, and at all events a mortal sin'. Closer to Nottingham's time, Sir Edward Coke in *Marriot v. Pascal* (1 Leonard 161) transformed the traditional case from rhetorical example to 'historical' instance to argue against granting the power of final determination to private conscience. It was a question to be decided within 'the course of the law'.

The casuists' fable of the judge who, though conscience-stricken, has the professional capacity to stay within the 'certain measures' of the court aligns with Lord Nottingham's proposition in *Cook v. Fountain*.[3] But there is a second aspect to the history of conscience as an English legal reality. It is a matter of the court of conscience rather than the conscience of the court. The Court of Chancery was, of course, known as the Court of Conscience, in distinction from the courts of law.[4] For at least two centuries before Lord Nottingham's term of office, references to conscience recur in Chancery records. Indeed, at first this Chancery conscience was 'not thought of as complementary with the common law but is rather set over and in opposition to it' (Yale 1957: xxxvii). This opposition rested on a historical association of conscience with the canon law so strong that the notion of conscience had seemed a foreign imposition on English common law (Barbour 1918: 835).

Yet, in English law too, conscience came to be associated not only with the status of litigants, defendants in particular, but with the person of the king. Because the king could not be sued in his own courts of law, the practice emerged of supplicating the Chancellor who thus acquired the status of 'keeper of the royal conscience'. From Bacon's reading on the Statute of Uses, Yale (1957: xl) cites a Tudor formulation distinguishing between the 'private conscience of the feoffee' and the 'general conscience of the realm which is Chancery'. That 'the idea of the Chancellor administering the royal conscience becomes one of the commonplaces of equity' can be counted among the outcomes of the successful attack on ecclesiastical authority by the royal power. A legal form of conscience was emerging that was impersonal and administrative.

In 1528 and 1530, Christopher St German, a barrister of the Middle Temple in London, raised the stakes in favour of the public legal conscience by printing his two famous dialogues entitled *Doctor and Student.* For Plucknett and Barton (1974: xx), 'St German's professed aim was to produce a work which should do something to remedy the lack of any collections of cases of conscience which took English law, rather than the civil law, as the secular law whose effect in conscience was to be considered'. Specifically, the 'author is setting out to demonstrate that the common law rather than the decrees of the Church should govern the consciences of Englishmen'. But this risked the common law appearing contrary to conscience, a risk compounded by Chancery's 'corrective' function. The solution was to stress the 'imperfection of human foresight and of human powers of expression' (Plucknett and Barton 1974: xlvi–xlvii), such that the equitable jurisdiction of the court of Chancery could make good the common law without finding that law to be bad.[5] As John Guy (1985: 19-20) summarises it, '[t]he key to St German's theory was that equitable interventions in the name of good conscience, which were sometimes necessary to mitigate the rigour of common law, were designed to reinforce, not to contradict, general legal principles'.

For St German, this arrangement was sealed by a divinely sanctioned moral anthropology: 'man received of God a double eye, that is to say, an outward and an inward eye'. This latter is 'the eye of reason, whereby he knows things invisible and divine'. On this basis St German's project was a strategic use of jurisprudential theory:

> It is possible that St German's primary goal all along in his *Little Treatise* [*Concerning Writs of Subpoena* (1532)], and in *Doctor and Student* itself, was not to explore equity's functions and boundaries as an exercise in practical jurisprudence *per se,* but was to do so as the essential theoretical precondition of attacking the independent jurisdiction of church courts and clergy in England as guaranteed by chapter 1 of Magna Carta.
>
> (Guy 1985: 89)

Thus St German set limits to religious conscience by relocating the effective norms of civil conduct into the historical sphere of the common law. Religious conscience was being dispossessed of its governing role. Having elaborated a theory to 'nudge English common law inexorably towards the apex of the jurisprudential pyramid' and having 'resolved the sixteenth-century conflict of laws in favour of English common law', no wonder St German was useful to Henry VIII at a time when endless disputes were generated around parliament's capacity to regulate religious matters from delapidations to liturgical practices.

In these circumstances St German's account of the relation of law and conscience was intentionally contentious. His *Little Treatise Concerning Writs of Subpoena,* a discussion of Chancery procedures, underscores the polemical identification of conscience with the historical grounds of English law, not the reverse. As Guy (1985: 89) writes, 'in concrete terms, conscience became the moral principle which gave the chancellor the cognitive and coercive authority to call parties before him, to pronounce decisions in his courts and to bind litigants to observe them'. This harnessing of conscience to external coercion is the very antithesis of the free and self-directing conscience proclaimed by Calvinist Puritans. Among other 'divers objeccions' that St German addressed was the unpredictability and excessive discretion of a jurisdiction based on one man's conscience:

> [I]n what uncertayntie . . . shall the kinges subgiettes stand when they shalbe put from the lawe of the realme, and bee compellede to be ordrede by the discrecion and conscience of oon man; and namelie, for as moche as conscience is a thinge of great uncertayntie, for . . . summe man thinkith that if he lak mony, and another hathe too moche, that he may take parte of his with conscience; and so divers men, divers consciences.
>
> (in Guy 1985: 123)

Given the fact of different men, different consciences, how was certainty to be established in the chancellor's judgment? The answer is that certainty lies in the historical laws of England. Inseparable from the 'lawes of the realme', the Chancellor's conscience is no longer an arbitrary private will. This procedural conscience of the court is separated from the uncertainties of an individual conscience:

> And thoughe summe men be disceyvede thorough a scrupulouse conscience, or an erronyouse conscience, or yn suche other manner, yet it is not to presume that the Chauncellor, whiche is alwaies appoyncted to his office by the kinge as a man of singuler wysdom and good conscience, wilbe disceyvede thorough suche errours yn conscience, having so strayte rules to thorder of his conscience as he shall have.
>
> (in Guy 1985: 124)

The mention of 'strayte rules' anticipates the 'certain measures' that guide the judicial conscience to which Lord Nottingham would refer in 1676.

St German's arguments did not dispel concern about an equitable jurisdiction based on an aleatory personal conscience. In the early 1600s, the lawyer and historian John Selden made his quip that 'Equity is a roguish thing': ''Tis all one as if they should make the standard for the measure we call a foot to be the Chancellor's foot. What an uncertain measure would this be. One Chancellor has a long foot, another a short foot, a third an indifferent foot. 'Tis the same thing in the Chancellor's conscience' (Selden 1927: 43). By contrast, where law is concerned, we 'have a measure' and 'know what to trust to'. But the cause of certainty was not helped by misguided attempts to use religious or moral conscience to settle what are legal problems. Hence Selden's remark that '[i]f once we come to . . . pretend conscience against law, who knows what inconveniency may follow' (Selden 1927: 35). For instance, an Anabaptist takes my horse but, when sued, replies that 'he did according to conscience; his conscience tells him all things are common among the saints'. Selden attributed to religious confession more generally an unpredictable quality: 'Religion is like the fashion; one man wears his doublet slashed, another laced, another plain; but every man has a doublet. Every man has his religion. We differ about the trimming' (Selden 1927: 117). When the larger question looms: '[I]s the church or the scripture judge of religion?', Selden answered: 'In truth neither, but the state.'

The same line is followed by another lawyer in Selden's circle, Sir Matthew Hale. A member of the Common Bench in Cromwell's time and Chief Justice of the King's Bench under Charles II, Hale distinguished a realm of conscience from that of law, but accorded no general supremacy to private conscience, 'for it sets up in every particular subject a tribunal superior to that of the magistrate'. Alan Cromartie (1995: 181) observes of Hale's proposition, 'No one could claim exemption from the magistrate's commands on the grounds they believed those commands to be morally wrong. Conscience must be obeyed in preference to any human power, but the government was perfectly entitled to punish sincere objectors to its will.'

In his *Prolegomena* or 'little treatise of chancery learning', Hale's protégé Lord Nottingham penned the following note on the rule *nullus recedat a cancellaria sine remedio*:

> And yet all cases that are without remedy at common law are not relievable in equity: nor is the rule *nullus recedat a cancellaria sine remedio* so to be understood, for some cases are only to be considered between a man and his confessor. As, for example, . . . the grand jury affirm a false verdict in an attaint, no court of conscience can help these cases. Yet the party is bound to restitution *sub periculo animae* . . . Yet God forbid a man should use no better conscience than the Chancery can compel him. However, the rule must always hold that it is not fit for a court of equity to do everything that is fit to be done: for there is a twofold conscience, viz. *conscientia politica et civilis et conscientia naturalis et interna.* Many things are against natural and inward conscience which cannot be reformed by the regular and political administration of equity. For if equity be tied to no rule all other laws are dissolved and everything becomes arbitrary.
>
> (in Yale 1957: xliii)

This self-limiting conscience of the court is the law's positivity, its delimitation of its jurisdiction and its objects of administration. A quite narrow set of procedures permits a legal judgment to take place that is socially binding by virtue of the institutional finality a State accords to law. Outside the law's domain, other conducts of life will operate, not least in the religious sphere where conduct is shaped 'between a man and his confessor'. Such an ordering is appropriate to the slow emergence with the early modern administrative State of specialised technical and social spheres, each with its expert functions and relative autonomy. However, this self-limitation – a court of equity will not do everything that is fit to be done – should also be seen against the backdrop of those Christian enthusiasms that sought to impose confessional conscience across the whole of life.

Within the legal sphere, Lord Nottingham displayed an English chancellor's conventional caution at intruding into the business of the courts of law, despite his own learning in the common law. Increasingly methodised and thus separated from an exercise of private conscience, equity was coming to be a regular part of English law.[6] This institutional process takes on a further historical interest when we recall that English equity, unlike the common law to which many unnamed officers of law contributed, was the cumulative achievement of individual chancellors.[7] Lord Nottingham's view on this, set out in the biographical note he wrote for Burnet, the biographer of Sir Matthew Hale, was to reduce equity 'to certain rules and principles, that men might study it as a science, and not think the administration of it had anything arbitrary in it' (in Yale 1957: cxxi). Once in place, the 'conscience of the court' meant that mentions of 'conscience' referred to a strictly legal reality. Rather than confessional, the conscience of the court is better described as professional. It was a major cultural acquisition, alongside Nottingham's other initiatives: systematic reporting of Chancery cases[8] and 'giving his solutions in every case a technical justification' (Yale 1957: cxxxii).

The 'Age of Conscience' made times difficult for political and religious moderates. But against its pressures, Nottingham granted conscience as a relation of legal propriety sufficient independence from conscience as a relation of Christian piety to make it possible to adjudicate legally rather than confessionally. Anglican voices warning against 'the domineering of [religious] conscience' suggest this was no small achievement:

> 'Conscience!', exclaimed Nathaniel Bisbie in 1682. 'Oh it is a good and tender thing; but withal it is many times proud and haughty, wilful and erroneous, disorderly and very rebellious'. Henry Dove [1682] agreed: the modish plea on behalf of 'private conscience' neglects to ask if it is 'an erroneous conscience'. William Falkner [1679] wrote that, for their 'passions and disorderly affections', the Dissenters 'substitute the name of conscience'. Truth these days, Bishop Laney lectured the King, is measured only by fervency of persuasion. His sermon of 1665 is a tirade against the popular jargon of conscience. There are complaints of our 'domineering over conscience', but we rather have cause 'to complain at the domineering of the conscience', for there is 'a great reason to restrain the conscience [and] there is no reason to give it liberty' when it errs.
>
> (Goldie 1991: 356–7)

Some recognised the problem posed by a religious enthusiasm which makes 'private conscience' the yardstick for all forms of life.

A moderate Anglican, Nottingham withdrew into his legal practice during the Commonwealth years. With the Restoration, he returned to public life. As Solicitor-General, he conducted the prosecution of the regicides. As leader of the Anglican party in the Commons, he has been judged 'the outstanding Churchman' of the Convention (Yale 1957: xviii). As to his disposition towards Presbyterians and Quakers, there is evidence of moderation. Describing Nottingham's judicial ability 'always [to] distinguish between a man's belief and the merits of his case', Yale (1957: xxxv) notes his response in a 1682 case concerning the charitable gift of a lectureship: 'Mr Attorney . . . harped much upon it that this lecturer was a Presbyterian and as soon as he had done in the church would run into a conventicle; and upon his repeating this matter so very often, the Lord Chancellor told him that he was not to be led or harangued with prejudice into a cause. It was not before him in this cause whether the man was a Presbyterian or not: he minded the matter only, not the man.' Such language, Yale observes, 'is not that of a religious fanatic'. We are reminded of Hobbes's contrasting the 'citizen' responsive to public criteria of order with the 'man' responsive to private religious belief, these personae marking two different lines of social organisation, the governmental and the religious.

Nottingham's half-sister Anne, Lady Conway – she was married to Lord Conway – converted to the Quakers. This 'persecuted sect owed much to Lord Nottingham' (Yale 1957: xxxv). But there is more to Anne Conway than her becoming a Quaker.[9] Richard Popkin (1992: 116–17), the leading authority on the post-Reformation scepticism that emerged in the face of now undeniable religious divisions and moral differences, finds her 'possibly the sharpest metaphysician in England during this period'. She lived in the company of the Cambridge Platonists and with 'the mystic Franciscus Mercurius van Helmont' pursued Boehme. Popkin considers a 'masterpiece' her work on *The Principles of the Most Ancient and Modern Philosophy, Concerning God, Christ and the Creatures, viz. of spirit and matter in general, whereby may be resolved all those problems which neither by school nor common modern philosophy nor by the Cartesian, Hobbesian or Spinosian could be discussed.*[10] Leibniz took the term 'monad' from Conway's work and based his system of metaphysics on her account of the universe as a living being, entirely governed by one 'infinitely perfect Deity, who is also all Spirit'. This vitalistic project exemplifies a philosophical 'Third Force' which, along with British empiricism and Cartesian rationalism, responded to post-Reformation scepticism. An intellectual ensemble whose combination of religion and science we now have difficulty conceiving, the Third Force sought to harmonise 'elements of empirical and rationalist thought with theosophic speculations and Millenarian interpretation of Scripture' (Popkin 1992: 90–1). Anne Conway's teacher and the Third Force's 'greatest theorist', the Cambridge Platonist Henry More, proposed a 'form of immaterialism best expressed by his friends, Lady Anne Conway and Isaac Newton'. No simple line can be drawn between the Newton who theorised universal gravitation and the Newton who worked urgently with More on deciphering the predictions in the Books of *Daniel* and *Revelation*. Urgency was appropriate. It was, after all, the 'climax of world history' (Popkin 1992: 101). The events accompanying the end of historical time and the second coming of Christ were actually beginning to happen. Ultimate certainty of things spiritual and material was being claimed by 'all sorts of religious preachers and prophets who were sure they were right and were sure they were in direct contact with the Divine world' (Popkin 1992: 103).

It was in this cultural setting that Lord Nottingham delimited a juridical form of conscience that was not religious but 'civic and political'. Meanwhile, his brilliant sister became a Quaker with the mystic Dr van Helmont. With More defending the Threefold Cabala and Newton defending his own interpretation of the seven Trumpets in *Revelation*, Anne Conway 'developed metaphysical theories that showed how their religious views could be part of one rational system—how acceptance of the new science and a belief in scriptural prophecies could be reconciled in a spiritual conception of the world' (Popkin 1992: 118). Against this unifying metaphysical backdrop the separation of a conscience that was legal and procedural from a conscience that was religious merits our appreciation.[11]

The vision of a universe underpinned by perfect reason points towards the Enlightenment. Popkin (1992: 119) makes this observation concerning the Third Force, that 'amazing combination of Millenarian, mystical, rationalist, and scientific views, based on a firm conviction that a New Heaven and a New Earth would soon appear'. Perhaps by concentrating too exclusively on the Paris *philosophes*, we have wrongly come to think of the Enlightenment as the antithesis of religion. In keeping with his larger project to restore visibility to the fundamentally religious disposition of early modern philosophers, Popkin asks us to take the Third Force thinkers seriously. Koselleck too invites us to cease treating Enlightenment as an irreligious rationality. These revisions seek to bring to light a critical Enlightenment that has functioned as a relay, not a rebuttal, of the great process of confessionalisation. The separation of a legal conscience that was 'merely *civilis et politica*' from the conscience that was confessional, like the separation of civil order from moral redemption, was a historical exception not the Western cultural rule.

4

THE COMMON LAW'S CRITICS

In early modern England, not only future-oriented Puritan salvationists criticised the common law.[1] Scholar-professors of civil and canon law at Oxford and Cambridge looked down on the clientelism and narrow craft of the common-law professionals in the Inns of Court and the courts of law, claiming for their own learned law a logical coherence and a jurisprudential certainty that eluded the commoners.[2] Searching to disinter the elements of a critical tradition within English law, Peter Goodrich (1992, 1994) calls up lost memories of these civilians and canonists who castigated common law for its formalist excess, feigned antiquity, unreformed archaism, foreign language, and isolation from the continental traditions of historical, philological and philosophical scholarship. Citing Cowell's (1583) description of the common law as 'a dark and melancholy science', Goodrich (1992: 204) appeals to a 'revised intellectual history of common law which placed the Anglican tradition within a continental context' and which could ground the English law in a coherent philosophical reason or a systematic theory.

As exemplary civilian and common law critics of the common law, Goodrich cites Sir Robert Wiseman and Abraham Fraunce respectively. Wiseman's *The Law of Laws; or the Excellency of the Civil Law* attacked casuistical reasoning from particular precedents and dismissed the common law: 'it being made use of frequently by false shows and colours to beautify the foulest and most deformed things'. Abraham Fraunce, author of *The Lawier's Logicke, Exemplifying the Precepts of Logic by the Practice of the Common Law* (1588), 'joined the other critics in belabouring the whimsical and haphazard method of English law and in berating the pervasiveness of professional abuses: the lack of learning, the delays, the profiteering, the poor rhetoric and linguistic obscurity, the fantasy, of the petty-fogging *voces venales* of the legal marketplace' (Goodrich 1992: 215). By way of remedy Fraunce proposed a methodical legal education based on Ramist lines and with a scholarly and multidisciplinary character. His proposal made no mark. But Goodrich (1992: 219) finds an 'enduring significance' in Fraunce's failure, namely the 'exclusion from the English law institution of any institutional place or role for scholarly examination and criticism of common law'.[3] However, if Fraunce scorns the 'grand little mootmen, who cast case upon case, as carters do billets, and for every collateral trifle, run over all the six hundred and thirty titles of Brooke's abridgment' (in Goodrich 1990: 30), perhaps this is one cultural milieu and its persona – the university and the contemplative intellectual – deprecating another.[4]

Goodrich's project is to disinter a forgotten ('repressed') continuity between these early critics of the common law and the present program of critical legal studies. The historical picture is clouded somewhat by his psychoanalytic incorporation of canon law into the same 'repressed' but always resurgent memory as the civil law. No doubt this aims to suggest an even deeper 'repression of the spiritual jurisdictions and the exclusions or closure of law to those other knowledges which were inherent in its classical designation as being also a form of justice, an art which mixed spirituality and temporality, body and soul' (Goodrich 1994: 14). However, the dialectical notion that 'the space of authority within the common law tradition is one which rests upon the conjunction of the material and the spiritual' (Goodrich 1990: 65) bears little relation to the historical disengagement of sectarian religion from the sphere of civil life and secular jurisdiction. Nor does the repressive hypothesis take account of circumstances in which a State might appropriately assert a supra-sectarian civil order. The 'defence of the established Church against the foreign popularising creed of Protestantism' (Goodrich 1990: 71) is taken as self-evident repression, as the 'democratic' note confirms. There is no hint of reformed Christians as a 'new elite' of sometimes fanatical perfectionists for the new moral order of the 'repressive Holy Commonwealth', to borrow Michael Walzer's (1963–4) memorable term.

The civilian Doctors and the courts of spiritual justice are thus rebaptised as a 'tradition of resistance' that forms a 'radical though repressed tradition in English legal scholarship'. But, Goodrich continues, 'even if there were not [such a tradition] the task of critical legal scholarship should be precisely that not of discovering but rather of establishing – of inventing – such a tradition of resistance' (Goodrich 1992: 200–1). Historical fact is jettisoned in favour of the critic's normative invention (or wishful thinking). The same move is made in relation to Wiseman's attack on precedent: 'Although the argument is not explicitly presented in the early positivistic legal doctrines [of common law], law, conceived as the form of sociality, can only be understood as a deep structure of social life, the presupposition of the identity of the social' (Goodrich 1992: 210).

These are exemplary demonstrations of how today's critical intellectuals elevate themselves above the historical given to a 'repressed' moral high ground that needs 'inventing'. From these reflective heights they see through the empirical circumstances to a 'deep structure' taken as the determining 'conditions of possibility' of actual laws and social relations.[5] Does this critical manoeuvre perpetuate the practice of the Calvinist officer in the 'new elite' who stood above the law in order to judge it from the viewpoint of a divine spirit as yet unrealised in this fallen world? The suggestion is not frivolous. In anticipating the deconstructive force of a 'radical hermeneutics' that 'suspends, though it does not necessarily deny the prior judgments of law's *regula* or calculus', Goodrich contemplates a future that does not exist:

> [T]o the extent that critical legal studies is a transformative enterprise it precisely reconstructs a history of a collapsed symbolic order from the place of the imaginary and necessarily addresses an audience that cannot be constituted within the horizons of the present, that has not yet come into being.
>
> (Goodrich 1992: 212)

Like the self-questioning Puritan, addressing oneself to a humanity that does not yet exist is an intellectual exercise that transforms one's mode of being in the old imperfect world. The contemplative one, unsurprisingly, takes no heed of the mundane fact that litigants actually chose the courts of common law to resolve their disputes. What matters to the critical intellectual is the imaginary overturning of existing institutions and the phantasmic installation of a new moral, theoretical or political order. To give this imaginary order some gravity, a whole tradition of critical resistance is retrospectively invented:

> It will be my argument here that the positive science of English law that emerged by the mid-seventeenth century was indeed predicated upon the repression of critical studies of common law and that by examining the texts which doctrinal history covered over, critical legal studies may go a long way not only towards reviving a tradition of resistance or non-conformism within English law but may also claim an inheritance of critique, a tradition of repressed texts within the institution of common law.
>
> (Goodrich 1992: 206)

Because this continuity of critique is an 'invention', its historicity depends on an ahistorical psychoanalytic recourse to the '"positive unconscious" of legal science' (Goodrich 1992: 201).[6] Without debating the probative value of repressed memory, we easily recognise the advantage this recourse allows the critic: a repressed tradition is one that the emancipatory intellectual can claim to de-repress. Goodrich draws a repressed past forward to legitimate today's mode of normative critical legal study. Koselleck, by contrast, historicises present critical practice back into its religious past.[7]

Thomas Hobbes was a mid-seventeenth-century critic of the common law, but one no less able to deliver a stinging attack on the university establishment and the clergy. In considering Hobbes in the former role, however, a figure appears whose theorising of politics might itself be theological in approach:

> Hobbes is in fact no professional theologian, but as was customary at that time, theology is naturally inherent in his thought. If we see him in

connection with the history of the theology of his time, this becomes clear very quickly.

(Reventlow 1985: 203)

If he separated Church from State and religion from government in the manner Koselleck describes, Hobbes did not preclude the State from using the Church as an instrument of government. The point is rather that the Church be subordinated to the political ends and needs of the State, as these arose. In this way Hobbes could emphasise allegiance to the Church of England, a posture that aligns with his commitment to 'absolute royal supremacy over church and state' but sits less easily with his plan to 'demonstrate from an anthropological perspective the need for an absolutist government of human society' (Reventlow 1985: 204–5). Hobbes also asserted that 'the way back to original purity began with the Reformation in England: first with the dissolution of papal power under Elizabeth I, then with the overthrow of bishops by the Presbyterians and, most recently, by the Presbyterians' fall from power' (Reventlow 1985: 220). This catalogue of serially falling clergy belongs to Hobbes's polemic against the 'confederacy of deceivers, that to obtain dominion over men in this present world, endeavour by dark and erroneous doctrines, to extinguish in them the light, both of nature, and of the gospel' (*Leviathan* 4: 44). The particular instrument of these deceivers of superstitious men and women was the misappropriation of the Bible to 'prove that the kingdom of God, mentioned so often in the Scripture, is the present Church, or multitude of Christian men now living' (*Leviathan* 4: 44).

Because the attack on clerical deception and academic pretension looms so large in *Leviathan*, it is much better known than Hobbes's attack on common law and common lawyers in *A Dialogue between a Philosopher and a Student of the Common Laws of England*. This was Hobbes's sequel to St German's *Doctor and Student*, a sequel that was anything but a faithful amplification of the earlier writer's apology for English law.[8] A nice complementarity is thus envisaged by a recent commentator: 'If *Leviathan* was directed to commoners and intended for use in reformed universities, perhaps the *Dialogue* was written for lawyers who skipped university to study directly at the Inns of Court' (Stoner 1992: 116). No matter that the legal profession served also as an instrumentality of State reason, on commissions and in giving counsel to the monarch (Jay 1994), it became the target of Hobbes's attack on any guild-like body for its actual or potential challenge to State unity. Other targets were the regimental military and the nascent scientific community whose dangerous power of 'independent judgment' had been asserted by the Royal Society.

On internal and external evidence, Joseph Cropsey (Hobbes 1971: 2) dates the composition of the *Dialogue* between 1662 and 1675, that is, four years before Hobbes's death in 1679. The work's genesis might lie in his friend John Aubrey's attempt to have him write about law by giving Hobbes a copy of Bacon's *Elements of the Law*.[9] However, Aubrey 'desponded that he should make any attempt (tentamen) towards this designe. But afterwards, it seems, in the country, he writt his treatise 'De Legibus', (unprinted) of which Sir J. Vaughan, Ld Chief Justice of the Common Pleas, had a transcript, and I doe affirm that he much admired it'. It is unclear if this 'treatise' is the *Dialogue*. But Aubrey's comment confirms that a manuscript by Hobbes could circulate at the highest levels of the English legal profession.[10] Indeed, Matthew Hale would write a tract in response.

At the heart of Hobbes's *Dialogue* is the charge that the common law had detached itself from the rule of natural law embodied in the sovereign temporal power whose authority is one and absolute. To the extent that they constitute an independent site of power, the common law judiciary become a target. Given that legal independency threatened sovereignty, Hobbes expresses not the slightest praise of the common law, whether for its general attachment to the Anglican settlement of Church and State, or for its general detachment from Puritan millenarianism.[11] At most, when in the *Dialogue* the Philosopher raises the issue of obtaining 'Peace at home', the Lawyer responds that such peace may be:

> expected durable, when the common people shall be made to see the benefit they shall receive by their Obedience and Adhaesion to their own Soveraign, and the harm they must suffer by taking part with them, who by promises of Reformation, or change of Government, deceive them.
>
> (Hobbes 1971: 57)

Here the Lawyer distances himself from the religious and political promisers. But later, when he observes that 'there be many yet, that hold their former Principles, whom, neither the Calamities of the Civil Wars, nor their former Pardon have thoroughly cur'd of their Madness', the Philosopher's response grants no immunity to lawyers:

> The Common People never take notice of what they hear of this Nature, but when they are set on by such as they think Wise; that is, by some sorts of Preachers, or some that seem to be Learned in the Laws, and withal speak evil of the Governors.
>
> (Hobbes 1971: 65)

Hobbes did not deviate from his usual argument for the absolute necessity of undivided sovereignty. Overshadowing all other experiences for Hobbes was that of civil war emergency. The Philosopher leaves no doubt, in opening the discussion 'Of Crimes Capital', as to the fundamental importance of the famous maxim: *salus populi suprema lex* – the security of the people is the supreme law.

The fact that the *Dialogue* indicts the common lawyers for arrogating to themselves an authority that properly rests only with the sovereign explains why the persona of Sir Edward Coke becomes the villain of the piece. As mentioned, Cropsey conjectures that the *Dialogue* was born from Hobbes's reacquaintance with Bacon's *Elements of the Law*. Hobbes's controversy with the dead Coke was, it seems, a continuation of Bacon's struggle against the living one. Coke had asserted the autonomy of the common law judges from the king and from Chancery, which Bacon took to be the vehicle for the royal exercise of ultimate power. In Bacon's time, what brought these constitutional issues to the boil was Peachem's case and Coke's threat to use the writ of praemunire against the chancellor. If in the *Dialogue* Hobbes in fact takes up Bacon's burden, then he does it anachronistically at least to the following extent: the much less overheated chancellor at the time the work was composed was Lord Nottingham for whom 'all cases that are without remedy at common law are not relievable in equity: nor is the rule *nullus recedat a cancellaria sine remedio* so to be understood'.

In the *Dialogue*, a Philosopher and a Lawyer treat seven sets of questions under the following heads: the Law of Reason, Soveraign Power, Courts, Crimes Capital, Heresie, Praemunire and Punishments.[12] There will be no need here to consider each of these sections. Nor is this the place to debate Cropsey's reading of the *Dialogue* as marking a shift in Hobbes from a politics of command to a politics of assent in which sovereignty lies not with the monarch alone, but with the monarch in Parliament.[13] Instead, to meet the purposes of this essay and to anticipate Sir Matthew Hale's response to Hobbes, the following observations are organised around three points: the establishment of civil peace, the demarcation of public action and private belief, and the status of legal reason and equity.

It is impossible to miss the intention of the *Dialogue*: to counter civil war. That the *Dialogue* wants to be more than another piece of jurisprudential speculation is the message we take from references already mentioned to *salus populi suprema lex*, the 'Calamities of Civil Wars', and the means of obtaining 'Peace at home'. The interlocutors are led to this same conclusion. The Lawyer raises the issue of bringing a 'Humane Law' to bear on the pre-civil condition where 'all things would be common, and this Community a cause of Incroachment, Envy, Slaughter, and continual War of one upon another' (Hobbes 1971: 58–9). The Philosopher accepts this diagnosis but asks: 'how can any Laws secure one Man from another when the greatest part of Men are so unreasonable, and so partial to themselves as they are, and the Laws of themselves are but a dead Letter, which of it self is not able to compel a Man to do otherwise than himself pleaseth, nor punish, or hurt him when he hath done a mischief?' The Lawyer gives the Absolutist answer: 'By the Laws, I mean, Laws living and Armed . . . 'Tis not therefore the word of the Law, but the Power of a Man that has the strength of a Nation, that makes the Laws effectual'. Constitutional powers are thus discussed in the light of civil war. To this the Philosopher adds the emergency of foreign invasion:

> How shall I be defended from the domineering of Proud and Insolent Strangers that speak another Language, that scorn us, that seek to make

> us Slaves? Or how shall I avoid the Destruction that may arise from the cruelty of Factions in a Civil War, unless the King, to whom alone, you say, belongeth the right of Levying, disposing of the Militia, by which only it can be prevented, have ready Money, upon all Occasions, to Arm and pay as many Souldiers, as for the present defence, or the Peace of the People shall be necessary?
>
> (Hobbes 1971: 61)

If the 'reason' of the common law precludes this emergency action under an absolute royal prerogative, ''tis reason also that the People be Abandoned, or left at liberty to kill one another, even to the last Man; if it be not Reason, then you have granted it is not Law'.

As might be expected if the *Dialogue* was meant to reform the denizens of the Inns of Court in the relatively more pacific 1670s, Hobbes confronts the issue of post-war peace and pardons. The interlocutors settle that the pardoning agent is 'the King in Parliament' (although the Philosopher insists that only the king can pardon 'Offences against the Peace' since these are injuries done not to the king's private person but to the public order of the king's peace and therefore to his subjects in general). The stakes are raised when the Lawyer observes: 'You see, by this your own Argument, that the Act of *Oblivion*, without a Parliament could not have passed; because, not only the King, but also most of the Lords, and abundance of Common People had received Injuries; which not being pardonable, but by their own Assent, it was absolutely necessary that it should be done in Parliament, by the assent of the Lords and Commons' (Hobbes 1971: 77). This is one of the rare points granted by the Philosopher. Yet if Hobbes has his Philosopher and Lawyer disagree as to the nature of sovereign authority, the end is not in dispute: the restoration of peace after civil war. This remains the supreme imperative of the science of Absolutist politics.

The second point concerns the demarcation of private belief from public action. Any derogation from the one sovereign authority implied a potentially schismatic power. As a private guild, the common lawyers would always threaten to become a factional interest liable to usurp public authority by asserting their independence of the sovereign power. To the extent he has peace safeguarded by a sovereign whose 'private' interests are not in conflict with the public interests of the realm, Hobbes relies on the constitutional fiction of a king's 'two bodies' whereby a supra-individual royal persona endures in perpetuity outside the contentious regime of private property relations.[14] By contrast, 'the private reason of the churchmen and common lawyers . . . lives always in some mysterious body of the profession, residing among individuals but never in the full possession of a single one'. Having drawn this characterisation, Stoner (1992: 130) continues: 'What makes the clerical and the common law mentalities dangerous is that their adherents, because they find their forms of thought in company, mistake their own opinions for common knowledge.' Rather than follow Stoner into *Ideologiekritik* – 'the clerics and the lawyers pretend some common standard as they hide, even from themselves, the private interests that make them tick' – we can follow him back to Hobbes's argument against any derogation from sovereign authority by a private group or community laying claim to a public political function. The private 'Mystery' or craft is the lawyers' point of leverage on the public conduct of subjects. For Hobbes, the mediation of subjects by so private a corporation is a fault that endangers the public order on which peaceful existence depends.

'The private priests of (legal) reason must be checked as the private priests of revelation needed to be checked'. Cropsey (in Hobbes 1971: 26) thus glosses the parallel Hobbes draws between lawyers and clergy. At issue in both cases is a challenge to the indivisible authority of the sovereign. The clergy had worked upon the people's 'opinion of things beyond reason', persuading them that death was preferable to damnation. The lawyers had worked upon matters of 'life and property':

> [T]here have been two great classes of indoctrinators, both private but usurping a public function of indoctrination, not to say legislation. The clerical indoctrinators or legislators have introduced a great punitiveness into the legal system particularly in connection with the crime or non-crime of heresy. The legistic indoctrinators or legislators have also contributed very much to making the punishments in English practice irrationally vengeful.
>
> (Cropsey, in Hobbes 1971: 40)

The reference is to Hobbes's discussion of heresy as an error whereby a private religious belief was made a publicly justiciable action under the penal law. In Germany Christian Thomasius would advance a similar argument.

The third point concerns the status attributed to legal reason and equity. The first section of the *Dialogue*, entitled 'Of the Law of Reason', opens *in medias res* with the Lawyer's question (Hobbes 1971: 53): 'What makes you say, that the Study of the Law is less Rational, than the Study of Mathematics?' Responding, the Philosopher indicates that he has read the laws 'not to dispute, but to obey them, and saw in all of them sufficient reason for my obedience, and that same reason, though the Statutes themselves were chang'd, remained constant' (Hobbes 1971: 54). This obedient disposition is to be expected from a Hobbesian persona. That said, a set of Coke's ideas is then dismantled. The idea that 'the Common Law it self is nothing else but Reason' is confronted with the idea that reason is what every man 'of right sense' thinks. Hence 'upon this ground any Man, of any Law whatsoever may say it is against Reason, and thereupon make a pretence for his disobedience'. The Lawyer is asked to clarify. As authority, he cites Coke's doctrine:

> *La.* I clear it thus out of Sir *Edw. Coke.* I *Inst. Sect.* 138. that this is to be

> understood as an artificial perfection of Reason gotten by long Study, Observation and Experience, and not of every Mans natural Reason; for *Nemo nascitur Artifex.* This Legal Reason is *summa Ratio*; and therefore if all the Reason that is dispersed into so many several heads were united into one, yet could he not make such a Law as the Law of *England* is, because by so many successions of ages it hath been fined and refined by an infinite number of Grave and Learned Men.
>
> (Hobbes 1971: 54–5)

Unwittingly, the Lawyer has given the Philosopher an opening for the argument that the reason of the common law is private (with all the dangers that privacy comports in Hobbes's scheme of things):

> *Ph.* This does not clear the place, as being partly obscure, and partly untrue; that the Reason which is the Life of the Law, should be not Natural, but Artificial I cannot conceive. I understand well enough, that the knowledge of the Law is gotten by much study, as all other Sciences are, which are studyed and obtained, it is still done by Natural, not by Artificial Reason. I grant you that the knowledge of the Law is an Art, but not that Art of one Man, or of many how wise soever they be, or the work of one and more Artificers, how perfect soever it be, is Law. It is not Wisdom but Authority that makes a Law.
>
> (Hobbes 1971: 55)

In reaching this familiar maxim, the Philosopher has drawn the boundary between public and private such that for all its history, the common law can be dismissed as the instrument of a private guild.

Are the common lawyers obedient to the sovereign? The Philosopher says they are not. Indeed, the independent authority claimed for the 'legal reason' of the common law must be displaced by the sovereign reason of the king as ultimate source of English law. Brushing aside the Lawyer's move to link common law to statutes, the Philosopher asserts that all law is reason, as it must be if it flows from the authority of the king that is right reason. The Philosopher's aim is double. First, since reason is a universal and public capacity, he himself can 'pretend within a Month, or two to make my self able to perform the Office of a Judge'. To the Lawyer's objection that the Philosopher will prove 'but an ill Pleader', he retorts: 'A Pleader commonly thinks he ought to say all he can for the Benefit of his Client, and therefore has need of a faculty to wrest the sense of words from their true meaning; and the faculty of *Rhetorick* to seduce the Jury, and sometimes the Judge also, and many other Arts, which I neither have, nor intend to study' (Hobbes 1971: 56).

The Philosopher's second aim is to refute Coke's account of the historical genesis of the common law:

> And whereas [Coke] says, that a Man who should have as much Reason as is dispersed in so many several Heads, could not make such a Law as

> this Law of *England* is; if one should ask him who made the Law of *England*? Would he say a Succession of *English* Lawyers, or Judges made it, or rather a Succession of Kings; and that upon their own Reason, either solely, or with the Advice of the Lords and Commons in Parliament, without the Judges, or other Professors of the Law? You see therefore that the Kings Reason, be it more, or less, is that *Anima Legis*, that *Summa Lex*, whereof *Sir Edw. Coke* speaketh, and not the Reason, Learning, or Wisdom of the judges.
>
> (Hobbes 1971: 62)

This principle of legal reason's identity with the 'Kings Reason' being established, the Philosopher takes Coke to task for magnifying the 'Learning of the Lawyers' when in fact 'the Kings Reason, when it is publickly upon Advice, and Deliberation declar'd, is that *Anima Legis*, and that *Summa Ratio*, and that Equity which all agree to be the Law of Reason, is all that is, or ever was Law in *England*, since it became Christian, beside the Bible' (Hobbes 1971: 62).

Now we can appreciate the Philosopher's repeated proposition ('remember this that I may not need again to put you in mind'): 'Reason is the Common Law' (Hobbes 1971: 56). This proposition constitutes a normative condition for correcting the historical patchwork of common law precedents and statutes by referring them to natural reason, equity and the unity of sovereign power. When the Lawyer fails to elucidate the distinction 'between Law and Right, *Lex* and *Jus*', the Philosopher obliges: 'my Right is a Liberty left me by the Law to do any thing which the Law forbids me not, and to leave undone any thing which the Law commands me not' (Hobbes 1971: 73). Right is equated with the freedom of the private realm ('Private, is in secret free'). This is confirmed in Hobbes's (1971: 116–17) discussion of suicide as a felony at common law, a view that the Philosopher finds contrary to reason and to right, and of Chancery as the supreme tribunal. Here a law that is 'nothing else but Equity' can properly revise decisions in the 'courts of law'. After a lengthy excursus on the etymology of *Cancellarius*, the discretionary nature of Chancery procedure is noted, the Chancellor having received the Great Seal 'without any Instruction, or Limitation of the Process in his Court to be used'. Thus the Chancellor can proceed with or without jury and determine how witnesses will be heard 'as he shall think fittest for the Exactness, Expedition and Equity of the Decrees' (Hobbes 1971: 92). The guiding proposition remains the same: an undivided royal sovereignty requires 'a Higher Court of Equity, than the Courts of Common Law, to remedy the Errors in Judgment given by the Justices of Inferior Courts, and the Errors in Chancery were irrevocable, except by Parliament, or by special Commission appointed thereunto by the King' (Hobbes 1971: 94–5).[15]

For those of the Philosopher's mind, the standard of right is whatever the sovereign authority deems will protect the peace of the State and security of the citizens. However, such a proposition can itself become normative to the point of losing touch with historical reality. This is not to paint Hobbes as some vulgar overreacher. But as Reventlow (1985: 208) observes (in a different context): if on specific political issues he 'could be quite restrained', it remained the case that Hobbes 'felt himself above all to be a philosopher, in that he kept aloof from the struggles of his day and instead wanted to develop an objective system on a 'scientific' basis, which in his view would provide each individual sovereign with a criterion for assessing his decisions'. There is a pathos in holding to the status of an aloof philosopher of reason while admitting the evidence of humans' urge to war in times when conscience has rendered slaughter moral. There is a pathos too in the image of the philosopher of pure reason reflecting critically on positive laws from which he sets himself aside. Hobbes's contemporary, Sir Matthew Hale, made just this point in his 'Reflections on Mr. Hobbes his Dialogue of the Lawe'.[16] Reading the 'Reflections', we recall Koselleck's Hobbes, who 'did not know that reason has a gravitation of its own' and so quite failed to anticipate that moral reason could itself become a fundamentalism.

5

THE COMMON LAW'S DEFENDERS

The manuscript exchange between Hobbes and Sir Matthew Hale was between the author of 'the first comprehensive and reasoned criticism of [the common] laws' (Holdsworth 1945: 500) and the author of a *History of the Common Law* that is, 'the first book with any pretense to be a comprehensive account of the growth of English law' (Gray, in Hale 1971: xi).[1] Hobbes's interlocutor was a great practitioner of the common law, appointed to the Court of Common Pleas in 1654, subsequently holding office as Chief Baron of the Exchequer and Chief Justice of the Court of King's Bench. Hale was the interlocutor that Hobbes's Philosopher could have had if Hobbes had not made the exchange between his general science of politics and a historical justification of the common law so complete a victory for the former. The 'Reflections on Mr Hobbes his Dialogue of the Lawe' defend the common law as a definite but limited exercise of reason, inseparable from the usages which historically constituted that particular legal conduct. Hale's response also raises an important possibility: Hobbes was less the positive realist of Koselleck's thesis than a philosophical fundamentalist promulgating a normative order abstracted from circumstance.

Organised under two headings, 'Laws in Generall and the Law of Reason' and 'Soveraigne Power', Hale's 'Reflections' begin the defence by depicting the common law as a specific mode of practical reason, before moving to the issue of the institutional normality of the English legal system. He opens with gentle agreement, admitting that the reason implied by the 'Congruity, Connexion and fitt Dependence of one thing upon another' is or may be 'antecedent to any Exercise of any humane Reasonable facultie' (Hale, in Holdsworth 1945: 500–1). Causal powers and mathematical relations are admitted 'though they were noe man in the world to take note of itt'. Even in 'Moralls though the objects thereof are more obscure', Hale allows that there may be a certain order 'antecedent to any Artificiall Systeme of Moralls or Institution of Laws' (Hale, in Holdsworth 1945: 501). This 'humane Reason' is manifest in Judgement or 'ye attainement of thinges to be knowne' and in Wisdom, Prudence and Skill or 'thinges to be done'. Hale thus recognises 'reson [as] a Facultie common to all reasonable Creatures . . . the common Engine or Instrument whereby all kinds of Knowledges or Arts are acquired. It is ye Same Facultie of Reason that Serves the Naturalist, the Phisician, the Lawyer, the Mathematician, the Mechanique, ye Plowman in all their severall waies and prosecutions' (Hale, in Holdsworth 1945: 501). Hale seems on the point of agreement with Hobbes on a higher principle of natural reason.[2]

Then comes the 'But . . .'. For the remainder of the 'Reflections', the argument is discriminating. It is the fact of different 'kinds of Knowledges or Arts' and 'severall waies and prosecutions' that sets the rule. Just as we might displace the notion of 'mind' as a universal faculty by a set of quite disparate 'mental' techniques having little in common, so Hale stresses that a man skilled in mathematics might be hopeless in 'Knowledge of Phisique'. Thus, 'sometimes men that could not give a tollerable account of ten words of Sence yett [are] strangely dexterous in Mechaniques and Sometimes in Musick' (Hale, in Holdsworth 1945: 501). Where Hobbes treats particular practices as transparent to a reason that is universal, Hale sees particular conducts of life distinguished by their locally 'habituated use and Exercise' of reason. It is the habitual character of a given practice of reason that makes practitioners 'excellent in their particular Arts'.

Hale prefaces his defence of the English common law by rebutting the claim by Hobbes's Philosopher that, thanks to his natural reason, he could master the legal art in no time at all.[3] A glance at Galen and Hippocrates, says Hale, will not make the mathematician a good physician. Likewise, 'if a Man that pretends himselfe and really be well Exercised in Natural Philosophy Shall run over the titles or Indexes of ye digest, or Code, [he] shall be . . . a weake Civilian, though possibly there might be a paritie in ye perfection or Degree of their reasoning Facultie abstracted from its habituation to its object' (Hale, in Holdsworth 1945: 502). The point is that we never meet with reason in the abstract, only in this or that 'habituation'. The natural philosopher is therefore to be placed, eclectically, alongside musicians and ploughmen, smiths, surgeons and lawyers, his reason being one particular art alongside theirs. Hale is now ready to reverse Hobbes's dismissal of existing law as an inferior practice of reason:

> Of all Kind of Subjects where about ye reasoning Facultie is conversant, there is none of So greate a difficulty for the Faculty of reason to guide it Selfe and come to any Steddiness as that of Laws, for the regulation and Ordering of Civil Societies and for the measuring of right and wrong, when it comes to particulars. And therefore it is not possible for men to come to the Same Certainty, evidence and Demonstration touching them as may be expected in Mathematicall Sciences, and they that please themselves with a perswasion that they can with as much evidence and Congruitie make out an unerring Systeme of Lawes and Politiques equally applicable to all States and Occasions, as Euclide

> demonstrates his Conclusions, deceive themselves with Notions which prove ineffectual, when they come to particular application.
>
> (Hale, in Holdsworth 1945: 502)

Hobbes had supposed his 'system' mathematically 'unerring' and universally valid for 'all States and Occasions'. Hale responds that this will not do for the particulars.

The focus then turns to 'Moralls' and 'Lawes for a Communitie'. The particularity of circumstances is not something Hale seeks philosophically to transcend but the reality he accepts. There might be a general notion of 'Just and fitt' but, in practice, it is not useful, given 'the greate difference in most of the States and Kingdomes in ye world in their Laws administrations and measures of right and wrong, when they come to particulars' (Hale, in Holdsworth 1945: 502–3). There follows a joust at 'men that pretend to be ye greate masters of Reason' and who 'perchance have this happiness to Shake and weaken one the others Principles or Conclusions'. However, as Hale puts it, 'when they Sett up their own positions they are weak and generally displeasing'. The target is Hobbes's claim that anyone who has reason can be a judge. Fortuitously this may happen:

> [Y]ett for the most part those men that have greate reason and Learneing which they gather up of Casuists, Schoolmen, Morall Philosophers, and Treatises touching Moralls in the Theory, that So are in high Speculations and abstract Notions touching Justice and Right, and as they differ Extreamely among themselves when they come to particular applications, So are most Commonly the worst Judges that can be, because they are transported from the Ordinary Measures of right and wrong by their over fine Speculacons Theoryes and distinctions above the Common Staple of humane Conversations.
>
> (Hale, in Holdsworth 1945: 503).

To let just any individual of reason exercise the office of judge would introduce the maximum uncertainty into the law, pure reason being arbitrariness itself unless conforming to 'Some certaine Laws and rules and methods of administration of Common Justice, and these to be as particular and Certaine as could be well thought of'. Recognising this, the 'wiser sort of the world . . . in greate measure avoided that jangling and Contradiction that would happen uppon the unstable reason of Men when once they came to particular Decisions'.

Taking up the cause of law's technical reason and working within the limits of a 'certaine and determinate Law', the prudential Hale is proof against perfectionist claims. Thus, 'it is a thing of greatest difficulty, So to Contrive and Order any Lawe that while it remedyes or provides against one Inconvenience, it introduceth not a worse or an equall' (Hale, in Holdsworth 1945: 503). The broad predictability of an established system is better: 'The Inconvenience of an Arbitrary is intollerable, and therefore a certaine Lawe, though accompanied with some mischiefe, is preferrable before itt. But it is not possible for any humane thing to be wholly perfect' (Hale, in Holdsworth 1945: 504). The predictability of the law depends on particular capacities. In making or interpreting a law, prudential foresight is a skill to be exercised: the 'Expounder must looke further than the present Instance, and whether such an Exposition may not introduce a greater inconvenience than it remedyes'. Such a foresight is halting and piecemeal, quite unlike the Hobbesian temporality for which, as Hexter (1980: 486) writes, 'there are only two fixed conditions—states of being linked by a transforming instant': these are 'the state of nature in which men live in a state of war and constant dread of sudden death' and 'the instant of magic transformation, the instant of the covenant in which men surrender to a sovereign will all their natural right to do what they will'.[4]

As Hale describes it, common law reason offers no such magic instant. On the contrary, it is the slow and unplanned aggregate of many judgments: '[I]t is a reason for me to preferre a Law by which a Kingdome hath been happily governed four or five hundred years then to adventure the happiness and Peace of a Kingdome upon Some new Theory of my owne tho' I am better acquainted with the reasonableness of my owne theory then with that Law' (Hale, in Holdsworth 1945: 504). Not derived from or dependent on some universal theory, this particular legal reason is inseparable from the national history. As 'the Production of long and Iterated Experience', the common law is opaque to any sudden speculative understanding. There is no short cut to lawyerly competence via 'Theoryes'. The alternative to theoretical breakthrough is more arduous and less exciting: 'it appeares that men are not borne Common Lawyers, neither can the bare Exerciss of the Faculty of Reason give a man a Sufficient Knowledge of it, but it must be gained by the habituateing and accustoming and Exerciseing that Faculty by readeing, Study and observation to give Man a compleate Knowledge thereof'. Even then, such a man 'cannot p'tend either to Infallibilitie in his Judgement or to a full attainment of all that is attaineable toucheing the Laws of England'. However, in being dependent on the mastery of certain arts and disciplines, competence in law is no different from competence in other fields of reason. It would be 'ridiculous' to expect someone who 'hath spent a Month in readeing Some of the Rudiments of Geometrie Should be as good a Master in the Mathematicks as he that hath made it the Study of his life'.

Hale can thus respond to Hobbes that the limits to the practice of English legal reason are no disadvantage, given the particular purpose of that reason:

> Such persons therefore that have had their Education in the Study of the English Laws have these Considerable advantages to render them fitter Judges and Interpreters of the Lawes of this Kingdome then any other whose Studyes and Education have intirely or Principally applyed to the Study of Philosophy or Mathematiques or other Studyes.
>
> (Hale, in Holdsworth 1945: 505-6)

As to the predictable philosophical retort that without a ground in principle or foundation in theory law will be incapable of coherent judgment, Hale explains that a professional practice made uniform by 'much reading, observation and study' provides the requisite consistency: '[T]his Conservation of Laws within their boundes and Limitts could never be, unless men be well informed by Studyes and readeing what were the Judgements and Resolutions, and Decisions and Interpretations of former ages, and of other Courts and Tribunalls, and therebye to keepe a Consonance and Consistence of the Law to it Selfe, which wold never be done without much readeing, and observation and Study' (Hale, in Holdsworth 1945: 506). By calling attention to the regularising effects of habitual practices that keep administration of the laws 'within their boundes and limitts', Hale rebuts the philosophical assumption that any empirical order must depend on a general theory or 'speculation'.

A brief anticipation of Hale's *History of the Common Law of England* helps reinforce the point. In the twelfth chapter, 'Touching trials by jury', he notes the role of such diverse factors as geographical organisation, cost control, administrative functions and professional routines in achieving a coherent system of law: '[T]he Preparation of the Causes in Point of pleading to Issue, and the Judgment, is for the most Part in the Courts at Westminster, whereby there is kept a great Order and Uniformity of Proceedings in the whole Kingdom, to prevent the Multiplicity of Laws and Forms' (Hale 1971: 161). The coherence of judicial rationality is addressed at the same level as the administrative arrangements that hold the English legal system together. Insofar as the system 'prevents Factions and Part-takings, so it keeps both the Rule and the Administration of the Laws of the Kingdom uniform':

> [F]or those Men are employed as Justices, who as they have had a Common education in the Study of the Law, so they daily in Term-time converse and consult with one another; acquaint one another with their Judgments, sit near one another in Westminster-Hall, whereby their Judgments and Decisions are necessarily communicated to one another, either immediately or by Relations of others, and by this Means their Judgments and their Administrations of Common Justice carry a Consonancy, Congruity and Uniformity one to another, whereby both the Laws and the Administrations thereof are preserved from that Confusion and Disparity that would unavoidably ensue, if the Administration was by several incommunicating Hands, or by provincial Establishments.
>
> (Hale 1971: 162)

So much for today's anachronistic critiques of the intellectual 'closure' of the early modern common law that overlook the institutional uniformities required for uniformity of judgment, including the critics' own. Such critiques proceed as if today's well-ordered circumstances also obtained in seventeenth-century England. Hale knew his times better. The problem was not some 'excess' of intellectual closure, but the struggle to achieve reliability of legal decision in support of a better civil order.[5] That the English legal system's means were practical and local, procedural and sociable, no doubt disqualifies them in the eyes of intellectuals fixed on recognising truth as the only unifier of a legal field. But then we should reiterate Milsom's (1981: 91) observation that, in the post-Reformation world, 'it was never again possible to believe whole-heartedly in the existence of a right answer to every dispute'.

Hobbes, too, knew his times. But neither in *Leviathan* nor in the *Dialogue between a Philosopher and a Student of the Common Laws of England* does he show the same historical interest as Hale in practical training, uniform administrative practices, or the importance of geography as conditions material to civil order. Rather he appeals to a conceptual presupposition of civil order: indivisible sovereignty as the single principle or truth to which he is absolutely committed.

The 'Reflections' suggest a Hobbes who was no pragmatist. Hale's view is stark: 'Such a Man that teacheth Such a doctrine as this as much weakens the Soveraigne Power as is imaginable and betrayes it with a Kisse.' Hale, like Hobbes, set civil order as the end of law and government, but the means to that end was England's balanced constitutional government. For Hale this becomes a 'Golden Knott'. Conversely, it was a knot that 'as by miserable Experience we have learned' can well be cut by political prescriptions such as Hobbes's, namely '[t]hat there is noe Law Soe Strictly and prudently Penned for the Secureing of his subjects Liberties and Properties, but they intrinsically have this Condicion implyed, tho' not Expressed. That when [the Sovereign] Judgeth itt fitt he may Suspend or abrogate them' (Hale, in Holdsworth 1945: 511). No doubt Hobbes's bad reputation contributed to Hale's assessment of these 'wild Propositions' as '[d]estructive to the Common good and safety of the Government'. Be that as it may, Hale's historical account of what English sovereignty actually was – the array of attributes that attach to the historical office of the English king and now define a royal prerogative bound by certain 'Qualifications' – is quite different from Hobbes's normative account of what all sovereignty ought to be.

Like government, law, too, needs protection from 'certaine Speculators that take upon them to Correct all the Governments in the World and to govern them by Certaine Notions and Fancies of their owne, and are transported with soe great Confidence and opinion of them that they thinke all States and Kingdomes and Governments must presently be Conforme to them' (Hale, in Holdsworth 1945: 509). Specifically, Hale confronts the philosopher's assertion that a prince who has to bargain with a parliament cannot guarantee 'Common safety':[6]

> I answer . . . that as Lawes So the Method and Modelling of Governments are to be fitted to what is the Common and Ordinary

> State of thinges ad Plurimum, because mankind have most Ordinarily to doe with Such Circumstances of affaires as most usually happen.
>
> (Hale, in Holdsworth 1945: 512)

This is a major turning point. Hobbes's prescription might suit the state of emergency and exception occasioned by foreign invasion or civil war, a state generalised in his moral anthropology as the condition of a humanity untransformed by obedience. Yet the emergency prescription will not do for 'the Common and Ordinary State of thinges':

> And it is a Madness to thinke that the Modell of Lawes or Government is to be framed according to Such Circumstances as very rarely occurre. Tis as if a Man should make Agarike and Rhubarb his Ordinary Dyett, because it is of use when he is Sicke which may be once in 7 yeares.
>
> (Hale, in Holdsworth 1945: 512)

By viewing everything in terms of emergency conditions, Hobbes risks disrupting the hard-won normality and order of ordinary life in the abstract name of a political theory and the unbounded generality of a moral anthropology.

Viewing existence from the perspective of emergency and exception teaches a sharp lesson: what, asks Hobbes, is the sovereign authority whose action brings law, government and morality into being in the first place and on which they thus ultimately rest? Hale, however, responds historically, asking whether such speculation is 'but an imaginary feare as appeares by Experience. For this Kingdome hath been now these 500 yeares govern'd by Laws made by a Parliamentary advise and noe time yett afford us an Instance wherein a Parliament might not be timely Enough called for such a Supply' (Hale, in Holdsworth 1945: 512). For Hale, committed to the historical balance of institutions in the English State, the emergency model fails to address normality, the secular year to year fact of English legal administration.

This raises the issue of Hobbes as 'positivist'. We read that 'Hale's short treatise is the most brilliant contemporary reply to Hobbes's theory of positive law' (Mintz 1962: 49). The characterisation of Hobbes as positivist is the usual view:

> Hobbes was the pure positivist. For Hobbes 'a Law is the Command of him, or them that have the Soveraign Power, given to those that be his or their Subjects, declaring Publickly and plainly what every of them may do and what they must forbear to do'.
>
> (Yale 1972: 123–4)

But two different Hobbeses have now appeared: a 'positivist' Hobbes for whom law derives from the enacted command of the absolute sovereign and, thanks to Hale, a Hobbes who was no positivist in the sense of one who works within the terms of the existing laws and institutions. This second

Hobbes had a capacity for philosophical abstraction from the 'ordinary measures' of legal living that made him less the positivist than the natural philosopher.

Norberto Bobbio (1993) explores this apparent contradiction in terms of the distinction – usual within the discipline of political science – between natural law and legal positivism:

> Thomas Hobbes belongs, de facto, to the history of the natural law tradition. There is no text on the history of legal and political thought which does not mention and analyse his philosophy, as one of the typical expressions of natural law theory. On the other hand, Hobbes belongs, de jure, to the history of legal positivism. His conception of the law and the state is indeed a surprising anticipation of nineteenth-century positivist theories.
>
> (Bobbio 1993: 114)

How is it possible, asks Bobbio, that Hobbes should be classed with Grotius, Spinoza and Pufendorf as 'one of the four great natural law theorists of the seventeenth century' and at the same time be the 'historical model' for legal positivists, the 'fervent adversaries of natural law theory'? Responding, he suggests that 'the Hobbesian paradox is genuine' (Bobbio 1993: 115). In other words, 'Hobbes does belong to the natural law tradition, and he does initiate the school of legal positivism.' The same question arises in relation to the State. Following a 'systematic hunting down of everything that can constitute a constraint or limit to the power of the state', Hobbes seems to reach the point at which he has 'eliminated all sources of norms (especially the common law) other than the law, that is, the will of the sovereign; and all legal orders other than that of the state (in particular those of the Church, of the international community, and of minor associations)'. But then we find a Hobbes who 'placed his state on the traditional pedestal of natural law' (Bobbio 1993: 117).[7]

Bobbio's solution to 'this fundamental antinomy of Hobbes's thought' is dialectical and rhetorical: Hobbes recognises natural law as the 'dictate of right reason' but grants reason a formal value only. By correlating natural law with the pursuit of a particular end rather than with actions independently good in themselves, and by stipulating that end as peace, Hobbes 'could reach a positivistic conclusion, even though he started from a premise derived from natural law theory' (Bobbio 1993: 121). Similar moves are made with regard to the relation between sovereign and sovereign, and between sovereign and subject. The sovereign is said to be bound by the law of nature. However, the law of nature is ineffective between sovereigns in the absence of an overarching power. As to sovereign and subject, the latter is accorded the right to resist an order of the sovereign that is contrary to the law of nature. But before partisans of natural law claim victory, Hobbes confronts them with the fact that subjects have waived their rights in granting absolute power to the sovereign.

Why does Hobbes go through this move so constantly? Bobbio allows a slight historical colour to the explanation. As a seventeenth-century rationalist, Hobbes was so 'concerned with the presuppositions of his inquiry' that he 'constructed a rational system of natural laws which could provide a ground for a positive legal order' (Bobbio 1993: 144). While accepting this need to demonstrate axiomatic grounds in the laws of nature, he conceded to them 'as little as a rationalist could'. This, says Bobbio, was not the position of an 'authentic natural law theorist'. For such a theorist more is at stake than locating a rationale for obeying positive law. It is the whole question of 'whether there exists another law side by side with positive law, that is equal, if not superior to the latter, and to which the citizen, the judge or another authority can appeal if positive law contradicts it' (Bobbio 1993: 144). Hobbes refuses the very notion of two levels of law. Instead, Bobbio argues, 'for Hobbes the law of nature is not itself a legal norm, but only a logical argument. The law of nature does not shape conduct, but demonstrates rationally the reasons why we must behave in one way or another'. Once again, while granting it a role as the ground of positive law, Hobbes achieves 'the dissolution of the law of nature in the classical sense of the term, that is, as a system of valid norms'. Thus 'no decisive argument against Hobbes's legal positivism ensues from the thesis that the fundamental norms of his system are laws of nature' (Bobbio 1993: 145).

There is an alternative assessment in the 'Notes on the controversy between Hobbes and the English jurists' by a German political historian, Martin Kriele, published in a collection co-edited by Koselleck. Hobbes, he argues, was the 'advocate of natural law, the English jurists were the legal positivists, not the other way round' (Kriele 1969: 215). This proposition emerges as the answer to his own initial question: 'Did Hobbes's political theory meet the political realities?' (Kriele 1969: 211). The question requires us to consider whether what we see in Hobbes is an intransigent theorist detached from local circumstance and particular fact. For Kriele, Hobbes conceived the authority which made law to be 'the sovereign power of his own conception', not the actual authority recognised by English law. And there was another breach with the facts: 'Hobbes did not see the danger of civil war in the given historical situation. Rather in abstract and theoretical terms he feared another *hypothetical civil war*, which English absolutism was meant to prevent' (Kriele 1969: 217–18). Kriele (1969: 216) prefaces these observations with his view that 'the principal controversy which had brought about civil war, and which was its *conditio sine qua non*, in terms of its actual historical development, was, namely, the *validity of constitutional law* or the ousting of constitutional law by the radical theoretical revolution of absolutist doctrine'.

Nor is that all. A further deviation from circumstance is signalled: 'Hobbes's theory of civil peace brought about by absolutist sovereignty was not gained from the analysis of the actual historical situation in England in the 17th century. Rather Hobbes had taken over and systematically expanded a theory which had been in circulation for some time; namely, the theory of the French *Politiques* of the 16th century' (Kriele 1969: 218). To import this theory from one political context to another was to be blind to the possibility that '*[i]n 17th century England* the doctrine had a quite different function from that which it had in *16th century France*':

> In France it was the answer to a civil war, which was actually raging, in England the doctrine preceded the war. In France it served to end the war by ascribing to the monarch the powers which enabled him to bring about religious *tolerance.* In England at the time of Charles I and Laud, according to the state of things, it was a vehicle for the tendency towards religious *conformity,* and because of this it could do nothing but arouse the embittered opposition of all dissenters and therefore the danger of a religious civil war.
>
> (Kriele 1969: 218)

In a seventeenth-century England whose political circumstances benefited from reduced regional and confessional conflict, the French theory of Absolutist sovereignty could generate the very disorder it was supposed to moderate. In other circumstances, imposed religious conformity might bring interconfessional warfare to an end:

> On the one hand [the Sovereign] can force the parties into living together in tolerance, or on the other hand he can align himself with one of the parties, subjugate the other party and if necessary liquidate it: then too the war is at an end. The French doctrine was a game of chance. The aim was that the absolutist monarch should pursue a policy of *tolerance,* but the risk was that he might adopt a policy of *subjugation.*
>
> (Kriele 1969: 219)

From the Edict of Nantes to its repeal by Louis XIV, French policy had shifted from tolerance to imposed conformity. With this repeal and the terror that followed, as Kriele puts it, 'the danger was revealed, which one had to resign oneself to in the desperate situation of civil war, in order to stand a chance of gaining peace'. His view of English royal policy is harsher still: in England 'the policy of subjugation was a definite intention, even if it resulted in the outbreak of civil war'.

As a theorist, Hobbes 'feared a civil war, but he was so strongly convinced that absolutism could prevent it, that he was prepared to tolerate a civil war for the sake of Absolutism'. In particular, 'Hobbes *did not foresee* what insistence on confessional conformity would mean in practice'. True, he 'recognised religious freedom of conscience and commended it to those in power' (Kriele 1969: 219), but without appreciating two overriding circumstances. First, freedom of conscience did not necessarily entail the freedom of confession that alone, for the *Politiques,* brought civil peace. As Kriele (1969: 220) observes: 'Even Cromwell and later Louis XIV respected conscience. Its freedom was expressly provided for even in the Edict of Fontainebleau (1685) which abolished confessional tolerance in France and which gave rise to all kinds of confessional terror'. Second, freedom of confession depended on 'legal assurance', not on the 'fortuitous morality and enlightenment of the ruler'. To recognise that in a given political circumstance a theory for peace could be the *causa belli* gives pause to the assumption that the best of theories can be adequate no matter where or when.[8] Hobbes did not pause. In the name of eternal peace, he denounced the legal administrators of the existing order. Kriele goes so far as to suggest that the theorist of peace, no less disdainful of the existing legal institutions than he was of the existing populace, was in reality one party to the conflict:

> If the supposition of the English jurists, that the Absolutists formed one *Civil War Party* (moreover the party which was causing the war), is right, then Hobbes's theory – whether he liked it or not – was in effect a party philosophy. The assumption that Absolutism could bring about peace, had the result that adherents of the Absolutist Party became fanatical and uncompromising and that the conduct of the war became radicalised. For this result is quite unavoidable whenever a party engaged in a war calls itself the 'peace party' and declares that it is only waging war for the sake of peace (Carl Schmitt).
>
> (Kriele 1969: 217)

If Kriele's contention is accepted, then Hobbes's theory exacerbated conflict.

As to the *Dialogue*, in his penultimate note Kriele proposes that, in the writings after 1651, Hobbes's aim, along with having Charles II renew his 'efforts towards Absolutism', was to ensure that '[t]he English should have a guilty conscience for not accepting his political philosophy already in 1640, and for not rejecting the common law and the conventions of constitutional law' (Kriele 1969: 222). This proposition nicely formulates the ethical notion that critical theory might work by producing guilt.

More specifically, Kriele (1969: 217) argues that in comparison with Hobbes's prescription, 'the theory of the English Jurists is not merely a party philosophy identical with that of the opposing side, but rather a "*third party*", comparable to the "*Politiques*" during the 16th century Religious Wars in France'. An important consequence follows: Hobbes, whose moral anthropology of brutish man was scandalously bleak, was '[i]n the eyes of the English Jurists . . . not *too* pessimistic but in fact not pessimistic enough and therefore not a realist'. Kriele explains how this could be by contrasting two Hobbesian themes: his blame of those who had not adopted his theory, the common lawyers central among them, as 'corrupt' and 'stupid', and his effusive praise, in the *Dialogue*, of 'the good King Charles'. As a result, Hobbes 'underestimated the dangers which a ruler and his counsellors can bring through their narrow-mindedness and fanaticism and their withholding information, etc.'

Kriele's picture of a Hobbes detached from the political realities is not idiosyncratic. Addressing the topic 'Thomas Hobbes and the law', Jack Hexter focuses on Hobbes's *Dialogue* and Hale's 'Reflections'. Aside from his doubt on the former's quality, Hexter's two conclusions merit attention.[9] The first concerns English political experience: 'If the common lawyers presented so serious a threat to the theoretical structure [of the moral and political science] that Hobbes treasured, why was he so long in confronting the threat?' (Hexter 1980: 488). By way of answer, Hexter offers an informed conjecture. Having seen off the common lawyers in chapter 26 of *Leviathan*, something must have encouraged Hobbes, at the age of seventy-five or more, to resume the attack. Through the 1640s and 1650s, civil war and Commonwealth oppression exposed the people of England to a terrible experience:

> [T]hey had dinned in their ears justifications of rebellion grounded on the claim that some law of God or nature stood over the sovereign and made disobedience to his claims legitimate . . . Well might Thomas Hobbes have believed in 1661 that his fellow countrymen had learned their lesson: that, weary of the incitement to rebellion of self-proclaimed men of religion, weary of the rebellious marching of self-proclaimed armies of saints, they would be ready to submit completely to the will of their undisputed sovereign, Charles II, by grace of God, King of England.
>
> (Hexter 1980: 488)

Given this circumstance, Hobbes might have believed his theory's time had come. But by the time the *Dialogue* was written, quite another political disposition was emerging that 'inseparably linked the common law through the rule of law, reason of law, and due process to the notion of due inheritance'. Given this sense of the common law as the safeguard of their liberties and property, '[t]here was no way that any large number of Englishmen would accept the view that the common law was nothing but the command of the sovereign, existing only by his will or sufferance' (Hexter 1980: 489).[10] Theories that would transcend circumstance have, it seems, their own circumstantial conditions.

Hexter's second conclusion brings the relation of philosopher and lawyer-historian to centre stage. For Hobbes, knowledge of human society is 'mathematical in aspiration if not in form', such that humans, 'reduced from their apparent intricacy to the essential simplicity of their true nature, their passions and their reason, are calculable atoms, the consequences of whose movements in a determined universe can be computed with something close to the certainty that Galileo achieved in computing the rate of movement of bodies in free fall'. Hobbes's application of mathematics to human society is striking in its originality:

> Hobbes may have been the first powerful mind in the history of thought to have been seized by the dazzling vision of a unified science capable of

> dealing mathematically with the physical world and man, and of achieving the same certainty, or nearly so, about the latter as about the former.
>
> (Hexter 1980: 483)

By contrast with this visionary theorist, Hale was:

> [The] proponent of a primarily historical mode of knowing about man . . . [and] may have been the first to espouse consciously an historical mode of knowing *over against* a mode that was consciously rooted in the new natural sciences and that used them as its universal model in method. Indeed Hale could have had few predecessors, since Hobbes was the first to universalise the scientific mode, and most of Hobbes' early opponents were too busy being shocked by his conclusions to pay much heed to his method.
>
> (Hexter 1980: 484)

For Hexter the stakes of the interaction between Hale and Hobbes are thus very high.[11] At issue are all 'ways of knowing *modo historico*' which do not 'let themselves be pushed into defining their claims within the boundaries set by the rhetoric of the natural sciences'. In Hale's historical account, the exercise of judicial reason in the common law depended on 'long study of particulars and of their multiple relations to other particulars', an 'erudite experienced alertness' and a professionally trained capacity to enter 'the minds of men of other times and climes, a necessity if one would discern their meanings, aims and intentions' (Hexter 1980: 485).

To support his account of Hale as a historian resisting the empire of rationalist philosophy, Hexter could have called on Pocock who had already recognised Hale's defence of the common law as historical reason against Hobbes's politics as science. Pocock (1957: 173) envisaged an English constitutional history in which a key agency was 'the myriad minds who, not knowing the importance of what they do, have, each by responding to the circumstances in which he finds himself, contributed to build up a law which is the sum total of society's response to the vicissitudes of its history and will be insensibly modified tomorrow by fresh responses to fresh circumstances'. Hale is characterised as the bearer of a 'lawyer's knowledge'. That is, in 'knowing the judgments and statutes of the past, he knows what ills they were designed to remedy and what the state of the law was which they remedied'. Given this openness to historical fact and change, Hale 'comes to see a greater part – never, perhaps, the whole – of the accumulated wisdom with which the refining generations have loaded it'.[12]

Hexter's (1980: 486) doubt about a Hobbesian critique disinterested in 'such prudence as the experience of daily life or studious investigation of man's past doings is said to impart' has found an echo in Anthony Kronman. As we saw at the outset of this essay, for Kronman what has all but annihilated prudential wisdom is the American Legal Realists' program for a scientific knowledge of law. This program is exemplified in Dean Langdell's search at Harvard for a 'geometry' of law grounded in a tradition of antiprudential thought running back to Hobbes. Again this is Hobbes the geometer, 'who more than anyone else may be credited with the invention of the tradition to which Austin, Bentham, and Langdell all belonged' (Kronman 1993: 175). Kronman's account of that 'curious essay', the *Dialogue between a Philosopher and a Student of the Common Laws of England*, sides with the Lawyer. In particular, he approves the latter's defence of the common lawyers' capacity to adjudicate 'by virtue of their "artificial reason", a craft mode of understanding that only those who have been professionally trained in the study of law possess' (Kronman 1993: 177). To understand the common law concepts slowly pieced together from the mass of case law, one needs to know 'what the precedents actually say, and this one can discover only by looking at the law as opposed to thinking about it' (Kronman 1993: 178).

Even if he did not share Hobbes's profound antipathy to the common law, Langdell was a Hobbesian geometer, seeking to turn common law into a teachable axiology by presenting it as grounded in 'a latent geometry of its own' (Kronman 1993: 182). The figure of latency gives the game away. It posits a crucial gap through which the theorist slips in, claiming to see the hidden structure or underlying rules that the pre-theoretical practitioner does not even know to look for. Yet the geometers are housed in a particular milieu. In describing how Langdell fashioned his geometry of law, Kronman (1993: 173) points to the special role accorded to intellectuals in the university milieu. This underscores Langdell's concern with a particular division of labour whereby the development of law as science 'should be viewed as being peculiarly within the province of university intellectuals rather than that of seasoned practitioners':

> [T]he greatest influence on Langdell's thinking [was] his desire to show the superiority of a university-based system of legal education to the old regime of apprenticeship training that had dominated the common law from its beginning. To show this, Langdell had to establish that university professors were better teachers of the law than their counterparts in practice. If one views the law as a scheme of axioms and analytic entailments, however, this conclusion follows naturally. For it is the academic lawyer, who has time to think and can proceed methodically, who is best equipped to master such a scheme – better equipped, in any case, than the practising lawyer who must rush breathlessly from one client to the next.
>
> (Kronman 1993: 184)

Building abstract systems – geometrical or moral – is recognisably a practice of university intellectuals, including some engaged in the presently prestigious practice of critique of law and government.

6

RELIGION, LAW AND CIVIL MANNERS

Alongside yet separate from the professional jurist was the pious Christian and, alongside yet separate from these, the gentleman. This is not at all how its author opens a recent intellectual biography of Sir Matthew Hale. On the contrary, Alan Cromartie (1995: 7) asserts that among 'Hale's great virtues was ignorance of the boundaries segmenting our own, more timid, mental lives'. A division of life into separate spheres has become the symptom of a flawed cultural history. Perhaps this is a mere rhetorical flourish. Yet Cromartie (1995: 232) concludes by observing that it is 'hard to read Hale's works without being struck by the seamlessness of his intellectual world'.

It is hard to approach early modern figures such as Hale without imposing a retrospective biographical unity on the separate personae through which they lived their often difficult lives. Hale's real achievement lay in a capacity to separate his religious convictions from his legal work, just as he published devotional and homiletic writings but not his works on law. This is not to question his profound Christian faith but to recognise that his religion was not for all his purposes. Seen in this pluralist light, Hale's virtue was not his 'ignorance' of our modern boundaries but his capacity to demarcate the religious and the legal spheres of life. In this way, the procedures of the law might be stabilised and lawyers safeguarded from religious enthusiasms that would otherwise have seen the secular law used for confessional ends.

To identify this limit is not to doubt Hale's piety. If not leading the 'revolution of the saints' (Walzer 1966), he was nonetheless a 'psychological Puritan'.[1] A more fervent Puritanism could easily sustain fanatical posturings: 'The dream that the saints could subdue the world and reshape nature was the excess and perversion of Puritanism. In more or less controlled forms, that disease had troubled Hale's times'. Hale's was the other side of Puritan piety, coloured by the doctrine of humanity's limited capacities and the 'awareness that only so much is possible within the structures provided by a working Christian's place and opportunity; that nature is only impressible, never transformable by grace' (Gray, in Hale 1971: xvi). Hence the need for coercive laws to regulate the public conduct of religion.

Even from this moderate perspective, Hale found such coercion essential, given circumstances in which 'the concerns of religion and the civil state are so twisted one with another that confusion and disorder and anarchy in the former must of necessity introduce confusion and dissolution of the latter'. At stake was civil peace: 'he that today pretends an inspiration or a divine impulse to disturb a minister in his sermon tomorrow may pretend another inspiration to take away his goods or his life' (in Cromartie 1995: 177). Piety was to be an inward matter, pursued via the private disciplines of conscience. On Sundays Hale set time aside for meditation. To fix his thoughts, he wrote down his reflections (Heward 1972: 126).[2] His *Contemplations Moral and Divine*, printed in 1676 without authorisation, praise the good derived from facing mortality and rendering to God a moral account of one's use of talent, time and money. Speculating that Hale wrote 'as a pious Christian, impelled, perhaps reluctantly, to share his meditations as a reasonable service to God', Gray (in Hale 1971: xxx) underscores an avoidance of extremes: 'Outside the law, Hale's associations were with men who in their sphere occupied the same "extreme center" that he held in jurisprudence. He was close to a number of churchmen who, in different ways, held out against religious narrowness.'

This 'extreme centrist' disposition was pertinent to Hale's rejection of Laudian fundamentalism (although in 1648 he had advised the impeached Laud) and Clarendon Code conformity. However, Hale was not unusual in regarding offences against Christianity as offences against the law of England. Hence his 1676 opinion (*Ventris* 1: 293):

> [S]uch Kind of wicked blasphemous words were not only an Offence to God and Religion, but a Crime against the Laws, State and Government, and therefore punishable in this Court. For us to say, Religion is a Cheat, is to dissolve all those Obligations whereby Civil Societies are preserved, and that Christianity is Parcel of the Laws of England; and therefore to reproach the Christian Religion is to speak in Subversion of the Law.
>
> (in Clark 1994: 179)

As Clark points out, this was Coke's opinion too. But when Coke aligned the common law and Christianity, it was in order to curtail a royal intervention into the lawyers' preserve. In fact Hale shared his predecessor's understanding of church jurisdiction as having legal force only insofar as ecclesiastical laws had been 'received' into the laws of England:

> Touching the power of making canons or constitutions ecclesiastical, observe: (a) That they could not make any canon or constitution contrary to the laws of this land . . . (b) They could not make any constitution to bind concerning any lay act or interest or anything that had a mixture therewith. Those constitutions did not nor could not bind till received and by usage incorporated into the laws and customs of the kingdom.
>
> (Hale 1976: 143)

Then Hale refers to 'ecclesiastical censures' and the 'power of the keys, viz. excommunication and absolution'. This power (*potestas clavium*) was 'double in respect of the double effect it had, *viz.* first *in foro interiori* upon the mind and conscience, secondly *in foro exteriori* as it introduced some civil charge in the person upon whom exercised' (Hale 1976: 145). As to action '*in foro conscientiae*, which is not properly a jurisdiction, because it is without any external coercion or charge in the party', Hale (1976: 146) indicates this is 'derived not from the Crown but from a higher commission'.[3]

If, for Hale, to 'reproach the Christian Religion' was to 'speak in Subversion of the Law', this convergence was none the less delimited by the lawyer's anticlericalism. For all his piety, Hale was suspicious of the 'reverence and respect which the Christian religion got in the hearts of men'. Here the bifurcation of spiritual and temporal is explicit:

> [W]hile in truth the civil right, *viz.* custom and admission, gave [clergy] their power as a civil thing, lest it should be subject to the same power in its dissolution or diminution, they subrogated and interwove into men's minds a pretence and opinion of a higher right, which did not only propagate the admission of their power, but did also fasten and establish it with the concurrence of a double principle, viz. the true and real civil right and admission, and the pretended and imposed divine authority.
>
> (Hale 1976: 146)

Whenever the civil magistrate questioned their 'higher right', the clergy's ploy was 'rather [to] choose to bestow it as a gift than to lose it by power'. In this way, they 'would seem to give what they could not hold'. Civil magistrates had nonetheless made political use of 'the power of ecclesiastical persons, and their power over the people', whether in 'mediations of leagues between different nations' or in 'cursing and excommunicating and preaching down factions and rebellions' (Hale 1976: 147).

As to the distribution of subject matter to spiritual and temporal jurisdictions, certain matters have by 'usage of the kingdom' contingently fallen to the ecclesiastical courts. However, 'no reason can well be assigned why incontinence, usury, etc. should be the subject of their jurisdiction, more than theft or any other offence, inasmuch as they all agree in this that they are offences against God, or why contracts matrimonial or testaments should belong to their jurisdiction rather than contracts between master and servant or gifts in lifetime'. As if to deny the historical contingency of their jurisdiction, 'the pretence of the clergy was a right of a higher nature, and hence, the last devolution was not to the king but the pope'. Conventionally anti-papist, Hale viewed Catholicism as a front for endless clerical power-plays against which 'the judge of the common law was the judge of the extent of their jurisdiction'. The ecclesiastical jurisdiction was 'only a subordinate derivative power', a view that Hale (1976: 163–4) sustains by medieval and Reformation examples confirming the 'subservience of the ecclesiastical power to the temporal'.

On church government, it was Hale's view – recorded by his friend, the tractarian Richard Baxter – that people should not 'be peevishly quarrelsome against lawful circumstances, forms or orders in religion' (in Heward 1972: 96).[4] The more latitudinarian Hale thus found matters that so concerned Dissenters 'inconsiderable'.[5] He wrote that he did 'not think that the essence of the Christian religion consists in this or in any other particular form of government':

> It is pitiful to see men make these mistakes; . . . one holding a great part of religion in pulling off the hat, and bowing at the name of Jesus; another judging a man an idolater for it; and a third placing his religion in putting off his hat to no one; and so like a company of boys that blow bubbles out of a walnut shell shall every one run after his bubble and call it religion.
>
> (in Heward 1972: 127)

This moderation risks displeasing all radical denominations. Yet the counsel is for prudence. In a further discourse, having regretted that '[p]ride, credit and reputation are commonly engaged in both parties to a controversy which make differences irreconcilable', Hale continues: 'When differences occur gentleness, mildness and personal respect quiet the passions and gain a hearing.' He concludes that 'men for their own sakes and for the honour of the Christian religion should use temperance, prudence and moderation in controversies about non-essentials' (in Heward 1972: 128).

The 'best-known episode in Hale's career' (Cromartie 1995: 237) ran religion and law together. This was the 1662 trial for witchcraft of two Lowestoft women at Bury St Edmunds Assizes, the women being sentenced to death by hanging for bewitching girls whom they caused to vomit pins. A religious wrong continued to be dealt with by the secular law.[6] The two spheres had not been separated. The complexity of the circumstance is underlined by contradiction in Hale himself. In a devotional essay composed on the eve of the execution, Hale approved the penalty for witchcraft, noting that 'the instrument, without which [the devil] cannot ordinarily work, is within the reach of human justice and government' (in Cromartie 1995: 238). This is in keeping with his advice to the 1662 jury that the existence of witchcraft and laws against it were affirmed by the Bible, the laws of other nations and English law, 'as appears by that Act of Parliament which hath provided punishments proportionable to the quality of the offence'. However, writing on the criminal law, he noted that the common law viewed witchcraft as a 'secret thing' (in Cromartie 1995: 239), that is, as a purely private error or belief, known to God and conscience but lying beyond the limits of secular legality.

That Hale acted as he did cannot be separated from the English political circumstance: confessional movements were throwing up religious phenomena such as the 'witch craze'. In this circumstance an existing law against witchcraft would most likely be applied. Second, the fact that in the case no clear boundary was observed between religious belief and legal action was less a function of Hale's superstition or the law's inadequate rules of evidence than of the English historical and political complex. In a relatively established State, there was less need to deny absolutely any ecclesiastical access to the civil scene. By contrast, as we shall see in considering Thomasius's 'de-criminalisation' of witchcraft, in war-torn Germany the combination of massive confessional mobilisations and weak or non-existent State authority would be remedied only by an absolute exclusion of religion from the legal regulation of civil life.

What of Hale as lawyer and jurist? He included the following resolutions in his code of judicial conduct: that 'in the execution of justice, I carefully lay aside my own passions, and not give way to them however provoked', and that 'I be not too rigid in matters conscientious, where all the harm is diversity of judgment' (in Heward 1972: 67). Methodical self-restraint oriented Hale's ethical-legal regime. Hence his further rules: 'That I never engage myself in the beginning of any cause, but reserve myself unprejudiced till the whole be heard' and 'That in business capital, though my nature prompts me to pity, yet to consider that there is also pity due to the country.'

Yet nothing would seem more contentious than Hale having accepted judicial office with both the Cromwellian and the Restoration regimes. Again this might be less a simple lack of logic than the complexity of the circumstances. There was no political consensus in the circle of the jurist and historian, John Selden, frequented by Hale (and Hobbes).[7] Following the execution of Charles I, Selden retired to private life for five years and did not take the Engagement oath of loyalty to the Commonwealth.[8] John Vaughan followed suit in 1649, remarking that 'it was the Duty of an honest Man to decline, as far as in him lay, owning Jurisdictions that derived their Authority from any Power, but their lawful Prince' (in Tuck 1979: 115). Hobbes left England for Paris.

Hale stayed and followed a different line. There was no doubting his allegiance to the king's party – he was counsel to Charles I, as well as to Lord Strafford, Archbishop Laud and other royalist nobles. Hale took the Engagement to the new regime in 1649. In 1654 Cromwell sought to raise him to the Bench. According to Gilbert Burnet's (1682) *The Life and Death of Sir Matthew Hale*, 'Hale did deliberate more on the lawfulness of taking a commission from usurpers; but having considered well of this, he came to be of opinion, "That it being absolutely necessary to have justice and property kept at all times, it was no sin to take a commission from usurpers, if he made no declaration of acknowledging their authority", which he never did' (in Tuck 1979: 116). Hale sought advice from fellow lawyers and from clergy. He was urged to accept Cromwell's commission by them and by 'all his friends, who thought that in a time of so much danger and oppression, it might be no small security to the nation, to have a man of his integrity and abilities on the bench'.

In fact 'Hale's dedication to the law looked very much like keen support for Cromwell' (Cromartie 1995: 84). So the dilemma remained:

> If a man of consequence arrives at terms with successive regimes in a revolutionary situation, must he not be convicted either of timeserving or, what is worse, of 'Hobbism'? Hale's real escape from that dilemma was probably to invoke his allegiance to the law. Regimes come and go, the common law abides. The duty of men called to the law is to keep it running, to preserve its continuity and quality when, despite political vicissitude, that remains a possible endeavour.
>
> (Gray, in Hale 1971: xiv)

In Yale's (1972: 144n) judgment, too, Hale 'justified himself on the ground that the ordinary civil and criminal law must continue to be administered "for the public necessity of the kingdom"'. Great questions of constitutional jurisprudence confronted Hale: Is there fundamental law?[9] Is legal allegiance owed to a *de facto* rule usurped by rebellion against a lawfully constituted government?[10] Can a non-king rule constitutionally? These were not comfortable abstractions. As soon as his Protectorate was instituted, Cromwell sought the advice of his judges on the crucial question. Responding, 'Mr. Hales and most of the rest of the judges answered that the three kingdoms could not by the fundamental laws or by the constitution of the government of the three kingdoms be governed by a less power and authority than that due to the title or person of a King or Emperor' (Sir Edward Nicholas, in Yale 1972: 143–4). As to his subsequent conduct on the Common Bench:

> [A]t first he made a distinction between common and ordinary felonies, and offences against the state; for the last he would never meddle in them; for he thought these might often be legal and warrantable actions, and that the putting men to death on that account was murder; but, for the ordinary felonies, he was at first of opinion, that it was as necessary, even in times of usurpation, to execute justice in those cases, as in matters of property.
>
> (in Tuck 1979: 116)

This is the conduct of one for whom maintaining a legally regulated civil life remained of paramount importance.

According to Richard Tuck (1979: 116–17), in an unpublished treatise Hale 'built on Selden's observation that the King and his people had sharply defined and separate bodies of rights, which neither could infringe and which could be transferred by their holders like any set of private rights'. Given this transfer, the fact of usurpation accorded the English people no more and no fewer rights against the usurper than against his predecessor, to the extent that the predecessor had not commanded his subjects to resist. As Hale went on to say, in England 'the last Change was by the Normans; which was a Conquest *in Regem*, but not *in Populum*; so their Rights remained. But what these were, we are not unhappy in not knowing.'

Hale and John Vaughan, a fellow common lawyer and Chief Justice of the Common Bench from 1668 to 1674, elaborated other aspects of Selden's thought, not least his theory of the state of nature. For Vaughan, the state of nature was one of 'complete amorality' (Tuck 1979: 114) and thus the foil against which to view the civil order. One of Vaughan's judgments – he left no written works – argues that but for the historical shaping of conduct by 'induc'd *Laws, Education*, and *Custome of Manners*, [incestuous copulation] had been as indifferent as with other women'. Since incest was possible, it could not be against natural law. The law of nature in the state of nature permits everything that it is possible to do, and forbids nothing except what cannot be done. Such was the Seldenian picture of nature prior to its historical taming by law and civil manners. Moral laws derived from historical interventions. Moral conduct was a historical achievement.

The issue of property was also debated. On the evidence of an unpublished *Treatise of the Nature of Lawes in Generall*, Tuck (1979: 162) sees Hale combining Grotius's theory of property and Selden's theory of obligation as dependent on the possibility of punishment. Of more specific interest is Hale's use of the triad of *justum* (law), *honestum* (religion) and *decorum* (manners):

> Altho' there were no instituted human government or lawes, but men were in that natural state wherein they were propagated into the world, yet even in that state there would be some things *justa honesta et decora*, and some things *injusta inhonesta et indecora*. Everything would not be lawfull to every man; and that imaginary state of war, wherein every man might lawfully do what he thinks best without any law or controll, is but a phantasy.
>
> (Hale, in Tuck 1979: 164)

Some minimum natural law obligations relate to 'things *justa honesta et decora*', that is, to legal, moral and political virtues. This natural law was 'not naturally intuited, but had been made known historically to mankind, first through the seven *praecepta Noachidarum* and then through the Decalogue' (Tuck 1979: 163). For Hale (in Tuck 1979: 163), the Decalogue was the divine gift 'to one particular nation, the jewish church; yet he made that nation signal and eminent and conspicuous to all the world by signs, wonders and observable providence, that they might be like a beacon upon a hill, like a mighty and stately pillar set up in the middle of the world to hang upon it those tables of natural righteousness, which might be conspicuous and legible to the greatest part even of the gentile world of many ages'. Moved by Hale's rhetoric, Tuck (1979: 163) describes this almost apocalyptic passage as 'one of the most eloquent expressions of the centrality of Hebrew studies which marks this whole English theory of natural law'.[11] But, historically speaking, a political limit was being set on theology: the Decalogue was a gift made 'to one particular nation'.

The Selden circle cultivated a 'turn to history', as Tuck (1979: 132) puts it, but this was 'no argument against the laws of England'.[12] Hale's *History of the Common Law* and his *History of the Pleas of the Crown* were in keeping with Selden's study of legal manuscripts and the English legal past.[13] Maitland (1911: 5) recognised in Hale 'the last great English lawyer who habitually studied records; . . . a student of general history [who] found relaxation in the pages of Hoveden and Matthew Paris, read Roman law, did not despise continental literature, felt an impulse towards scientific arrangement, took wide and liberal views of the object and method of law'.[14] Hexter (1980) makes Hale an originator of the *modo historico.* Isaiah Berlin (1991: 53) links him to a crucial cultural pluralism: 'Jurists like Hotman in France and Coke and Matthew Hale in England, who rejected the universal authority of Rome, developed the beginnings of a view that, as customs, ways of life, outlooks differed, so, necessarily, did the laws and rules by which various societies lived, and that this expressed deep and basic differences in their growth as distinct and at times widely dissimilar social entities'. Gray (in Hale 1971: xii) discerns in Hale '[a] penumbra of attitudes that can be called historical', attitudes that adhere to the English legal system 'where precedent has been given conscious value and doctrine was transmitted orally and unofficially within the guild of practitioners'.

Before Hale, Coke and his colleagues 'knew about the past, talked about it, and exploited it, as earlier lawyers had not'. Coke had made an advocate's expedient use of the past, a move that Gray (in Hale 1971: xx) captures well: 'Historical awareness was put to the ahistorical use of establishing the immemorial character of the common law and hence its title to represent the ultimate in achievable social wisdom.' By contrast, a half-century later, Hale displays a different disposition to the legal past:[15]

> By the time [Hale] wrote, restraints had been imposed on mythmaking in legal history. Scholarship had extended the range of information and scrutinised uncritical conclusions. Civil war had called attention to the danger of polemical history. The prescriptive standard of right had been challenged openly. Hale's instinct was to defend that standard from a tenable base in history and theory.
>
> (Gray, in Hale 1971: xx–xxi)

To represent the common law's historical continuity, Hale adopted the image of 'the Argonauts Ship [that] was the same when it returned home, as it was when it went out, tho' in that Long Voyage it had successive Amendments, and scarce came back with any of its former Materials' (Hale 1971: 40).[16] This image justified the law's present form while admitting the impossibility of knowing 'the Original of the Laws':

> From the Nature of Laws themselves in general, which being to be accommodated to the Conditions, Exigencies and Conveniences of the

> People, for or by whom they are appointed, as those Exigencies and Conveniences do insensibly grow upon the People, so many Times there grows insensibly a Variation of Laws, especially in a long Tract of Time; and hence it is, that tho' for the Purpose in some particular Part of the Common Law of England, we may easily say, That the Common Law, as it is now taken, is otherwise than it was in that particular Part or Point in the Time of Hen. 2. when Ranulf de Glanville wrote, or than it was in the time of Hen. 3. when Bracton wrote, yet it is not possible to assign the certain Time when the Change began.
>
> (Hale 1971: 39)

The lesson is that 'Exigencies' have seen 'Use and Custom, and Judicial Decisions and resolutions, and Acts of Parliament' alter old laws into new laws 'which we now take to be the Common Law itself, tho' the Times and precise Periods of such Alterations are not explicitely or clearly known'. However, the fact of alteration has not prevented continuity:

> But tho' those particular Variations and Accessions have happened in the Laws, yet they being only partial and successive, we may with Reason say, They are the same English Laws now, that they were 600 Years since in the general.
>
> (Hale 1971: 40)

The metaphor of the ship rebuilt as need arose condenses Hale's argument for an English legal system that had adapted to historical experience yet retained its congruence. In part this was thanks to the continuity of the political realm within which those legal alterations were made.

Hale was committed to a transhistorical English constitution grounded in consent and custom. His was a Norman 'Conquest' *in regem* not *in populum* that assured an organic continuity with the pre-existing legal order of English life. This idealised continuity helps Hale refute Hobbes's theory of sovereignty and the pre-legal act of power that founds the State. Indeed, for Hale '[a]ny amount of material change would have been compatible with the "formal" continuity of the *Grundnorm*' (Gray, in Hale 1971: xxviii). But does this breach Hale's otherwise sharp sense of legal particulars and historical circumstances? Does he here reveal the lawyers' blindspot: the high-minded assumption that their law had governed the English State from the very start? This is where the lawyers claim too much. Hobbes might have been a poor theorist of normal law and orderly times but, as a great theorist of sovereignty, he was sighted where Hale was blinded by the phantasm of a timeless, self-creating legal system. For Hobbes, before there could be a legal system – or a morality – an act of sovereign power had to found a State.

In fact Hale's transhistorical constitutionalism had its own historical circumstance. He was responding to the controversy generated by Coke's proposition that the English law and constitution were largely unchanged since Saxon times, a controversy which had 'torn apart the nation and threatened the foundations of law'.[17] As Postema (1986: 20) then adds, for Hale the evidence of 'the link between present law and the far reaches of the nation's past is the *present sense or conviction* of this continuity'. Present usage is the crucial factor, but it cannot be grounded in ultimate historical fact since the original laws, as Hale (1971: 37) puts it, are 'as undiscoverable as the Head of Nile'. How then is legal identity across time confirmed? Postema's answer is by 'nothing but the present practice of regarding it as the same'. In other words, 'the law rests ultimately, in Hale's view, on an important social fact: a widely shared practice of regarding certain rules, regulations, institutions, and procedures – both substantive and formal or constitutional – as historically validated law of the land' (Postema 1986: 23). English legal institutions are thus 'grounded in an invisible substratum, the custom and practice, the common life, of the community at large' (Postema 1986: 27). There are two objections to this historicism that so neatly bonds law with community. First, what becomes invisible here is the law's dependence on a technical apparatus of enforcement. Second and more broadly, no less than religion, the effects of a legal system are contingent not on 'community at large' but on the particular historical and political setting in which any actual community exists.

In fact Hale was not dismissive of the technical apparatus of common law. His turn to history was not a turn away from professional concerns such as the evidentiary environment or the process of law reform. In his *History of the Common Law of England*, Hale's preference for trial by jury rather than by civilian procedure responds to his conviction that it was the means which 'beats and boults out the Truth much better than when the Witness only delivers a formal Series of his Knowledge without being interrogated' (Hale 1971: 164). Jury trial was more than a simple matter of listening for witnesses who contradict one another.[18]

Hale's writings on law reform display his prudential disposition. In *Considerations Touching the Amendment and Alteration of Laws*, he distances himself from reformers who imagine only perfection:

> And hence if there once occur any inconvenience in a law, presently away with it, and a new frame or model must be excogitated and introduced, and then all will be well. But this is a great error; for it is most certain, that when all the wisdom and prudence, and forecast in the world is used, all human things will still be imperfect.
>
> (Hale, in Heward 1972: 157)

This is so 'because it concerns the manners of many men, which are so various, uncertain and complicated, both in themselves and the circumstances adhering to them, that they are not possibly to be exactly fitted'. These comments are directed at those like Hobbes who 'think the laws are foolish; because if they were reasonable things, they must understand them without study, as they do the force of an argument'. For Hale, however, '[t]hey that are but half sighted in the business of the law, are more ready with speed and peremptoriness to pronounce for its alteration, than they that look about them and see this whole business before them' (in Heward 1972: 158). Hale was a prudent reformer of the law, able to anticipate the possibility that a new arrangement might prove more 'inconvenient' than the present one. Moreover, for new laws to be effective, the citizenry must be made ready: 'let the time that [new laws] shall be put into execution have such a prospect as men may not be surprised by the change of things, but may be fitted and prepared for it' (Hale, in Heward 1972: 160).

The historical circumstances – what Hale termed 'the whole business' – were an essential element in any successful reform. This marks his distance from a pure exercise of philosophical intellect: 'All that I contend for is not to render laws of men like laws of nature fixed and unalterable, but that [amendment] be done with great prudence, advice, care, and upon a clear prospect of the whole business' (Hale, in Heward 1972: 159). In a treatise exploring the advantages and disadvantages of a national register of conveyances of land, Hale observes:

> 'Indeed, it is a fine thing in the theory and speculation, and a man that fixeth his thoughts upon the good that might come by such an expedient, without troubling himself with the difficulties that lie in the way of it, may drive it on very earnestly; but he that shall consider the difficulty of it, will easily see that it is but a notion and speculation and cannot be effected or reduced into practice, at least not without immense confusion'.
>
> (in Heward 1972: 165).

Practical difficulties ranged from the administrative problem of good titles for which the deeds were destroyed in the Civil War to the geographical problem of where to locate a central register.

In his 'Reflections' on Hobbes's *Dialogue*, Hale warned judges against the theories and abstractions of 'reason at large'. The warning is extended to the 'high Speculations, and abstract notions touching Justice and Right', such as are pursued by 'Morall Philosophers, and Treatises touching Moralls in the Theory' and which work above the 'Common Staple of humane conversations' (in Holdsworth 1945: 503). These latter are among the social competences on which a civil life depends. By comparison with the 'comely countenance' of a Coke, the pious believer and threadbare jurist that was Hale seems all too unworldly. But alongside the pious believer and the professional jurist was a third persona. In his *Social History of Truth*, Steven Shapin (1994: 81) describes the emergence of the 'Christian gentleman', a 'major preoccupation of much English courtesy literature from ca. 1580 to ca. 1680'. Shapin grants real importance to the cultivation of gallant manners. He associates the attribute of 'gentle truthfulness' particularly with Sir Robert Boyle, but this habitus of 'Christian gentility' (Shapin 1994: 156) applies well to Hale, also a member of the Royal Society. Alongside but distinct from *honestum* (divine grace and morality) and *justum* (sovereign law and coercive legality), *decorum* introduces a sphere of social conduct grounded neither in internal religious or moral absolutes nor in external legal force. *Decorum* governed actions in accordance with norms of civility and peaceful sociability, a prudent middle way between religion and law.

From the viewpoint of historical ethics, *decorum* represented a definite new ordering of life. It built less on higher principles than on a scatter of available models for a secular ethos. Along with the non-theological courtesy literature and court philosophy to which Shapin (1994) refers, another such model for the times was found in neo-stoic *exempla.* Hale translated Cornelius Nepos's life of Pomponious Atticus, the Roman stoic renowned for his 'political neutrality by living through the Roman revolution on terms of friendship with all the major antagonists' (Gray, in Hale 1971: xiii–xiv). Hale's constancy of service to the law across divergent political regimes and through no small theological storms may have found a practical support in Atticus's ethical ideal of *apatheia* or prudent restraint of otherwise ungovernable personal passion.

From the unifying viewpoint of a history of ideas that cannot read Hale's works 'without being struck by the seamlessness of his intellectual world', Cromartie (1995) shows how to miss this historical and ethical point.[19] In dealing with an early modern individual of several persons – the religious, the legal and the gentle or well mannered – we can do more than recognise the independence of the legal from the religious. Unlike the historian of ideas, we can also take manners seriously. Of the Fall, Hale wrote that it set 'the lower faculties in rebellion against the superior; so that the wiser and more morate part of mankind were forced to keep the generality of mankind in some sort of order'. In a footnote on 'morate', Cromartie (1995: 235) cites the OED definition of 'morate' as 'mannered, well-mannered, respectably conducted, moral'. But he adds: 'It seems just as likely, however, to be "moderate", misprinted'. Surely not. It is our over-intellectual habit of mind that too easily dismisses the historical achievement of the 'morate' sphere.

Civility in public life was a real accomplishment. Prior to his death in the Tower of London in 1584, the barrister Thomas Norton drafted thirteen orders 'for the better government of the fower [four] howses of court'. Included in these orders was the following recommendation:

> [T]he young gentlemen should be incouraged to acquaint themselves with fencing, riding, dauncing, singing, . . . so that the said delightes be taken in christian sorte, and the better enabling of themselves to all honourable services, and not to feede themselves with the pleasure thereof.
>
> (in Prest 1972: 170)

Norton's proposals were not taken up. But his statement nicely offends our habit of drawing a fundamental distinction between external manners such as the good 'dauncing' of a courtier and the inner moral sense of the self-directing man or woman of conscience. We are dealing with a less than intellectualist matter of cultural geography: a sociable lifestyle available in the capital city of London where the lawyers of the Inns of Court rubbed shoulders with the courtiers. As Prest reminds us:

> [A]lthough historians have been impressed by links between the inns and parliament, contemporaries were probably more aware of their connections with the royal court . . . Parliament was at best an intermittent event, but the court exercised its attractions as arbiter of taste and fountain of preferment all the year round, not just for the gentleman students who followed its lead in dress and deportment, but for any member who sought advancement and patronage.
>
> (Prest 1972: 223)

It is immediately important to resist a trivialising impulse if we wish to recognise court society, in its role as 'arbiter of taste and fountain of preferment', as central to the 'civilising process'.

This proposition has been argued by the historical sociologist, Norbert Elias. In *The Court Society* (1983), together with *The History of Manners* (1978) and *Power and Civility* (1982), Elias accords the system of court manners a major role in the civilising of Western humanity. To say just this is to hint at a larger project: Elias's history of manners poses a challenge to Kant's philosophy of morality. It is worth recalling just how dismissive Kant was of achievements in what he termed mere 'civilisation':

> We are *civilised* to the point of excess in all kinds of social courtesies and proprieties. But we are still a long way from the point at which we would consider ourselves *morally* mature.
>
> (Kant 1970: 49)

For the critical philosopher, all spheres of positive conduct – courtly, legal, administrative, military, commercial – become no more than 'semblances of morality'. The enlightened one measures their shortfall against the standard of absolute inner self-direction exercised by a pure will. Elias's history of how courtly manners changed 'external compulsion into internal compulsion' renders the Kantian schema eccentric, but this schema remains all-powerful in critical circles. Along with his account of court society, Elias proposed a tripartite model of social change in Europe as the outcome of monopoly formation, depersonalisation of power, and the Königsmechanismus or kingship apparatus. Welcoming Elias in part because he avoids 'the teleology and moralisation that tends to beset much of Marxist historiography', Koenigsberger (1986: 9) recognises the pertinence of the Königsmechanismus: 'the English monarchy had broken down much of English regionalism and had greatly weakened or even abolished the autonomy of provincial, urban and ecclesiastical corporations'.[20]

The key to this mechanism is the physical relocation of particular men and women when, '[a]t a certain stage in the development of European societies [some] individuals are bound together in the form of courts, and thereby given a specific stamp' (Elias 1983: 39). New forms of conduct were shaped by an ethical process that Elias terms 'courtisation'. Drawing them away from their regional estates into the royal centre, court life transformed men from dangerous warriors and difficult bishops into pliant courtiers. This 'civilising process' involved a discipline as punctilious as a monastic regimen. The 'gentle' ideal of the courtier rested on mastering the infinity of niceties set down in the 'courtesy literature', those manuals of court manners of which Erasmus's *De civiltate morum puerilium* and Castiglione's *Il libro del cortegiano* are the best known. If Machiavelli's *Il principe* exemplifies the art of politics for rulers, these seemingly superficial guides to courtly manners of speech, posture, dress and most every other aspect of the courtier's daily comportment carry the detailed art of court.

On one side, Elias attaches court conduct to the historical process of state formation and the centralisation of a feudal nobility away from their regional power bases, a process best realised in the French court of the *ancien régime.* On the other side, he attaches this minutely programmed behaviour to an ongoing psychological process of taming the instinctual drives. Elias (1983: 91–3) captures the electric ambience of court society, describing it as a 'stock exchange' of reputations where 'the value of the people present in each other's opinion' rose and fell. Fluctuating and dangerous, court society called for its members to calculate their conduct in what was 'an especially intense and specialised competition for the power associated with status and prestige'. In such a milieu, '[e]tiquette . . . needs no utilitarian justification' (Elias 1983: 103). Here, where 'everyone depended on everyone else, and all on the king', a princely aristocracy developed a 'court rationality' distinctive in its attention to the minutiae of manners:

> The intensive elaboration of etiquette, ceremony, taste, dress, manners and even conversation had the same function. Every detail here was an ever-ready instrument in the prestige struggle and this elaboration served not only for demonstrative display and the conquest of status and power, that is, external distancing, it also created graduated internal distances.
> (Elias 1983: 111)

Internal reflection and external manners became equivalent modes of conducting oneself, their usage contingent on the given circumstance. The crucial skill was that of observing others and disciplining oneself: 'This courtly art of observation is all the closer to reality because it never attempts to consider the individual person in isolation, as a being deriving his essential regularities and characteristics from within. Rather, the individual is always observed in court society in his social context, as a *person in relation to others*' (Elias 1983: 104). There was a practical reason for avoiding self-deception: the courtier 'must know his own passions if he is to conceal them effectively' (Elias 1983: 105).

Our present interest lies in the fact that court rationality was a form of sociability dependent neither on an inner religious conscience nor on external legal regulation. It represents the third sphere of action alongside those of *honestum* and *justum*, that of *decorum*. Here individuals worked to perfect their social manners. Elias takes these routines of courtesy as seriously as principles of morality. Kant would insist, however, that the confrontation of manners and morality marks the fundamental critical threshold where actual behaviour faces the normative principles of how men and women ought to be.

Let us put Lord Nottingham into this cultural setting. 'Black and funereal' though his family dynasty was said to be (Yale 1957: ix), through his profession Nottingham was connected to the more coloured lifestyle of the royal court.[21] Samuel Pepys, a government official of some standing and a posthumously famous diarist, recorded a visit to Kensington on 14 June 1664. He had much enjoyed 'going into Sir H. Finche's [Lord Nottingham's] garden, and seeing the fountayne, and singing there with the ladies, and a mighty fine cool place it is, with a great laver of water in the middle, and the bravest place for musick I ever heard' (Pepys, in Yale 1957: xxii). Previously, on 16 August 1661, Pepys had 'dined today with Sir H. Finch, reader at the Temple, in great state' and later seen King Charles at the theatre. This was the 'last day of Heneage Finch's autumn reading that year, which was generally accepted to have been one of the most splendidly celebrated on record'. The festivities continued for six days, the Duke of York and Prince Rupert were admitted to the Society of the Inner Temple and, on that final evening, 'the King and a distinguished company dined to the sound of twenty violins' (Yale 1957: xxii–xxiii).

Yale (1957: xxiii) regrets that contemporary chroniclers 'tell us much about the lavish nature of the entertainment, but unfortunately all too little about the reading itself'.[22] Of course we see why he might wish for less entertainment and more legal analysis of Nottingham's reading of a Tudor statute, 39th of Elizabeth, concerning the vexed issue of a Crown debt. But the contemporaries' scale of interests is itself interesting, as suggested by Barbara Shapiro:

> A fairly substantial portion of the upper classes who were associated with the Inns of Court were exposed to the fashionable pursuits of the day. These included not only attendance at sermons and theatrical performances but the study of anatomy, astronomy, geography, history, mathematics, theology, and foreign languages. Thus, those who would actually enter the legal profession, as well as those who simply used the Inns as a fashionable club, were likely to be familiar with the substantial scientific activities and contemporary literature.
>
> (Shapiro 1983: 170).

For the early modern Inns of Court in London, lack of contact with the theological ethos of the university might be a positive condition. Academic critics make an easy target of 'the aristocratic parlour-game disputations of the Inns of Court' (Goodrich 1987: 435). Max Weber (1968: 784–5), a century ago, contrasted 'law as a craft' (English common law) with 'law as a science' (university-based civil law). He then elaborated this distinction between the 'guildlike English method of having law taught by the lawyers' in the Inns and 'modern legal education in the universities', that is, in Germany. There is no suggestion that, for some purposes, detachment from universities might be advantageous.

In London and away from the theological faculties at Oxford and Cambridge, the Inns were side by side with court society. Prest (1972: vii) re-establishes the Inns' historical functions by 'relating developments within their walls to the wider world outside'. The earliest recorded account of these unique institutions, Sir John Fortescue's *De Laudibus Angliae* (*c.* 1470), identifies the practical distinction between the Inns in London and the universities at Oxford and Cambridge, the former needing a competence in French for the study of the common law, the latter teaching only in Latin. Fortescue also recorded a social distinction whereby, as Prest (1972: 2) comments, '[t]he students at the inns of court were virtually all noblemen. Tuition in dancing, music and other courtly arts was available, so many great men enrolled their sons there, "although they do not desire them to be trained in the science of law, or to live by its practice, but only by their patrimonies"'. The connection to courtly manners is clear.[23] From the 1550s, the Inns' physical environment was altered by 'the growing concern for order, proportion and regularity, the conversion of fields and orchards to formally laid-out gardens, all suggest[ing] a conscious attempt to transform the former lawyers' hostels into the semblance of aristocratic, collegiate institutions, "the nurserie for the greater part of the gentry of the realme"' (Prest 1972: 20). *Decorum* becomes an instrument whereby the realm, through its gentry, becomes more civil.

The Inns' location made them 'ideally suited to introduce young men to the exciting world of London, already the mecca of ambition and talent, the kingdom's administrative, commercial, cultural and political hub'. True, their academic work was 'confined to the common law, barbarous by definition, lacking any respectable classical pedigree and hence rigidly excluded from the curricula of Oxford and Cambridge' (Prest 1972: 21). However, as Prest (1972: 116) goes on to say, the Inns 'could introduce students to a far wider range of informal cultural and intellectual pursuits than the two universities, isolated in their provincial market towns, were able or willing to provide'.[24] In fact two modes of life overlapped in the Inns, that of the civil gentleman and that of the professional lawyer:

> [T]he young gentlemen had every incentive to adopt attitudes and patterns of behaviour which would clearly distinguish them from the

> common lawyers with whom they were nominally associated. Hence the aggressive insistence on their own gentility, fully echoed by the poets and dramatists whom they patronised; hence also the competitive aping of court modes in dress and taste, the cult of wit, the incessant versifying (for private circulation, not mercenary publication), even perhaps the obsessive drinking, gambling and womanising.
>
> (Prest 1972: 41)

In time the professional formation became the dominant function. Prest (1972: 44-6) cites mid-seventeenth-century expressions of concern that in a gentleman's expected cursus vitae the traditional spell at the Inns of Court was being replaced by the Grand Tour of Europe with a private tutor. However, he warns against exaggerating this mutation, since 'the inns continued to serve the landed classes by providing younger sons with a respectable alternative career to the church and army'.[25] Something endured of Fortescue's fifteenth-century view of the Inns as a 'kind of academy of all the manners nobles learn'.

A certain community of social interests and cultural pastimes bound the members of court society and Inns of Court, finding expression in such practices as granting courtiers honorific enrolment in the societies. Shared banquets also served this end – 'such gargantuan gastronomic events as the banquet customarily given for newly-called serjeants in the Middle Temple hall (counted the third feast in England after the coronation and St. George's feasts . . .), the Grand Day feasts held on All Saints and Candlemas day, and the twice yearly readers' dinners' (Prest 1972: 226). Just as spectacular were the masques which the Inns produced either in-house – with the Inns 'all turned into dancing schools' (in Prest 1972: 154) – or by using professionals. But '[w]hether masques were staged at court, or like William Browne's *Masque of the Inner Temple* in 1614, "done to please ourselves in private", courtiers were sure to be among the audience, which meant the chance of advancing suits and seeking preferment' (Prest 1972: 223–4). Whilst enhancing the participants' social and professional interests, such activities also helped sustain the secular metropolitan culture of the times.[26]

The broader issue remains: how to conceive the relation between courtly forms of decorous self-cultivation and what we might term inner moral sense? Once a habitual intellectualism is set aside, two possibilities emerge. First, thanks to Elias, a better light falls on both court society and the Inns of Court. The motley training routines adopted in the Inns, the customary 'uses' and technical 'exercises', formed an intellectual practice legitimate in its own right, regardless of the style of theological, philosophical or contemplative rationality that was prestigious in the university.[27] The geographical distance of the Inns of Court from Oxford and Cambridge echoed their distance from theology and philosophy. Away from the universities but in contact with the court society, common law as a gentlemanly accomplishment can be associated with a relatively non-sectarian professional ethos.[28] The courtly norms sustained the mannered persona of the courtier, as depicted in the portrait of Sir Edward Coke in Fuller's *Worthies*: 'the jewel of his mind was put into a fair case, a beautiful body, with a comely countenance, a case which he did wipe and keep clean, delighting in good cloathes, well worne, and being wont to say, that the outward neatness of our bodies might be a monitor of the purity of our souls'. This was a truly decorous figure. With Elias's help we accord it also an independent ethical value.

Second, however, we return to a key theme: the historical division of life into separate spheres, specifically the separation of spiritual discipline and religion from secular law and civil government. For today's historians of ideas, as we saw, this division too easily becomes the symptom of a flawed cultural history. The critical urge is to return to unity. But viewed in the light of the political, religious and social history of confessionalisation, the splitting of *honestum* from *justum*, the theological from the legal and governmental, demands a new attention. The separation is more muted in the Anglican settlement with its relatively peaceful acceptance that State controlled Church. However, in French and German territories savaged by uncontrollable confessional civil war, Absolutist de-theologisation of government meant a far more radical separation of religion from government and morality from law. It meant a separation whose ethical dimension we have difficulty appreciating, given our own exposure in the university to the prestige of post-Enlightenment critique.

7

SEPARATION OF POWERS

The need to secure civil peace from unstoppable religious civil war occasioned an extraordinary displacement in political rationality: the installation of a State with absolute powers over the confessional contestants. The shock wave of this displacement is still passing over us. *Raison d'état* remains an outrage to moral sensitivities ignorant of its historical justification. The grant of ethical autonomy to governmental and legal institutions still seems intolerable, as does the notion that the 'laws are not moral because they correspond to an eternal legality of morals, although they may do this; they are moral because they have originated in a commandment derived directly from the political situation'. We still have every difficulty comprehending that moral arrangements might depend on the establishment of a State in which '[i]t is not a frame of mind or a correct measure that makes a virtue out of virtue, but its political foundation' (Koselleck 1988: 37).

Religious war ran on in Europe into the seventeenth century. Until mid-century 'there was no year of peace at all' (Bonney 1991: 188). As to the state of things in France, 'we are confronted, not so much with a succession of distinct battles as with a continuing battle, not so much between distinct and disciplined armies as between compatriots and neighbours, consumed with religious and political hatred' (King 1974: 51). Jean Bodin (1529–96), jurist, historian and *Politique* (as distinct from *dévot*), was a rallying point for French and other Absolutists in search of ways to end uncontrollable religious war. Citing Bodin's taut formula: 'Nothing can be public, where nothing is private', Stephen Holmes (1988: 5) suggests that '[l]iberal beliefs about the proper relation among law, morality and religion first acquired distinct contours during the wars of religion that ravaged France between 1562 and 1598'. Like Schmitt and Koselleck, Holmes argues that what we habitually conceive as fundamental 'liberal' rights were in actuality historical creations of strong political States:

> Generalising from the English and American cases, we ordinarily assume that liberal ideals initially emerged in a struggle against the politics of absolutism. Rights, we tend to think, are shackles upon a restive

> sovereign. The relation between power and freedom, however, was never so unequivocally antagonistic as the storybook account makes it appear. In crucial cases, rights were created and maintained *by* the modern state to promote the goals *of* the modern state.
>
> (Holmes 1988: 6)

The right of religious freedom was thus 'inextricably linked with the consolidation of dynastic rule, especially in France'. This reverses the 'storybook' account of rights by relocating the 'origin' of the freedom that liberalism now defends in a purposive act of the Absolutist State. That act required a de-politicisation of religion and a de-theologisation of government:

> By the 1570s, a disjunction of temporal and spiritual domains was already being advocated as a technique for strengthening the sway of secular rulers over nonreligious matters. Privatisation of religious disputes or the withdrawal of public officials from theological controversies was acclaimed as sovereignty-enhancing. Important theorists urged the government to steer clear of 'the religious thicket', so to speak, in order to augment effectiveness and credibility in other domains.
>
> (Holmes 1988: 6)

From Bodin's (1576) *De republica*, Holmes (1988: 6) teaches Americans a tough lesson: that there has in fact been a 'mutually supportive relation between state power and individual freedom'.

The discussion of Bodin's problematic parallels Koselleck's account of Hobbes's politics.[1] Once again, '[t]errible concentration of power is justified as the one acceptable alternative to religious civil war. Mutual butchery of citizens was Bodin's *summum malum*, the uttermost evil to be avoided at all costs' (Holmes 1988: 7). To this end the 'sovereign' had legitimate exercise of an absolute and indivisible authority, manifested in a unified order of command. Bodin's preferred form of sovereignty was a centralised monarchy, since 'an absolute king is best equipped to prevent the sedition, faction and civil war that are perpetual threats to every commonwealth and that have become particularly perilous to France during the Catholic–Huguenot struggles' (Holmes 1988: 8).[2] That said, although above the civil law because he makes it, as in the Justinian maxim *Princeps legibus solutus est*, the prince is nonetheless subject to the laws of God and nature. He is subject also to the constitutional laws of the kingdom, such as passage of the crown to the eldest male heir and interdiction on private appropriation of the public domain.

In this 'tension' of an 'unbound sovereign' who is not free to act entirely arbitrarily, Holmes discerns an essential element of Bodin's approach to the State's grant of religious freedom. Dismissing readings that see in Bodin only an incoherent aggregation of 'medieval constitutionalism with modern absolutism', Holmes (1988: 12) promotes a more sophisticated Bodin who 'embraced limitations on state power as techniques for enhancing state power'.

The operative slogan is: '*limits strengthen*'. Far from incoherence, Bodin's originality was to 'rethink traditional limits on royal power as conditions for the *successful* exercise of royal power' (Holmes 1988: 14). In practical terms, 'the less the power of the sovereignty is (the true marks of majesty thereunto still reserved) the more it is assured' (Bodin 1962: 517).

Bodin thus elaborates a doctrine of explicit limitation of State powers, the aim being to enhance the regulatory capacities of the sovereign. At the heart of this art of government was the grant of religious freedom, a grant intended to deflate religious passions and thus secure civil peace in historical circumstances we now have difficulty grasping:

> Ordinary men and women in sixteenth-century France did not understand the need for separating religious and political allegiances. Many preferred civil war to sharing their country with heretics. First-hand experience of self-destructive dispositions on the part of the people may have made Bodin somewhat less scornful of paternalism than we tend to be today.
>
> (Holmes 1988: 25)

These dispositions generated the St Bartholomew's Day Massacre and started the fourth French war of religion in 1572.[3] Scripture and Eucharist, adult baptism and church regiment were true causes to kill or be killed for.[4] Bodin proposed a political alternative to confessional conflicts: the sovereign must dispense with 'the traditional view that social cohesion required all subjects to share religious beliefs'.[5] If Bodin was right, '[t]he king should cease attempting to save souls, punish heretics, or eliminate religious dissonance'. Instead, recognising that civil war was bred in the conflict of uncompromising religious confessions, he should seek 'the lesser goal of establishing a *modus vivendi* between conflicting groups':

> In rejoinder to his *dévot* critics, Bodin could well have said: Lower goals serve higher ones. Instead of futilely attempting to confer moral perfection or Christian redemption on his subjects, the monarch should attempt to 'avoid commotions, troubles, and civil war' (IV, 7, 537). If the king keeps the peace, his subjects can pursue a wide variety of spiritual objectives. The state is a legal framework in which moral antagonists can coexist and cooperate in secular undertakings. Sectarian religions can also flourish, but only so long as they adapt themselves to the rules of peaceful coexistence.
>
> (Holmes 1988: 26)

In a Machiavellian note, Bodin recognised that '[t]he utility of religion does not hinge upon its truth'. Public toleration of religious confession as privatised belief did not aim to extirpate religion but rather to use and channel it. In Bodin's commonwealth even a 'false religion is nevertheless useful because it "doth yet hold men in fear and awe, both of the laws and of the magistrates, as also in mutual duties and offices one of them towards another" (VI, 7, 539)' (Holmes 1988: 28). Attempts at imposing conformity would be counterproductive, radicalising those whose confession was suppressed and thus endangering civil peace. Hence Bodin's advice, cited at the outset of the present essay: 'that religion or sect is to be suffered, which without the hazard and destruction of the state cannot be taken away'. In Holmes's (1988: 31) summation, '[r]eligious unity remains an ideal, but, in the circumstances, religious diversity is the only realistic option'.

Bodin approved the Peace of Augsburg that in 1555 ended strife between Lutherans and Catholics and calmed public dispute on confessional matters. As he wrote in the 1570s, when in Germany 'no man should upon pain of death dispute of the religions. Which severe punishments, after that the German magistrates had inflicted upon diverse, all Germany was afterwards at good quiet & rest: no man daring more to dispute of matters of religion (IV, 7, 536)' (Holmes 1988: 37). This 'good quiet & rest' did not last, whether in the German territories whose momentary peacefulness impressed Bodin or in France itself. The Augsburg Treaty, great though it was, had no way of compelling the rival confessions to abandon the belief that, given time, they would each become the one true universal Church.

In 1576, the year of publication of the *De republica*, the Huguenot rebellion was under way, joined by Henri de Navarre, the first prince of the blood, on his escape from arrest by the pro-Catholic royal authorities.[6] Two attempts at religious pacification were made. The Peace of Monsieur ended a rebellion by the Catholic Malcontents under the Duc d'Alençon, younger brother of King Henri III. On the Protestant side, the Edict of Beaulieu made concessions to the Huguenots in relation to the exercise of Calvinism in France and thus ended the fifth French war of religion. A consequence of this peacemaking was the emergence of the first Catholic League. As a Catholic moderate, Bodin sought reconciliation with the Protestants. This was the position of the *Politiques.* Their programme was one of religious toleration and a strong State, since 'not only could a strong State afford religious toleration, but (as in French conditions) a State had to be tolerant in order to be strong' (King 1974: 53). In the event, the uncompromising combat of religious confessions continued, super-heated by communal hatreds, dynastic claims and foreign interests.

In these circumstances, the separating of religion and confessional conscience from the government of civil life seems apposite, as does the international politics of a Richelieu whose sense of State interest overrode confessional communities and their damaging mutual hatreds (Collins 1995: 59). As for the state of law in France, the flowering of natural law study known as the 'elegant jurisprudence' – associated with the names of Budé and Bodin, Cujas and Doneau – was overpowered by the turmoil of religious civil strife. Faced with the Huguenot Wars, many French jurists left for Dutch or German universities. Others such as Jean Domat (1625-96) remained in

France. A contemporary of Hale and Nottingham, he probably encountered Hobbes in the Jansenist milieu in Paris. One option, as taken by Domat in his *Les loix civiles dans leur ordre naturel*, was to speculate on a natural law superior to circumstance because universal in its order. In 1681, four years before the revocation of the Edict of Nantes and Louis XIV's shift from toleration to conformity, Domat thus proposed to Louis this systematic restatement of the laws of France. He gained his pension and pursued his intellectual project unhindered by other tasks until his death in 1696. Far from separating theology from law, Domat took theology to provide the fundamental truth that grounds the law and, indeed, the whole hierarchy of knowledge (Stromholm 1989: 56).

More interesting is Domat's Jansenist connection. It is less a question of Jansenism's theological interest as a Catholic equivalent of Calvinism – Jansenists held the doctrine that post-lapsarian humans could know grace only through divine revelation – than its adoption by a particular stratum of the French nobility. This was the *noblesse de robe*, ennobled through the holding of administrative office, unlike the *noblesse d'épée* or upper nobility distinguished through prowess in war. The nobility of office was an enduring juristic stratum whose independence even 'the revolutionary political course of events was unable to interrupt' (Stromholm 1989: 54). The Jansenist stratum operated as an elite spiritual enclave or illumination society supporting intellectual exercises in the style of Domat's *Loix civiles* but also as the historical estate whose sons would become the personnel of public office. Just as there was no break with theology, so the social order of the nobility of office maintained itself into and through the Absolutist phase.

In the more differentiated view of the early modern French State emerging from current historiography, the high judiciary of the royal courts is a relatively closed caste. They attended the Jesuit *collèges*, rather than university (Collins 1995: 13). In the universities, the faculties of law passed students through endless textual exegesis, principally by dictation in class. The course in law was 'excessively erudite' (Brockliss 1987: 289), Roman law requiring skills in Latin etymology, canon law requiring the massive bibliography of ecclesiastical history. The great issues of the day could hardly be avoided. However, these were still times when theses propounding the independence of the temporal realm could be found 'contrary to the word of God'. Debate on the relations of Church and State was generally managed within the theory of 'the two separate and independent gloves but the secular power had been given a larger hand, necessarily so in order that it could fulfil its protective function' (Brockliss 1987: 329).

Meanwhile, beyond the learned sphere, confessionalisation proceeded with the spiritual disciplining of the population. Thus 'by 1700, after years of persevering effort, a situation had been achieved in which religion was presented as a personal choice, a decision of the heart and mind, a road to salvation, but in which everyone, or nearly everyone, was nevertheless involved in church attendance, with people showing a degree of punctuality never previously attained' (Delumeau 1989: 148). Salvation and religion as 'personal choice' went with a new capacity to regulate oneself, for instance a new compulsion to be punctual. Having people worry about getting to the church on time was a step towards having large numbers of people reflect more constantly on the state of their soul. It was a matter of acquiring 'constant motives', to use Max Weber's (1930: 119) term.

However, the actual propagation of the Word was uncertain. With her usual measure, Natalie Zemon Davis (1972: 208) observes how Calvinists attempted to spread their message in books and pamphlets carried into the countryside by 'evangelical peddlers'. Yet they failed, in part because of the high-minded inflexibility that marred initiatives such as the new *Calendrier*, printed in Geneva in the late 1550s, which replaced saints' days by 'historical' references: 'March was the month of Martin Bucer's death, July that of Edward IV. Constantinople was taken by Mahomet II May 29, 1453. On August 27, the "reformation according to the truth" took place in Geneva. Under October was remembered Martin Luther's attack on indulgences' (Davis 1972: 204). For peasants who organised their lives by saints' days, this earnestly didactic calendar was useless. But 'zealous Protestants could overlook all that, could face the possibilities of destroyed merchandise and even death for the sake of "consoling poor Christians and instructing them in the law of God"' (Davis 1972: 205). Despite these evangelising efforts, 'the little spark of Protestantism had burned out in the countryside' (Davis 1972: 208). Theology and fanaticism lost out to local circumstance.

The historical ambivalence of confessionalisation is here. On the one hand, confessionalisation acted as a form of social discipline in alliance with the State's own interests. On the other hand, in its demand for complete community adherence to the one true faith carried to the point of death, confessionalisation posed an explosive threat to an always fragile civil order.

8

THE CONFESSIONAL STATE

In the sixteenth century two separate organisations of living emerged and then converged, one spiritual, religious and directed by the Church, the other worldly, political and administered by the State. Heinz Schilling has termed this convergence 'confessionalisation', displacing the notions of Reformation and Counter-Reformation in favour of a more variable and continuing series of exchanges between religion and politics. Confessionalisation is proposed as an 'independent paradigm of social history' where '[s]quarely in the centre stands the connection between ecclesiastical and religious forces and the rise of the early modern state with its modern social discipline' (Schilling 1988: 265–6). Far from there being a necessary contradiction between Church and State, 'ecclesiastical, political and social developments combined to form politically significant confessions'.

Confessionalisation was a process of 'Christianisation', complicated by the split into competing 'confessions': post-Tridentine Roman Catholic, Lutheran and Calvinist. Each one of this plurality of faiths was itself deeply anti-pluralist in matters of faith. Each purported to be the one universal and true rationale for living and, more important, for dying in a state of salvation. It is hard to grasp how violent inter-confessional disputes over matters such as the nature of Christ's existence on this earth could be. But confessionalisation was not only metaphysical speculation. It was a social discipline. Each confession was a programme to form whole communities by installing a new concern for the detailed moral ordering of worldly life. Schools, seminaries and universities were built for the new humanity. The social reality of confessional religion lay in the populations that it produced: committed, hyper-religious, ready to die for salvation and therefore to kill for it too. Religious difference meant the most profound social disturbance: civil war.

Noting that '[o]ne of the most striking features of the Reformation is the great number and variety of new theological systems which were devised and which found adherents in Europe within a very few years after Luther had first challenged the established Church', Koenigsberger (1986: 170) recalls the appearance on the European scene of 'dozens of would-be religious reformers, each convinced that he held the key to the only, and unique, way of attaining salvation'. The sheer number of their ecstatic followers, Koenigsberger (1986: 170) continues, militates against any purely doctrinal explanation: 'When so many men were willing to follow so many different religious leaders, the theology of even the most outstanding of them is not likely to explain this phenomenon.' In the welter of activity designed to 'turn the [spiritual] ideal of the few into the daily life of all' (Delumeau 1989: 149), the constants were the centrality of the Bible and communal hatred between rival Christian confessions.[1] In fact, such conflict was not new. Fratricidal fracturing had always been the Christian way:

> [W]e have looked at the Reformation the wrong way round. We have assumed that the theological and ecclesiastical unity of Catholic Christendom was its natural condition and that, in consequence, the Reformation [was] a dramatic break in this condition which ran counter to all previous Christian experience and which, in a sense, destroyed the natural order of things.
>
> (Koenigsberger 1986: 171)

'But', Koenigsberger asks, 'was the long existence of a unified Church really as natural and inevitable as it was assumed to be?' The answer is that 'Christians remained distressingly prone to engage in deadly wars with each other'. If we then ask how the Church survived 'as a unified institution', the response is that there was no such unity. The Church had held together as an administrative repository of 'highly specialised skill . . . needed in every part of Christendom' (Koenigsberger 1986: 173). Christian 'unity' was 'not an inevitable and eternal form necessarily derived from the Church's universalist claims' (Koenigsberger 1986: 177) but its historical monopoly on what today we would call multinational management expertise.

At its height in the thirteenth century, the Church's monopoly of administrative skill entered into decline as a new political force emerged: the modernising and court-centred monarchy that began developing its own territorial monopoly of administrative competence, its own chanceries or secretariats and, in the English case, its own secular legal system.[2] The administrative construction of territorial States aimed to consolidate a unified political regime and sovereign power in the face of the collapsing political order of the old German empire. Centralised administration of a unified territory and uniform social discipline were impeded by the traditional social estates and their ancient privileges, residues of feudal rule. Justified by the imperative of defence against other princely States, these Statist undertakings were to maximise the territory's wealth. The State's aim was not salvation for souls but security for its citizens. The population was redefined as a potential asset, its welfare and gainful employment becoming prime objects of government. The instruments of State building were administrative. Hence the term 'cameralist' State, that is, a State based on the *Kammer* or bureau which deployed the administrative expertise codified by administrator-theorists like

Johann von Justi, specialists in State management. Such expertise was a matter of diverse competencies, having to deal with the different technical spheres of education, health, transport, agriculture, economy, public safety and defence. The generic term for this array of bureaucratic instruments was 'police' or 'policey' (or our modern 'policy').[3]

Confessionalisation extended the spiritual order and moral discipline favoured by the congregation of the faithful to all members of the community. Territorial State building extended the political order and civil discipline favoured by the ruling prince and his court to all members of the population. Common to the religious and the Statist aspects of confessionalisation was the extension of discipline to ever wider sectors of the population. The conduct of the growing urban stratum was made a particular problem and target for improvement by both Church and State. Their overlapping religious and political programmes constituted the distinctive feature of a hybrid form – the 'confessional State'. There were mutual benefits to both sides, the spiritual and the temporal. The construction of a unified State required a uniform population. The religious ideal of instilling one true faith could thus find common cause with the political objective of building a citizenry whose shared identity was grounded in new habitual loyalty to a 'sovereign who stood above ordinary mortals', including the old regional noble and religious estates. The practical achievement of the confessional State rested on the pastoral offices of the Church and 'the formation of a bureaucracy differentiated by function', their joint aim being 'the development of a unified, disciplined – perhaps we should say "tamed" society' (Schilling 1986: 30). Addressing physical and moral welfare problems like drunkenness and disorderly conduct, inadequate childcare and schooling, in public places and in private households, the alliance of 'pulpit and administration' engineered a complex interaction between evangelising religions and centralising States. Souls could be administered through the pulpit, citizens through the city hall.

The overlap between the Protestant sects and the apparatus of the early modern State came near a universal distribution of that inner sense of moral responsibility we know as conscience. Yet the confessional State remained a marriage of convenience between two different programmes of life. Each used the other as its platform. The Churches' initiatives in the disciplining of sinful or immoral behaviour obtained support from the technical expertise of organised bureaux that found common cause with the confessions because they were themselves 'permeated by the same spirit of religious and moral discipline' (Schilling 1988: 271). The State also offered political protection. Its programme for unifying the territory and harmonising the population chimed with the exclusivity of the confessionalisation process. When it came to actual conflict between rival confessions – this would happen as the century advanced – the State provided military force.

From the State's side, a territorial prince might advance his political programme by adopting a particular confession. Advantage could be derived from the regularity of habits that religious discipline had imposed on congregations for redemptive purposes. When the confessional Churches 'incorporated all subjects into a system of pastoral and moral influence and control' they also 'promoted the formation of a uniform body of princely subjects' (Schilling 1988: 266). The fashioning of a moral community thus coincidentally aided the Statist programme. No less valuable to the State was the affective bonding achieved by confessional religion. When it came to mobilising the population around the single prince, the habit of one true faith – no matter which – and the communal sense of spiritual exclusivity and perfect religious animosity that went with an aggressively partisan confessional mentality were major assets for a State in competition with its rivals.[4]

In practice there was no exact correlation between Roman Catholic, Lutheran and Calvinist doctrines on the one hand, and States' political arrangements on the other. In 'Between the territorial state and urban liberty: Lutheranism and Calvinism in the county of Lippe', Schilling (1988) publishes in English translation the case study and an outline of his conclusion from *Konfessionskonflikt und Staatsbildung* (Schilling 1981). In Lippe we do not find the expected correspondences between religious ideology and political regime: Calvinism with active pursuit of individual rights within the political apparatus, Lutheranism with passive acceptance of the authoritarian status quo. Yet this is 'the alignment taught by historical science and classical sociology of religion – Calvinism and bourgeois freedom, Lutheranism and princely authority' (Schilling 1988: 267). Whatever normative political theorists and moral theologians might wish to believe or claim, once State interest had separated itself from religion the relations of political reality and religious ideology ceased to respect any single theory. They had become expedient, varying according to the local pattern of winners and losers.

In the Westphalian county of Lippe, 'Calvinism allied with the early modern authoritarian state and Lutheranism with civic autonomy and freedom, both corporate and individual' (Schilling 1988: 267). A key factor was the presence of Lemgo, a city enjoying traditional commercial and legal freedoms as a member of the Hanseatic League. Resistance by an individual city could win it freedom. In Lemgo a Lutheran disposition was first manifested during a church service when German Evangelical hymns were spontaneously sung. However, the territorial prince, Count Simon V, remained Roman Catholic. A majority of Lemgo's city council adopted his anti-Lutheran policy and no Lemgo priest turned Lutheran. Thus, 'lacking a local clerical leader, the Lutheran reformation here acquired the character . . . of a communal movement of the citizenry' (Schilling 1988: 268). In this way, a religious movement generated a moral community which forced the city administration to embrace reformation. The result was a city, strengthened in its Lutheran confession, confronting a count who had failed to unite his subjects behind his own Catholicism. His successor, Bernard VIII, converted to Lutheranism, more in recognition of political realities than as an act of confessional State building. Not until the early seventeenth century was this latter task taken up again, when Count Simon VI 'tried once more to create in Lippe the type of princely state that was already well advanced in other German territories' (Schilling 1988: 269). Although the principle of *cuius regio, eius religio* was embodied in the imperial Peace of Augsburg (1555), when the count converted to Calvinism and adopted Calvinist confessionalisation as his instrument of State building, conflict ensued. Lutheran nobles resented the centralising pressures of the prince's Calvinist court. On the other hand, rural peasants and the city dwellers of Lemgo found other reasons for non-compliance. Yet, as Schilling (1988: 271) underlines, '[t]he conflict-ridden nature of the confessional transformation nonetheless gave the prince a chance to break the autonomy of estates and towns, which the Lutheran Reformation had strengthened, and thus to force, through the instrument of Calvinism, the formation of a unitary territorial state with a uniform body of subjects'.

As elsewhere, the conflict of confessions was damaging. Nearly ten years of strife 'brought the city and the territory close to financial and economic ruin'. The Lippe conflict took place '[i]n the tense times on the eve of the Thirty Years War, when the confessional fronts confronted one another with irreconcilable ideological, political and military enmity' and 'every confessional conflict was liable to act like a spark in a powder keg' (Schilling 1988: 274). The wider resonance of the local struggle is evident: the Lutheran and Calvinist sides sued one another in the supra-regional imperial courts and sought to co-opt their co-religionists in other territories. Finally, a settlement was reached that went against the unifying State. In 1617, in the Röhrentrup Decree, the city of Lemgo's Lutheran confession and autonomous status gained formal recognition from the Calvinist territorial government of the count. If peace was thus achieved, it was not a matter of principles winning through but because 'confessional conflicts out of control could plunge the region, the Empire, and even all Europe into chaos' (Schilling 1988: 275). Unstoppable by any existing political or legal means, war 'out of control' would be the terrible setting for the Absolutist separation of confessional religion from government, moral absolutes from law.

From the case study, Schilling (1988: 276) draws six conclusions, three of which pertain to the present essay. First, confessionalisation cannot be separated from an 'overarching social process, which may be described as . . . the development of the institutionalised territorial state with its uniform body of subjects'. Following Schilling, we might amend Elias's 'monopolisation' thesis: in Protestant States, the State monopolised the Church before it monopolised military power and taxation, the two focus points for Elias.

Second, unlike taxation, confessional conflicts touched entire societies. Thus 'the question of religion and confession formed a crystallisation point around which other important social problems settled' (Schilling 1988: 277–8). With confessionalisation, religious differences came to 'form the core of competing political programs'. Each confession understood itself as the only programme for living in this world and getting to the next. Radical disagreement concerned the true way forward to God's kingdom, an issue whose urgency was both cause and effect of 'new age' visions of the end of time and the second coming of Christ. Given their claim to exclusivity, confessions 'made social conflict in principle incapable of resolution. The confessionally shaped mentality of conflict thus differed qualitatively from that of a pluralistic society, which must constantly keep open the possibility of compromise'. The result was an 'acceptance of total confrontation, even when socially destructive'.

The third conclusion – Schilling's sixth and last – compares the two Reformations, the Lutheran and the Calvinist, and suggests just how much will run through the cultural channel established by the Calvinist confession. Unlike traditionalistic Lutheranism but like the territorial bureaucracy with which it had 'a qualitative, and not merely a functional, affinity', Calvinism was 'convinced . . . of the need for changes':

> In this respect it is important that, on the basis of the practical enforcement of the Second Reformation, Calvinism could also attract persons who had little interest in theology or religion. For this reason crypto-Calvinism and Philippism in Germany became gathering points for physicians, literati, and jurists – that is, for humanists from faculties other than theology.
>
> (Schilling 1988: 283).

However, Schilling adds, 'the cultural, literary and scholarly consequences of this movement remain to be investigated'.

The confessional State marked a temporary overlap of political interests and religious visions. It 'drove forward the modern secularisation of political life'. Yet confessionalisation also led to 'the long years of the great religious wars of the earlier seventeenth century, when Europe was plunged into chaos' (Schilling 1988: 265). Schilling nonetheless offers a positive assessment of the hybrid religious and political State:

> [T]he German type of early modern development had its roots in a combination of Christian education – in its various confessional forms – as a means of social control with the sophisticated, intensive activities of the state. The latter was known in contemporary political thinking as 'law and order' (*gute Policey*). This combination of confessional education and law and order produced results, the evaluation of which – good and bad – depends in part on individual opinions. For my own part, the education of civil servants to a special sense of duty toward and responsibility for the common good (*das gemeine Beste*) seems to me a positive achievement.
>
> (Schilling 1986: 30)

But the mutuality of Church and State proved one-sided. In the event sectarian spiritualisation overwhelmed secular administration. It was not just the disproportion between a stairway to heaven and good government. By the 1600s the State's promise of welfare lost out to the Church's promise of salvation as the State itself was absorbed into the conflict of rival *Konfessionskirchen.* As Schilling (1986: 22) writes, each confession 'formed a highly organised system, which tended to monopolise the world view with respect to the individual, the state, and society, and which laid down strictly formulated norms in politics and morals'. The city hall was conscripted to the pulpit in the higher cause of human redemption. The administrators lost out to those preaching salvation. The political apparatus of the territorial State succumbed to the moral principle of the confessional community. Peace lost out to religious civil war.

We must assume enthusiasm for the unprecedented slaughter of confessional rivals that occurred in the Wars of Religion, notably in Germany in the Thirty Years War (1618–48). For Schilling as for Koselleck, this historical fact is the record of religion as a social reality. The present essay brings this record to the notice of those critical theorists who, heirs of their confessional forbears, long to displace today's political State by a new society and today's legal system by a new moral community. Hence the history lesson. When the early modern administrative State lost civil governance to spiritual salvation, all were engulfed by a war that none knew how to end.

The political response was princely Absolutism and *raison d'état.* Securing the State and its citizens became a higher imperative than redeeming the community of souls. To this end the several spheres of State action – politics, law and administration – now emerged from religious domination as separate secular realities, immune to the normative claims of theology and the former civil powers of the Churches. Without reserve Koselleck endorses the achievement of Absolutism. This will not find easy acceptance, given our own constant exposure – through German Romanticism and critical theory – to moral criticism of the State. What Albion Small wrote in 1909 holds true today: 'To Americans, absolutism is so unthinkable as a principle of political philosophy, that nothing tolerable can be credited to theories in which such a postulate is a factor.' Small added his note of regret: 'But Americans would have become much profounder political philosophers than they are, if they had been patient enough to learn a little more about the part which the fiction of absolutism has performed in the process of civic evolution' (Small 1909: 15).[5] Following the long years of confessional civil war, the Absolutist State responded by a de-theologising programme that separated religion from government, morality from law, theology from public administration. The purpose of this separation was to achieve civil peace in circumstances where communal hatreds and religious enthusiasms were intensified to the point that 'irreconcilable, total confrontations . . . endangered social life as such' (Schilling 1988: 265).

Against this danger, the Absolutist State 'required new forms and new guidelines for public behaviour' (Oestreich 1982: 157). But to establish such guidelines something other than the confessional regimen of Christian education was requisite. One alternative was the Stoic model of discipline whose early modern revival Gerhard Oestreich (1982) attributes to the Dutch philologist and rhetorician, Justus Lipsius (1547–1606). In *Neostoicism and the Early Modern State*, Oestreich (1982) records Lipsius's fashioning of a non-theological civics as part of the 'Netherlands movement' that also produced Hugo Grotius (1583–1645). Two of Lipsius's books – together with his edition of Tacitus – became standard manuals for training a new elite of civic officers. These were his 1584 *De constantia libri duo qui alloquium praecipue continent in publicis malis*, a discourse 'on constancy in evil times', followed in 1589 by *Politicorum libri sex*, translated into English as *Sixe Bookes of Politickes or Civil Doctrine* (1594).[6]

De constantia was written against 'the actual state of civil war and the almost unbearable conditions in [Lipsius's] own country, the Netherlands' (Oestreich 1982: 13). In the form of a conversation between the author, fleeing from Louvain, and an older friend committed to the Stoic doctrines, '[i]n the triad *constantia, patientia, firmitas* (steadfastness, patience, firmness) Lipsius gave to his age, an age of bloody religious strife, the watchword for resistance against the external ills of the world' (Oestreich 1982: 13). The aim of constancy was to achieve a 'right and immoueable strength of the minde, neither lifted up, nor pressed down with externall or casuall accidentes' (Lipsius 1939: 79). The aim of patience is to resist the importunities of passion and, in particular, to avoid one's reason being overtaken by *opinio*, that is, by 'vain imagining' (Oestreich 1982: 19). How to stand firm in the clash of reason and 'imagining' was the essential neo-Stoic art of living.

An international bestseller, *De constantia* was a prudential survival manual '*in malis publicis*', for times of public ill: civil war, confessional fanaticism, blind love of country. Describing *De constantia* as an 'utterly serious tool for living (*instrumentum vitae maxime serium*) . . . more practical psychology than abstract ethics, more direct guidance for wise living than theoretical moralising', Oestreich sums up its ethical message:

> The ideal individual in the political world, as portrayed by Lipsius, is the citizen who acts according to reason, is answerable to himself, controls his emotions, and is ready to fight. The ideal of Lipsius was so in tune with the political spirit of the age that agreement was soon achieved between his anthropology and the form of the state. For the Lipsian view of man and the world, carried over into the realm of politics, entails rationalisation of the state and its apparatus of government, autocratic rule by the prince, and strong military defence.
>
> (Oestreich 1982: 30–1)

In the *Six Bookes of Politickes or Civil Doctrine*, Lipsius set out the positive prescriptions for 'the new state and . . . the men who should hold responsibility within it' (Oestreich 1982: 30).[7] In this programme, prudential wisdom acquires a crucial role. 'Roman Stoicism,' writes Oestreich (1982: 7), 'as reconstructed by Lipsius, furnished a philosophical basis for a change in mental and spiritual attitudes'. Religious passions were to be muted:

> Lipsius met the religious needs of the age by supplying a religious, yet undogmatic base and, finally, by adapting it in some measure to Christian piety, but he openly declined to become involved in theology. In this age of confessional conflict, his appeal to ratio, to moral forces controlled by reason, liberated human piety and religious sentiment from dogmatism. Reason is called upon to create a world of self-control, moderation, pious yet active faith, and genuine reverence for God.
>
> (Oestreich 1982: 33)

It is hard to read these lines without recalling Matthew Hale, another 'extreme centrist' and 'Christian gentleman' who also took a Stoic model as an ethical guide to civil conduct in times of public ill.

The Lipsian programme rested on the 'disciplining process' outlined in *Of Constancie* and the works on military, legal and administrative training. The neo-Stoic man of constancy was a secular alternative to the contemporary enthusiasm for Christian models. Oestreich recognises Lipsius's contribution to the Dutch achievement of producing personnel for military, juridical and administrative offices, men equipped with a capacity to set aside their religious beliefs in order to perform official functions for the State.[8] This 'de-theologising' of soldiers, lawyers and administrators was all the more remarkable, given the circumstances:

> Deep religious emotions affected individuals and groups, united or divided territories and populations, cutting through families as well as nations. Theology held undisputed sway over men's lives. The layman was more firmly committed to his confession than any voter now is to his party, and the religious strife cut deeply into the life of individuals.
>
> (Oestreich 1982: 266)

The State's reason slowly became the official's professional rationality. The neo-Stoic aspect of this rationality is well caught by Bonney (1991: 314), following Oestreich: Lipsius 'thought it better for the subject to "endure any kind of punishment" meted out by the tyrant rather than to precipitate civil war'.

Absolutist separating of religious enthusiasm from civil government drew also on other non-Christian sources, ranging from Erasmus's cultivation of courtly manners to Machiavelli's art of politics, from Bodin's theorising of sovereignty to neo-Aristotelian political science. The practical need for non-theological competences in State administration and city commerce saw new modes of training for law and other fields. Viewed in terms of this administrative agenda, Absolutism has less to do with the notion of divine right than with a concrete response to the experience of confessional civil war. The issue was to disengage the demands of spiritual life from civil government, the dictates of moral conscience from law. This historical disengagement – if Koselleck is right – was to provoke post-Enlightenment moral critics into their still continuing attempt to restore the moral community of the old confessional State around the new figure of humanity and its inalienable rights.

The notion of Enlightenment as religion by other means invites us to revise habitual notions of Enlightenment as unpious irreligion. As Joachim Whaley (1981: 112) puts it: 'Enlightenment and piety went hand in hand. Progress was on the side of the angels.' Among Lutherans and Pietists, there was an attempt to 'formulate a code of social ethics based on the conviction that the church and its clergy should play a central role in the education of their congregations in the duties of responsible citizenship within the confines of an authoritarian state'. However, appointment to a function in the unitary State apparatus, no matter how honourable, transformed clergy into a cadre of civil servant.

For Americans used to the idea of Christian Churches as private associations, Churches that are agencies of the State will seem themselves in need of some redemption.[9] John Stroup (1984) has sought to redeem the Lutheran clergy of northwestern Germany, drawing attention to their moral protest against the centralising pressures of the State. The protests, he says, found expression in a practice of spirituality associated with a moral duty of personal *Bildung*. This practice of ethical self-fashioning, subsequently identified with philosophical and literary personalities, came to be trained in the critical humanities academy and is now emerging in the law school.

9

CONFLICT OF CONFESSIONS; CONFLICT OF FACULTIES

When confessionalisation possessed a territorial State, government became a programme of redemption. Given the conflict of confessions, the result was civil war fought for Christian principles but uncontrollable by any known legal or administrative instrument. The Absolutist State was the remarkable political response: a concerted attempt by administrative intellectuals and Statist lawyers to separate religion from government, morality from law, theology from public administration. The State or prince was not absolute in the sense of resolving ultimate questions of theology or pursuing the salvation of souls. They were absolute in the sense that their political judgments had social finality in the form of a *raison d'état* which made the peace and the order of the State the ultimate value. The received idea of Absolutism merits revision in two respects at least.[1] First, absolutism did not reduce to a doctrine of divine right of kings and their personal power. Second, although centralist, the Absolutist State was also pluralist in that it inherited the cameralist mode of governing the territory and 'policing' the population through multiple expert bureaux or administrative departments. Unlike a confessionalised community, the Absolutist State was not reducible to one theological doctrine or moral principle.

This is not the liberal division of powers (legislature, executive, judiciary). Nor is it derived from the liberal grant of primacy to the conscience and fundamental rights of the moral person that set limits to government. The history suggests something else: these limits derived from the State's self-limitation – as Bodin understood it – for the purpose of controlling dangerous religious zealotries and ending endless spiritual war. To aid citizens' survival, the Absolutist State installed a new division of powers. By disconnecting spiritual redemption from worldly government, the State undid the bond imposed when confessionalisation mortgaged government to religion and community. This separation was Absolutism's historical solution to confessional civil war. But it has since been intellectualised and inflated into humanity's metaphysical problem of 'divided' being.

The Absolutist State reset the roles of Church and State. Heavenly salvation was one thing, worldly political order was quite another. As always, there was more than one way of doing things. The French State under Louis XIV might have set out towards confessional freedom but ended by pursuing a policy of religious conformity to eradicate the Huguenots. In Kriele's (1969: 219) words: 'then too the war is at an end'. But the Prussian case is the interesting one. Here the State made itself indifferent to individuals' religious beliefs. Disengaging the spiritual from the political, distancing salvation (controlled by Church, confession and moral conscience) from civil life (controlled by State, government and worldly law), the Prussian State no longer took itself to be ruling in the name of the one true faith. Peace was imposed on fanatical divines and their inflamed communities by a State which set religious differences aside from worldly government.

Undoing the confessional knot that had bonded government to religious conscience aimed to remove the Church from any place in civil society. The most breathtaking achievement was the privatisation of conscience. As Koselleck (1988: 30) writes: 'conscience was not a subjective matter, but an act of deliberate judgment'. The 'political neutralisation' of religious zealotry was a step to peace. But it was also the crucial step towards religious freedom. This sounds paradoxical. The Absolutist State redefined individuals' religious beliefs as a purely private matter, entirely neutral as far as the State was concerned. Freed in this way, however, religious conscience lost its hold on the processes of civil government. This was not religious toleration as a fundamental moral advance whereby a natural human right – freedom of belief – was at long last recognised by a more enlightened society. It was 'purposive toleration', a political instrument for reserving the sphere of civil life entirely for civil government, positive law and secular administration. The confessions would no longer have a role in political government. Religious difference would no longer find expression in public disturbance.

Once the spheres of public conduct had been reserved for government, new secular institutions had to be founded to equip a governing elite to administer the business of the State. Civic universities were established, for instance at Halle in Brandenburg-Prussia in 1694. Halle was not a traditional university. As the public instrumentality of a modernising Absolutist State, its mission was not universal and spiritual but local and practical: to equip a new educated stratum with the interests and capacities appropriate to service in the civil offices of State. Political, legal and administrative skills (and a commitment to the Prussian State) would distinguish the Halle graduates, rather than confessional devotion (and a commitment to the imperial cause). An important academic reform went with this reorientation: the faculty of law displaced the faculty of theology as the locus of intellectual authority within the university.

In fact a variety of conflicting forces were in contention, associated with the personalities of three of its founding figures:

> Halle, the university of the rising Brandenburg-Prussia state, received an impress especially from three men: the jurist Christian Thomasius –

> who introduced the study of jurisprudence – the theologian A.H. Francke, and the philosopher Christian Wolff.
>
> (Paulsen 1908: 44)

Paulsen depicts Christian Thomasius (1655-1728) as 'the first teacher of the theory of natural rights at a German university . . . a man of the new culture represented at the French court . . . the editor of the first monthly magazine in the German language . . . the first to use that language in the lecture room'.[2] Thomasius served as head of the faculty of law. The students he drew formed the nucleus of the new university. From 1710, he was president for life. An anecdote points to his political disposition: 'On a visit to the princely library of Wolfenbüttel in 1707, Christian Thomasius discovered a partial print of the Political Testament of Dr Melchior von Osse, who had been a chancellor to the Elector of Saxony in the mid sixteenth century. This was a manual on the government and administration of a German territorial state. Thomasius decided to have it printed in full, and accordingly it appeared in 1717 in a fine quarto volume of over 500 pages "for the use of Thomasius' audience"' (Oestreich 1982: 155). The incident signals an intellectual orientation to practical politics: a professor of jurisprudence promoting a manual devoted to mundane matters of policing and civic administration. If Thomasius was so interested in a 150 year-old 'police' manual, we can take it that he shared Osse's concerns with cameralist matters such as hygiene and health, street-cleaning and fire-prevention, building codes and traffic regulation, Sunday observance and sorcery, cursing and perjury, weddings and funerals, begging and almsgiving. These are the concerns of social duty.[3]

As civic jurist, Thomasius sought to separate theology from jurisprudence while pairing law with civility. This too was an eminently practical tactic:

> One of the leading educational modernisers of early eighteenth-century Germany, Christian Thomasius, sought [at Halle] to combine the educational desiderata of a gentleman (including riding, fencing, foreign languages, and the new sciences) with the state's formal requirements for civil service education. Thanks to this clever mixture of cosmopolitan spirit and modern legal training, Thomasius began attracting law students from the wealthier classes from all over Germany.
>
> (McClelland: 1980: 34–5)

The mix echoes the London scene, where cosmopolitan life in court society and legal formation in the Inns of Court overlapped.[4] The recruitment of nobles to the Halle faculty of law to train for public office shows a traditional estate succumbing to the State on the civic, educational and professional front. Thomasius's 'clever' combination of law and courtly arts – dancing and music can be added to the list – was in part opportunistic: the new university was based upon an existing *Ritterakademie* or 'knight's academy', where sons of the aristocracy received their 'finishing' schooling in martial arts, social graces, foreign languages and mathematics (McClelland 1980: 34–5). Of course, from Halle's standpoint, nobles also 'paid considerably higher fees than commoners and brought a certain prestige to the university'.

There is also a philosophical side to Thomasius's art of disarticulation. In a manner that typifies the anti-war politics of the post-war Absolutist intellectuals, he drew conceptual boundaries to expel theology from jurisprudence and proposed divisions to mark philosophical morality off from positive law. These boundaries and divisions rested on a new demarcation between private and public, that is, between conscience and government. They were defended in treatises and pamphlets designed to remove the Church from public life and establish law on a basis amenable to State interest rather than theology.

The point – Thomasius's 'political neutralisation' of organised religion as a force in civil government – can be made by reference to his later work, the *Fundamenta juris naturae ex sensu comuni deducta* (*Foundations of the Law of Nature and Nations Deduced from Common Sense*). We again encounter the division of *honestum*, *justum* and *decorum* that Sir Matthew Hale adopted to organise his thinking on the relations between religion, law and social manners. The *honestum* is the sphere of moral conscience and governs our actions by inner piety and the spiritual pangs of conscience. The *justum* is the sphere of law and governs our actions by public legal sanctions. The *decorum* is the sphere of manners and politics, governed by social norms. The three spheres did not form a hierarchy in which *decorum* and *justum* were steps towards morality or *honestum*. On the contrary, Thomasius's aim was to insulate law and manners from the devastation that religious conscience and moral absolutes had wreaked when pursued into reality.

Schematic perhaps, these categorisations were crucial intellectual devices to bring students to terms with the new political reality in which one's religion was to be a private matter, and in which worldly law and social manners shouldered responsibility for achieving peace and maintaining social order. Rendered independent of theology, positive law was to secure the practical conditions of survival. Such law sheds any transcendental standpoint of adjudication in theological truth. Thomasius thus argued for legal limits to the public exercise of church law, the *ius circa sacra*. The sovereign's positive law was absolute in the territorial State. Indeed, had clergy not usurped it, this power would still be recognised as belonging to sovereigns, for it was originally theirs.[5] The treatises that Thomasius published at Halle attest to his preoccupation with containing ecclesiastical powers: in 1695 *De iure principis circa adiaphora* (*On the Right of the Prince Concerning Things Indifferent*),[6] in 1696 (with Enno Brenneysen) *Das Recht evangelischer Fürsten in theologischen Streitigkeiten* (*On the Right of Evangelical Princes in Theological Controversies*), in 1697 *Problema Juridicum An haeresis sit crimen?* (*On the Juridical Problem Is Heresy a Crime?*) and *De iure principis circa haereticos* (*On the Right of the Prince Concerning Heretics*), and in 1712 *Cautele circa praecognita jurisprudentiae ecclesiasticae* (*Precautions concerning the Principles of Ecclesiastical Jurisprudence*).

Thomasius's reasoning can be illustrated by indicative comment on some of these works, with a passing mention of his 1712 *De origine ac progressu processus inquisitorii contra sagas* (*On the Origin and Progress of Inquisitorial Procedure against Witches*). In *On the Right of Evangelical Princes in Theological Controversies*, Thomasius delimited the capacity of clergy to determine matters pertaining to the public sphere, the legal jurisdiction of the prince alone, organised religion having no place in civil government. As Christian, the prince obeys the will of God, listens to inner conscience and hopes for personal salvation. As worldly magistrate, however, the prince obeys only the *raison d'état* which is directed not to salvation but to the peace of the State and the survival of its citizens. The distinction is made more complex by an intermediate status: the prince as man, bound to the law of nature.[7] Yet civil peace is the practical precondition of self-preservation (the law of nature) and thus of concern with one's soul (the law of God). The prince thus subordinates his roles as Christian and as man to his role as prince. The same arrangement has general application. To achieve civil peace, it is not necessary that individuals act according to their innermost conscience. It is imperative, however, that they act in accordance with the territorial laws designed to protect that peace.

Thomasius also drew the boundary between the religious and the legal spheres in relation to law about heresy and witchcraft. Here too he rolled back theological jurisdiction. *Is heresy a crime?* (1697) argues that heresy should be immune to penal sanctions since it was an error of understanding, not an error of will and thus not a crime. To impose secular sanctions on heretics was to grant religion standing in the sphere of public government. Correcting religious beliefs was not the role of criminal law.

A parallel case is made against penal sanctions on witchcraft in *On the Origin and Progress of Inquisitorial Procedure against Witches* (1712). Again it is a case of recognising that positive law did not regulate religious belief. However, in specifying the jurisdictional limits, Thomasius's point was not to curb that law in the name of human rights but to free it from religious interference. This was not 'humanisation' but advocacy of a politically neutralised religious sphere and a de-theologised civil sphere, an argument intelligible in the historical circumstances of a German Absolutist State that totally rejected any power-sharing with organised religion. As to the specific issue of witchcraft, a statutory offence derived from times when no clear demarcation had existed between the sphere of religion and that of civil life. In times of confessional mass mobilisation, the secular courts would be pressured into an ecclesiastical concern: witchcraft as the devil's work. Through this door religion obtained a place in civil government, endangering peace by again imposing one creed on all. Hence Thomasius's 'de-criminalisation' of witchcraft as an error of private religious belief and his rejection of witch-burning as a religious interference in a sphere where the Church should be allowed no public jurisdiction. The English history was different. Chief Justice Hale had sentenced the two witches at Bury St Edmunds in 1662. In England, the secular courts could still be pressured into what was, for Thomasius, strictly a confessional concern. Thus, in England, for all the philosophising on fundamental liberties, law still hanged witches.

For Thomasius, however, witchcraft was a matter for the *honestum*, a religious belief whose handling belonged to private conscience with which the positive law – *justum* – had no business. Distinguishing between religion and law, Thomasius also had to take his distance from traditional natural law, separating positive law – typically legislation by states – from theological doctrines and moral absolutes. Dreitzel (1996: 19) recognises Thomasius as having reached the point of a major disarticulation: 'Positive law is the only law; "natural law in the strict sense" contains only maxims for legislation and judgment. There is no natural law as God's legislation – only as advice for living (*Lebensführung*) as Christ preached.' The State and its law were thus detached from a natural law framework as they were from theology. The order of positive law was an end in itself. In this light juristic studies could be refashioned to serve not for ultimate truths but for the non-theological training of an administrative elite.

Thomasius could build on what Richard Tuck (1987) terms the 'modern natural law' theory of Grotius. This theory faced the fact that religious division was a horizon for any politics but still sought a law of nature on which to base moral conduct and civil order. Religious division had generated confessional war. As Tuck (1987: 115–17) notes, 'many of these modern natural-law writers turned to a powerful and – in our terms – illiberal state to protect intellectual freedoms from mistaken or dogmatic philosophers arrayed in churches'. They knew the post-war State as the guardian not the predator of religious freedom. Drawing on a 'substantial element of descriptive ethical sociology' and linked to actual diplomatic and commercial activities,[8] Grotius proposed a natural right to self-preservation and a natural wrong of inflicting wanton death (Tuck 1987: 115–17).[9] In formulating this 'minimalist core of universal moral principles' pertaining to all humans no matter where or when, Grotius sought a natural law immune to confessional difference.

Linked also to court civility, this 'minimalist core' of natural law had sufficient social gravity to enhance Thomasius's anti-theological jurisprudence. Yet he was always up against the 'maximalist' Christian ethos that empowered its enthusiasts with an incorrigible sense of ultimate moral right. Tuck (1987: 118) identifies the threat: 'It would, I think, be impossible to overestimate the importance to these [natural law] writers of their sense that large areas of life needed defending from fanatics, that is, from people who believed in more extensive moral obligations than those contained in the minimalist core'. Given this threat, the natural law theorists 'saw it as part of their duty to defend a relatively pluralist intellectual and aesthetic culture against its enemies – notably the Calvinist and Catholic churches'. Surprisingly, Tuck does not apply the term 'fanatic' to those whom he identifies as the barrier to our own understanding of the natural law minimalists: today's advocates of a 'post-Kantian history of morality'.

With the fashion for studies in the law of nature, the sons of the German upper classes enrolled in the 'modern legal training' at Halle with no sense of demeaning themselves (McClelland 1980).[10] The cultivation of *decorum* – polite manners and civility – was an important factor. Among the elements confected by Thomasius into an eclectic civic ethos for the post-war times were an Epicurean ethic and neo-Stoic conduct, as well as the *honnête homme* or the 'gentleman' modelled in 'court philosophy'. Along with Castiglione, a source was Baltasar Gracian y Morales, the improbable Spanish Jesuit who wrote 'galant' conduct manuals such as *El Héroe* (1637) with its portrait of the ideal courtier, *L'arte de ingenuo* (1642) with its guide to the 'precious' manner, and *Il Discreto* (1646) with its directions for the knowing 'man of the world'. This worldly persona is the Thomasius who founded and edited *Monatsgespräche* (*Monthly Conversations Entertaining and Serious, Rational and Unsophisticated Ideas on All Kinds of Agreeable and Useful Books and Subjects*). It was the first such periodical in German and only slightly later than the original periodical of style, the French *Mercure galant* of 1672 (later the *Mercure de France*). Thomasius followed the *Mercure* in appealing to women readers. Then, as now, Parisian style counted. In *Von der Nachamung des Franzosen* (1687), Thomasius recommended 'imitation of the French', citing Madeleine de Scudéry, author of the *précieux* novel *Clélie*, on the worldly arts of *politesse* and the good taste of the *salon*. These skills of social rhetoric were conceptualised as *decorum*, the repertoire of civil manners appropriate to life at court or in diplomacy. They enabled peaceful sociability between men of different religious confessions and moral customs in the absence of any universal morality of the sort envisaged in the theological domain of natural law (Rüping 1968: 50–3). Like positive law, *decorum* was thus an end in itself, not a step on the stairway to more spiritual being. *Decorum* did not pretend to theological truth. Better, if Elias (1983) is right, it made a contribution to the Western civilising process.

At Halle Thomasius had rivals. Not least was the Pietist theologian August Hermann Francke (1663–1727). At first Halle benefited from their co-presence. McClelland (1980: 34) explains that in the early eighteenth century Pietism was still a 'dynamic force in Germany, a religious doctrine stressing active faith and emotional commitment more than scholastic subtlety'. This dynamism was not limited to an intensification of the citizens' inner spirituality. It took shape in radical social reforms in Halle – the Pietist orphanage and schools, publishing and trading companies. Hence the Pietists teaching at Halle were 'not implacably opposed to the vita activa and thus did not place major obstacles in the way of other faculties'. Not at first. By 1713, however, Pietist intolerance had succeeded temporarily in curtailing Thomasius's activities in the faculty of law.

More was at stake in this confrontation between the faculty of law and the faculty of theology than Thomasius's argument on the historical and non-universal character of the injunction against polygamy. A biblical crime was not inevitably a civil crime. In his history of Pietism and State formation in Brandenburg-Prussia, Carl Hinrichs (1971) relates this particular dispute to a more general conflict between Thomasius and Francke. By charging that Thomasius endorsed polygamy, the Pietists had the king silence him on questions which they held to be the preserve of theologians. The broader charge that Thomasius's jurisprudence was atheistic marks this as a nasty conflict of university faculties.[11] The theologians sought to suppress the jurist on issues that they deemed fundamental and thus their own, that is, on religious, ecclesiastical and moral questions. In principle, a demarcation of this sort was quite in line with Thomasius's separation of religion from law. But it was also a practical question: who was to instruct the future officers of the State? Hinrichs (1971) sees in the conflict of the Halle faculties of theology and law a competition between an older theological and a newer civil programme of life brought about by the emergence of the Absolutist State. As representatives of these programmes, Francke and Thomasius did not stand in an exact antithesis. Both accepted the Pietist doctrine of the Fall and its consequence: humanity's incapacity to know the divine essence of things. Thomasius used this limit to justify the need for purely worldly measures to make life civil for the citizens of the territory; Francke pursued the transformative path: a spiritual renewal that would save the individual and, ultimately, the world.

For the theologian, it is a matter of completing the second Reformation by pursuing piety in every aspect of the world. For the jurist, historical law and worldly manners achieve the best in the circumstances. The discipline of law and the cultivation of manners were not one and the same. Hinrichs (1971: 358–9) records Thomasius's observation that university training should not stress manners to the point where intellectual learning becomes inadequate. However, when decorum is neglected, as in the faculty of theology where spirituality takes absolute precedence, the result will be graduates who are 'useful for nothing; who are a burden to themselves and others; who need neither man nor God; who wish to reform and improve everything but are in themselves the most miserable people; with whom one can have no rational intercourse; who trample all reason under foot and with an irrational so-called conscience torment themselves and others.' This zealous Pietist, lacking social graces and thus unsuited to worldly occupations of which he is nonetheless so critical, is the converse of Thomasius's cosmopolitan young noble trained for service in the State's administrative elite. The conflict of the faculties of law and theology ended by damaging Halle's reputation. As McClelland (1980: 35) observes, '[o]nly when these two rather different traditions – the worldly noble and the Pietistic – came into conflict did Halle's fortunes decline'.

In fact the academic conflict at Halle was three-cornered. The faculty of philosophy, in the person of Christian Wolff, was equally engaged. In Paulsen's

(1908: 45) view, Wolff's contribution to Halle was of the 'greatest significance':

> The aim of philosophical instruction up to this time had been to inculcate the scholastic Aristotelianism, primarily as a preparation for the study of theology. The new philosophy now defiantly appealed to its own reason. Wolff's *Vernünftige Gedanken*, the general title of his German works, positively denies the dependence of philosophy upon theology. Basing himself upon the modern sciences of mathematics and physics, he declares that philosophy should seek the truth free from all assumptions, regardless of what may happen to the theologians. Similarly as in the case of theoretical philosophy, the theological basis of practical philosophy was also positively repudiated: law and morals, he declared, must be based upon a rational knowledge of human life and society'.
>
> (Paulsen 1908: 35)

This was a declaration of war by philosophy on both theology and law.[12] At Halle the battle of the 'new philosophy' and Pietistic theology ended with Francke's success in having Wolff banished to Marburg from 1723 to 1740, when Frederick the Great allowed him to return to Halle. For their part, Thomasius and his followers were just as keen to attack the philosophers.

In Paulsen's account, law was as much the target of philosophy as theology. Like theology, law was said to lack a fully rational knowledge of its own conditions. Like the theologians, the jurists were thus to be demoted in favour of practitioners of the one discipline 'free from all assumptions', namely philosophy. As Paulsen (1908: 393) put it, 'The essential prerequisite for applying the law is not merely a familiarity with the statutes but rather a mastery of the rational principles of all law'. Between the philosopher's claim to know these metaphysical principles and the minimalist natural law jurisprudence of Grotius and Thomasius the contrast could not be clearer. For the philosopher, what matters is 'to recognise the inherent necessity of legal norms and institutions, to find their teleological explanations in the conditions essential to both state and society' (Paulsen 1908: 395). But only philosophy can know these prior conditions, being 'free from presuppositions, the absolutely unbiased science, because it is its function to examine the presuppositions of all the rest' (Paulsen 1908: 239–40). But then, as a foremost neo-Kantian, Paulsen would be expected to say just this.

Thomasius's concern was primarily practical: to equip his students and the educated stratum with an ethos appropriate to a civil life. Like his advocacy of reason of State and legal proceduralism, his differentiation of *honestum*, *justum* and *decorum* was not to accord a fundamental truth to theology or philosophy. It was his instrument for disarticulating religion from law and social life. In this schema, the philosophy of reason was denied the power to reunify the separated spheres of life.

The issues that provoked the academic battles at Halle were still unsettled at the end of the eighteenth century. They remain unfinished business. Kant laid down his resolution in the *Conflict of the Faculties*, three essays on the relations of the philosophy of universal reason to theology, law and medicine. Published in 1798, this late work still sets terms for moral critique of law, depicting an ideal hierarchy of critical consciousness in which lawyers – along with clergy and doctors – are assessed from a standpoint above and beyond their historically compartmentalised interests. A similar hierarchy, Kant argues, should mark the division of the university into faculties: on the one hand, the faculties of theology, law and medicine (the 'higher' faculties); on the other hand, the 'lower' faculty of philosophy.[13] The former are simply creatures of the State which sets their terms of action: to train professional clergy, lawyers and doctors as 'tools of the government' (Kant 1979: 25). The faculties of theology, law and medicine are bound to the teaching of officially sanctioned 'writings'. Thus 'the biblical theologian draws his teachings not from reason but from the *Bible*; the professor of law gets his, not from natural law, but from the *law of the land*; and the professor of medicine does not draw his *method of therapy as practised on the public* from the physiology of the human body but from *medical regulations*' (Kant 1979: 35). But the faculty of critical philosophy is different in kind:

> It is absolutely essential that the learned community at the university also contain a faculty that is independent of the government's commands with regard to its teachings; one that, having no commands to give, is free to evaluate everything, and concerns itself with the interests of the sciences, that is, with truth: one in which reason is authorised to speak out publicly. For without a faculty of this kind, the truth would not come to light (and this would be to the government's own detriment); but reason is by its nature free and admits of no command to hold something as true (no imperative 'Believe!' but only a free 'I believe').
>
> (Kant 1979: 27, 29)

The others fall short of the faculty of philosophy. Indeed, they must, since this faculty alone derives its teachings from the 'free play' of pure moral reason that has not been tied to this particular instrumental purpose or to that particular utilitarian interest.

Philosophers' privileged access to moral right and critical reason allows them to illuminate the limits of any present jurisprudence. Conversely, the jurist is bound by contingency and convention:

> The jurist, as an authority on the text, does not look to his reason for the laws that secure the *Mine* and *Thine*, but to the code of laws that has been publicly promulgated and sanctioned by the highest authority (if, as he should, he acts as a civil servant). To require him to prove the

> truth of these laws and their conformity with right, or to defend them against reason's objections, would be unfair. For these decrees first determine what is right, and the jurist must straightaway dismiss as nonsense the further question of whether the decrees themselves are right.
>
> (Kant 1979: 37, 39)

Indeed, the jurist must obey the inferior imperative of the State's 'external and supreme will'. Not to do so 'on the grounds that it allegedly does not conform with reason would be absurd; for the dignity of the government consists precisely in this: that it does not leave its subjects free to judge what is right or wrong according to their own notions, but [determines right and wrong] for them by precepts of the legislative power' (Kant 1979: 39). The critical philosopher demotes the work of these 'officials' for whom the highest form of conduct is obedience to the 'dignity' of government directives. Against this 'external obedience' Kant (1979: 45) elevates philosophical reason as the sole site of truly free judgment, the disinterested voice of the one faculty that exposes the contingency of all the others. 'A department of this kind', he writes, 'must be established at a university; in other words, a university must have a faculty of philosophy. Its function in relation to the three higher faculties is to control them and, in this way, to be useful to them, since *truth* (the essential and first condition of learning in general) is the main thing, whereas the *utility* the higher faculties promise the government is of secondary importance.'

It is truly a grand programme. However, since for the time being the 'people' will remain 'incompetent' (Kant 1979: 25), the theology, law and medicine that regulate their external conduct cannot yet be replaced by the philosophy of reason that speaks to the universal mind. Given this temporary deficit, for the present the 'conflict can never end, and it is the philosophy faculty that must always be prepared to keep it going' (Kant 1979: 55). Whatever the given circumstance, it will be challenged by the critical philosophy. This never-ending critique of existing institutions takes itself to be the intellectual answer to the historical and sociological scepticism generated by the evidence of irreducible religious difference and insurmountable moral variation. To this end religion is quite redefined, de-theologised and de-historicised. It is no longer 'the sum of certain teachings regarded as divine revelations (that is called theology), but the sum of all our duties regarded as divine *commands* (and, on the subject's part, the maxim of fulfilling them as such)' (Kant 1979: 61). The fact of historical difference is transcended when 'morality' displaces the actual plurality of confessions:

> As far as its matter or object is concerned, religion does not differ in any point from morality, for it is concerned with duties as such. Its distinction from morality is a merely formal one: that reason in its legislation uses the Idea of God, which is derived from morality itself, to give

morality influence on man's will to fulfil all his duties. This is why there is only one religion.

(Kant 1979: 61)

Or one morality. Unlike historically divided confessional religion, in this moral reason that alone 'deserves to be called religion, there can be no division into sects (for since religion is one, universal and necessary, it cannot vary)'. As a result, 'a division into sects can never occur in matters of pure religious belief. Wherever sectarianism is to be found, it arises from a mistake on the part of ecclesiastical faith: the mistake of regarding its statutes (even if they are divine revelations) for essential parts of religion, and so substituting empiricism in matters of faith for rationalism and passing off what is merely contingent as necessary in itself' (Kant 1979: 85, 89).

In this Kantian manoeuvre, a de-theologisation of religion would overcome sectarianism. Religions would be replaced by a universal moral law on which any future State must be grounded. This was Kant's weapon in the contest with statists' arguments. In their manoeuvre, too, as in Thomasius's programme, sectarianism is overcome by a de-theologisation. But here religion is not replaced by a higher moral law; it is displaced by a State on whose political interests – civil peace above all – the moral code itself depends.

Kant's commitment to the one all-transcending end – humanity's advance to the pure rationality of moral reflection – responds to sceptics' recognition of historical difference as final fact. All actually existing practices become provisional modes of being, pending our ascent to morality. Only critical philosophy is spared, spanning as it is said to do from the contingent to the necessary. In glimpsing the *a priori* principles, the faculty of philosophy transcends the faculty of 'merely contingent' positive law as surely as it does the faculty of merely 'biblical' or historical theology. The terms of this challenge to positive institutions have become habitual. Whether against State or government, bureaucracy or the existing legal system, the critical claim remains the same: to see through the practice in question to its formal conditions of possibility. These, by definition, are hidden to the practitioners but visible to the critic's 'eye of reason', as St German might have put it. Positive institutions are thus rendered transparent to theoretical critique that anticipates the higher moral ends of which existing practices have lost sight but to which the insightful critic now recalls them. Law is rejoined to a morality it had forgotten.

Beyond the chapter title, 'The conflict of the philosophy faculty with the faculty of law', Kant's collection is silent on actual law. It is, rather, an extended meditation on the topic: 'An old question raised again: is the human race constantly progressing?'. In *The Metaphysical Elements of Justice* (*Metaphysische Anfangsgründe der Rechtslehre*), Part One of *The Metaphysics of Morals* (*Metaphysik der Sitten*), Kant proposed a 'general theory of justice' as the application of the principles uncovered in the earlier *Foundations of the Metaphysics of Morals*. Recalled to 'supreme principles', 'ultimate criteria' and 'concepts preliminary' to action, law becomes an extension of thought about morality. Legality is subsumed into moral rules:

> The mere agreement or disagreement of an action with the law, without regard to the incentive of the action, is called *legality*; but when the Idea of duty arising from the law is at the same time the incentive of the action, then the agreement is called the morality of the action.
>
> (Kant 1965: 19)

A fundamental threshold is installed between a merely prudential jurisprudence and a truly critical philosophy. Such a jurisprudence is then adjudged a failure to realise universal enlightenment, as if this was an appropriate criterion for historical law and professional lawyers. From this enlightened standpoint, empirical legal arrangements are of interest primarily as prelude to the contrast: 'But it is otherwise with moral laws . . . [or] with the instructions of morality', given that the latter 'command everyone without regard to his inclinations, solely because and insofar as he is free' (Kant 1965: 15).

Bathing in this critical light, Kant rewrites the history of the Absolutist State with a truly moral vengeance, obliterating all trace of the fact that freedom – religous freedom in particular – was a peace-keeping initiative of the State. Instead, the State is simply a derivative reality of man's exercise of his natural freedom:

> [W]e cannot say that a man has sacrificed to the state a part of his inborn external freedom for some particular purpose; rather, we must say that he has completely abandoned his wild, lawless freedom in order to find his whole freedom again undiminished in a lawful dependency, that is, in a juridical state of society, since this dependency comes from his own legislative Will.
>
> (Kant 1965: 81)

Having established self-directing man as the maker of social order, Kant (1965: 84) dismisses historical approaches to the State and its law as 'pointless' on three different grounds. First, it is intellectually futile to seek historical explanations for what is metaphysical necessity: the *a priori* conditions of morality. Second, it is politically dangerous to do so. Such questions 'threaten the state with danger if they are asked with too much sophistication by a people who are already subject to civil law; for, if the subject decides to resist the present ruling authority as the result of ruminating on its origin, he would be rightfully punished, destroyed, or exiled (as an outlaw, *ex lex*) in accordance with the laws of that authority itself.' Transcendental morality gives way to rank intolerance, perhaps displaying Kant's dismay at events in Revolutionary France. Third, to safeguard the rational integrity of his schema, Kant refuses to countenance that the politically 'supreme legislation' could 'contain a stipulation that it is not supreme'. Thus, he argues, '[i]t is the people's duty to endure even the most intolerable abuse of supreme authority' (Kant 1965: 86).

In his 'Supplementary explanations' to *The Metaphysical Elements of Justice*, Kant justifies total obedience to a worldly law that, by his own account, is a mere historical appearance, not a perfect constitution: 'Although the [actual] constitution may contain grave defects and gross errors and may need to be gradually improved in important respects, still, as such, it is absolutely unpermitted and culpable to oppose it' (Kant 1965: 140). Such opposition breaches the 'Idea of a political constitution' that Kant terms 'holy and irresistible'. His mode is gracious: to apologise for the present state of the world even at its best.

It is not difficult to imagine the civilian jurists whom Weber described as 'automatons of the paragraphs' being denigrated as one-sided formalist technicians. It is not difficult to imagine Lipsius's self-denying neo-Stoic officers denigrated as alienated instruments of State power. Yet this is to deny the achievement of fashioning a personnel of men and women able to operate within the relatively impersonal procedures of the law and its administration, curbing their individual discretion the better to adhere to the 'course of the law' and arriving at judgments possibly at odds with their own religious views. It is also to gloss over the social discipline needed to treat State service as honourable. Nor is it difficult to imagine Thomasius's gentlemen-lawyers denigrated as unprincipled *galants* too superficial and morate to attend to humanity's spiritual transformation. Yet this comfortably omits the contribution of positive law and civil manners to the social order whereby the State ended confessional strife by granting a space for freedom of religion.[14]

Nor is it hard to appreciate why, already in the eighteenth century, Friedrich Schiller set about redressing what he took to be Kant's one-sided stress on formal reason by a balancing return to the sensuous life that resisted rational programming. This now well-practised move from formalism to dialectical play was perfected in a nineteenth-century German academy where metaphysical philosophy was dominant and where Hegel and Marx projected Schiller's aesthetic dialectic into a developmental philosophy of history that has generated powerful images of future humanity as a moral community. It remains the favoured device of today's critics of law and government.

Neither Kant's unifying moral reason nor Schiller's dialectical aesthetic wholeness tolerated segmentation in the style of Hobbes's differentiation of man and citizen as discrete personae or Thomasius's separation of religion, law and manners as independent positive spheres of life. To heal the historical separation of religion from government, these intellectual exercises sought to forget the separation that came with the neutralisation of belligerent confessional conscience. In particular, the Enlighteners rewrote the actual history of the State's grant of religious freedom. To recall Koselleck (1988: 73): 'Protection by the State was replaced by protection from the State.' A contest was thus initiated between critical modes of thought and positive history.

Into this unresolved contest it is worth introducing Michel Foucault's (1991) account of 'governmentality'. Given his thoroughly revisionist recognition that exercises of power have been productive not repressive of new human capacities, Foucault easily admits the achievement of seventeenth-century government: the emergent sciences of 'police' that saw multiple fields of technical expertise begin their transformative work on territory and population. However, as he tells it, the developmental work of these relatively autonomous fields was left incomplete, blocked by a sovereignty that expressed the will of the Absolutist prince. Foucault thus diverges in two respects from Schilling and Koselleck. First, he neglects the role of religion in fashioning a State that was both governmental and 'confessional'; second, he depicts Absolutism as the political accompaniment of the early modern 'police' State, not as the political response – in the form of a de-theologising *raison d'état* – to the confessional monopolisation of that State and the consequent onset of uncontrollable civil war.

Foucault's account is perhaps more a theoretical position than a historical description. To establish a threshold against which to set his own social theory, he unifies the Absolutist system into what he terms the 'juridico-discursive',[15] a bloc against which the new expert governmental discourses of cameralism failed to assert themselves as a brake on State power. The break came later, with the emergence of a quite new political order, the 'disciplinary society' or 'archipelago'. Foucault programmatically distinguished a before and an after, an epochal break from a regime of singular power exercised via the spectacle of Absolutist sovereignty to a regime of plural powers exercised via normalising but invisible disciplines that 'escaped the rules of jurisprudence' (Foucault 1979: 88). This theoretical distinction aimed to contrast perfectly antithetical ways of exercising power. On one side, there was public execution, dismemberment and the full majestic ceremony of a law whose single purpose is to repress whomsoever violates the sovereign's will. On the other side, there was the web of less conspicuous yet ubiquitous disciplinary institutions working away in schools, hospitals and families – below the threshold of the law. This division between the 'juridical' and the 'normative' reduced the confessional State and the Absolutist response to a convenient foil for a 'modernity' that Foucault wished to theorise in his own terms of 'polymorphous' normalising disciplines. These latter, he wrote, render law 'utterly incongruous with the new methods of power' (Foucault 1979: 89) by ushering in 'a society which, from the eighteenth century to the present, has created so many technologies of power that are foreign to the concept of law' (Foucault 1979: 109).[16]

The concept of the 'juridico-discursive' marked Foucault's adherence to a 'command' theory of law. It assimilated all of law to interdiction and the criminal penalty: 'law cannot help but be armed, and its arm par excellence is death; to those who transgress it, it replies, at least as a last resort, with that absolute menace' (Foucault 1979: 144). Against the 'juridico-discursive' Foucault (1980: 102) issued his emancipatory imperative: 'We must eschew the model of *Leviathan* in the study of power. We must escape from the limited field of juridical sovereignty and state institutions, and instead base our analysis of power on the study of the techniques and tactics of domination.' This was an invitation for critical theorising to continue, uninterrupted. Yet, in contrasting a negative and repressive pre-modernity – the 'juridico-discursive' – with his own counter-conception of the disciplines as modern and 'productive' governmental power, Foucault applied to law precisely the negative concept of power that he seemed to have rejected. Locked into this general antithesis, he neglected the constructive effects of the legal order, notably the manner in which law ascribes to individuals (and non-individuals) forms of legal agency that allow entry into civic, economic and personal capacities. Analysis of power relations cannot get far without recognising this enabling side of law.

To enhance his picture of 'polymorphous' forms of modern disciplinary power, Foucault counterposed it to an image of law assimilated to the unitary power of the sovereign. The Absolutist State indeed sought to unify territory and population, to centralise rule and administration. But when we look at the historical circumstances, what we see is quite different. In England, with Coke, the common lawyers engaged in their resistance to the sovereign. In France, far from a unitary centre of royal power, we see an eclectic array of jurisdictions: royal, aristocratic, ecclesiastical, parliamentary, regional and local.[17] As an academic notion, it is true, the unity of the laws dated back to the sixteenth century and Hotman's project; Domat worked on an *Institution* of French law in the 1600s; from the later eighteenth century, Bourjon and Pothier worked to distil unity from the scatter. But that unity took form only with the *Code Civil des Français* of the Napoleonic commission. The dispersed German territories, too, displayed a unity at the academic and theoretical level – codification and synthesis were artefacts of university law faculties – but a disunity (or absence) of effective legal institutions. Far from resting on a solid juridical unity, these territories struggled to centralise adjudication away from the dispersed sites of traditional power: noble estates and *Lände*, imperial and ecclesiastical authorities, regional and municipal customs, feudal remnants.

The point is not that Foucault's *Discipline and Punish* would have been a better work had it referred to all this. It is simply that the 'juridico-discursive' is less history than philosophical presupposition. Foucault's concept functions as the foil for his new social theory of governmentality and the disciplines and sustains his depiction of an epoch of sovereign power and law definitively superseded by an epoch of disciplines and liberal government. In *Discipline and Punish*, law was reduced to 'theatrical remnants' (Foucault 1977a: 184) mortgaged to sovereignty, an outdated form of power. Hence the epochal warning in the first volume of *The History of Sexuality*: 'We have entered a phase of juridical regression in comparison with the pre-seventeenth-century societies we are acquainted with; we should not be deceived by all the Constitutions framed throughout the world since the French Revolution, the Codes written and revised, a whole continual and clamorous legislative activity' (Foucault 1979: 144). Yet contradictory texts can be culled from Foucault's oeuvre. In 'Governmentality', having referred to the 'triangular' relation between sovereignty, discipline and government, Foucault (1991: 102) wrote that we should not think 'in terms of the substitution of a society of sovereignty by a disciplinary society and the subsequent replacement of a disciplinary society by a governmental one'.

Perhaps a positive gloss on these inconsistencies can be found. To Richard Tuck's (1987) observation that early modern natural law thinkers turned to an 'illiberal State' to protect their freedoms and Stephen Holmes's (1988: 6) lesson that the historical record in fact shows a 'supportive relation between state power and individual freedom', we can add Foucault's admission: what we now take to be 'liberal' rights in matters of religion and economy derive not from a restriction but from the broadening of government responsibility that occurred when the State excluded religion from the public sphere. This being granted, as history, Foucault's (1991) account of liberal governmentality remains a brilliant dialectical projection in which exemplary oppositions – constraint and freedom, directive State and self-directing population, government and self-government – endlessly play off one another in the usual manner of critique.

To see the building of social order as a positive achievement is not Foucault's theme. Conversely, he offers exquisite formulae inciting us to 'think otherwise' and to 'separate out, from the contingency that has made us what we are, the possibility of no longer being, doing or thinking what we are, do or think' (Foucault 1985: 46). Perhaps law and lawyering are simply too gritty and positive, too much part of given circumstances to register as interesting to the other-worldly Foucault who confessed: 'I would like to produce some effects of truth which might be used for a possible battle, to be waged by those who wish to wage it, in forms yet to be found and in organisations yet to be defined' (Foucault 1989: 191). Given this sort of disposition, determinacy in social conditions can register only as impediment or oppression, not as cultural achievement. This is why, in approaching the ancient techniques of self as aesthetic rather than purposive, Foucault misses what his sometime critic Pierre Hadot (1990) sees: in times of worldly chaos nothing might be more 'other' than the ethos of those engaged in producing order. But social stability as cultural achievement is a difficult theme for critical intellectuals. The abandon with which 'difference' and 'transgression' are now discerned in Foucault's work for consumption as cathartic intellectual stimulants is a measure of how critics can become mindless of the ordered civic existence that makes their form of life possible.

Defining 'disciplinary society', Foucault (1977a: 223) was at pains to treat the 'universal juridicism' of modern society as nothing but a mask for the exercise of domination 'on the underside of law'. Despite this retreat into conventional ideology critique, it would be wrong to consign Foucault entirely to the critical basket. He was also the author of descriptive genealogies –

'grey, meticulous and patiently documentary' (Foucault 1977b: 139). Yet it is probably through others than Foucault that we might best broaden discussion into the fields of historically inflected sociology and philosophy.

Max Weber has provided the formulations 'conducts of life' and 'departments of existence'. This is not the Weber of general theories of modernity, rationality or domination but the one 'reconstructed' by Wilhelm Hennis (1988), for whom Weber's 'central theme' is the formation of 'personalities' fitted to existence in definite 'orderings of life' (*Lebensordnungen*), particularly the methodical orderings of professional life. The crux is the match between the properties of personae and the properties of specific cultural settings. Investigation of a persona in an order of living entails attending to the practical techniques for living a given 'conduct of life' (*Lebensführung*).

Of Weber's historical studies of personae, the Puritan is the most famous. This was the persona housed in the distinctive order of living associated with the Protestant sects where life was methodically conducted by daily Bible reading, constant keeping of spiritual account-books or journals, intense monitoring of one's spiritual progress through each day and through life. The ideally self-governing persona fashioned in this manner and for this milieu was not restrictive of human freedom but augmented lives with new interests and capacities. Along with the Puritan, Weber explored other personae and their cultural settings: the bureaucrat in the administrative office; the intellectual in Weimar literary society; the peasant in the agrarian life order of Eastern Germany; the university scholar in defeated post-war Germany; the common lawyers and the civil lawyers in their respective settings, the English Inns of Court and the continental law school. Nor should we forget the persona of the singer in the German choral society:

> A person who is used daily to let powerful feelings flow out of his breast through his larynx without relation to his action – without therefore adequate abreaction of these powerful expressed feelings in powerful actions – that is a person who, in short, very easily becomes a 'good citizen', in the passive sense of the word. No wonder that monarchs have such a love of these sorts of performances. 'Where they sing you can peacefully settle down.'
>
> (in Hennis 1988: 57–8)

Weber's lesson concerns the extraordinary work that has gone into fashioning novel personae to meet the exigencies of particular cultural settings. There is no general relation – of integration or alienation – between personae and their spheres of life. As happened in Lemgo, choral singing might not always give monarchs peaceful reassurance. There is no theoretical breakthrough here. As Hennis (1988: 24) says: 'It is not so much the complexity, but rather the *simplicity* of Weber's problematic – confronting us in our modernity, poised upon our intellectual heights – that is an obstacle to its comprehension.' Asking what this image of Weber implies, Hennis (1988: 104) answers that to a theory-oriented social science which, in Weber's words, sought 'to shift its location and change its conceptual apparatus so that it might regard the stream of events from the heights of reflective thought', these 'special sociologies' of personae and their life orders would have little interest. Conversely, once able to descend from such heights, we might find these sociologies important.

The historical particularity of personae also figured in Weber's famous 1919 address on 'Politics as a vocation'. He put this question:

> But is it true that any ethic of the world could establish commandments of identical content for erotic, business, familial and official relations; for the relations to one's wife, to the greengrocer, the son, the competitor, the friend, the defendant?
> (Weber 1946: 18–19)

Only by being not of the world could an ethic claim such universality. Weber then drew the lesson for his audience: 'We are placed in different life-spheres, each of which is governed by different laws' (Weber 1946: 123). To grasp their historical particularity, it is vital to see that these different 'life-spheres' do not constitute a ranking or continuum of human cultural development.[18] We are at the antipodes of Kant's 'only one religion', the universal moral law that was the ground and destiny of all other fields.

However, as if repeating Kant's demotion of mere officials, we easily rank the bureaucrat or judge and the man or woman of conscience. This habit of mind belongs to a particular conduct of life – that of the philosophical intellectual – in a stratum historically excluded from power in the administrative State and thus, like Koselleck's Masons, committed to developing their inner life into the universe:

> The salvation sought by the intellectual is always based on an inner need, and hence it is at once more remote from life, more theoretical and more systematic than salvation from external distress, the quest for which is more characteristic of non privileged strata. The intellectual seeks in various ways . . . to endow his life with a pervasive meaning, and thus to find unity within himself, with his fellow men, and with the cosmos. It is the intellectual who conceives of the 'world' as a problem of meaning.
>
> (Weber 1968: 506)

On this basis arises a 'demand' we recognise: that 'the total pattern of life be made subject to an order that is significant and meaningful'. A kind of hermeneutic salvation is promised from the plurality of personae that organise lives across the 'different life-spheres'.

No ultimate moral or philosophical justification for a given form of life is possible 'because the different value systems of the world stand in conflict with one another' (Weber 1989: 22). Between these 'value systems' there is battle between gods of different religions: '[D]estiny not "science" prevails over these gods and their struggles. One can only understand what the divine is for one system or another, or in one system or another' (Weber 1989: 23). The absence of a universal moral norm is the contingency that modern Western scholars must have the intellectual honesty to face. It is therefore no fault if the routines of legal training and professional practice fail to furnish ultimate moral answers; they succeed in fashioning a persona dependent on legal means. In Weber's (1989: 11) words, 'Personality is only possessed in the realm of science by the man who serves only the *needs of his subject*, and this is true not only in science.' As for those who would follow a single god despite the plurality of spheres, this monotheistic disposition is delusory as long as the battle of the gods is inconclusive. Weber invited his audience to be 'polytheistic', to take on the persona particular to the professional sphere of life in which they had engaged themselves. The virtue of the specialist disciplines is to have formed their own personae that do not depend on some global moral personality. Weber (1989: 11) was direct as ever on this point, lambasting that literary intellectual lifestyle whose 'idols are "personality" and "personal experience"', in which 'meaning' is sought by pursuing experience 'for its own sake'.[19] Now only in the sphere of private feelings does 'something pulsat[e] that corresponds to the prophetic *pneuma*, which in former times swept through the great communities like a firebrand welding them together' (Weber 1946: 155).

Perhaps we are less vulnerable to religious prophets. But, like Weber, we recognise the intellectual discomfort of living in a culture of 'parcellisation' (Hennis 1988: 69).[20] Weber did this without 'falling under the influence' of the usual unifying schemes: the whole personality, the moral–political community, the historical process, the dialectical synthesis, the deconstructive play. In this way, he had his listeners take as a serious cultural and ethical achievement the mode of conduct – prosaic, reliable, non-prophetic – that comes with technical competence in professional practices.

Given his focus on such untheoretical antiquities as character formation and cultural settings, the 'reconstructed' Weber's argument that each of our 'life-spheres' is 'governed by different laws' will not have persuaded everybody. However, from a different intellectual tradition, the American Aristotelian, Amelie Rorty, also invites us to respond positively to the fact of plural personhood. This means breaking with the habit of thinking that one among the several personae we may happen to occupy in our passage through social institutions must be the fundamental form of personhood, the point of unity. It is therefore a mistake to address legal personality in the terms – theological or philosophical, literary or critical – used elsewhere to address the unified or 'whole person'.

This raises the question: 'Why, then, is there such a metaphysical longing for one concept [of "the" person]? Or is it a longing for one metaphysical concept?' Rorty proceeds to answer in both philosophical and historical terms:

> Perhaps the explanation is that the various functions the concept plays are unifying functions: 'the' locus of liability; 'the' subject of experience; 'the' autonomous critical reflector or creator. Since these various functions are unifying functions, there might be a strong temptation to look for their unified source. But this is an elementary error . . . A desire for unity cannot by itself perform the conjuring trick of pulling one rabbit out of several hats: a transcendental unity of the concept of person, unifying the variety of distinct, independently unifying functions that each regional concept plays.
>
> (Rorty 1988: 44–5)

The 'error' of a unified concept of person lies in its failure to recognise that the concept has quite different functions in different cultural contexts or social 'regions'. Given their 'regional' character, personae and their definite but limited settings must not be left 'under-described'. If they are, we fail to see that each has its own history and distribution, has fashioned its own ethos, and is directed by its own techniques and to its own ends. Conversely, it is only 'under-description' that enables normative generalisations about 'the' person – whether the self-directing individual or the moral community.

The historical response to the persistent longing for unity returns to the religious dimension. The figure of '"the" autonomous critical reflector' has a Christian genealogy:

> The modern Western conception of persons derives many of its characterisations – that persons are reflective responsible agents – from Augustine. But his account appears within a theological frame that defines the primary concepts and tasks of the post-Adamic condition. Augustine held that our basic activities are directed toward integrating the divided and corrupt psyche of the natural, fallen condition, so that we can freely consent to being the agents of God's purposes. Augustine used his analysis of the doctrine of the Trinity – his account of how the three persons of the divinity form a single substantial unity – to explain how persons can be simple unified agents despite the diversity, and sometimes the conflicts, among their faculties and powers.
>
> (Rorty 1988: 7)

But ours is a multi-regional existence in which the word of God is no longer the letter of the law. Like Weber, Rorty is concerned to avoid a 'theocratic' unification. When she says that a single rabbit cannot be lifted from several hats, she is inviting us not to be lured into a theological game. In effect she is proposing that we abandon the long-established spiritual anthropology which furnished the image of fallen man, 'parcellised' in his faculties, divided from himself by sin, cut out of paradise by God but dreaming of return to unity. This anthropology has generated extraordinary images of personal salvation and social transformation. Rorty calls it into question by citing evidence from cognitive psychology that shows mental functioning as 'multiple' in character, as in the phenomenon of self-deception. But, above all, she recontextualises 'the' unified person in its Christian history, establishing a limiting historical circumstance for what is a quite particular confessional formation, not a fundamental truth.

When she addresses the issue of our differentiated personae, Rorty is not joining the familiar moral chorus against what are said to be the fractured lives of modern people. These personae are not a sign of existential fragmentation. Their difference does not represent some postmodern shattering of meaning, paranoiac or liberating. Nor does Rorty propose a counter-politics for a new community in which law is reunified with conscience or individual morality and State with society or moral community. Instead, the plurality of civil personae that emerged with the early modern separation of religion from government is simply a historical fact to be faced. The anti-Kantian message is clear: do not elevate the reflective moral persona to the status of a general ideal.

Finally, it is worth pausing on the response – the longing for unity – that Rorty invites us to abandon. It is the response of those post-Enlightenment intellectuals for whom 'the universality of an enlightened ethic crossed all the boundaries so painstakingly drawn by [Absolutist] politicians' (Koselleck 1988: 41). It is the response of the 'moral judiciary' that treats all the spheres of life as transparent to its own de-localised adjudication. The result of imposing such transparency is that 'the concerns of one context are imported to another, in the premature interest of constructing a unified theory' (Rorty 1988: 7). In this way, a 'misguided attempt' is made to 'derive decisions from "the" (illicitly decontextualised) concept of a person' (Rorty 1988: 7).

By way of example, Rorty takes the intractable debate on abortion. Given the fundamentalists' recourse to ultimate religious principle in defining 'the' person, the debate has stirred 'conflicting intuitions on the primacy of theological, biological or sociopolitical criteria for personal identity'. This conflict, she argues, is not solved by imposing a theological criterion on the political context or, for that matter, a moral criterion on the legal context:

> Even if a particular sectarian theology classifies the fetus as a person, nothing follows about the propriety of importing that particular theological conception to legal and political contexts. However detailed and articulate it may be, a theological doctrine does not, by itself, establish the propriety of its dominance in a non-theocratic legal system.
>
> (Rorty 1988: 8)

It would be possible to dissolve the problem of plural personae by moving to 'legislate one central notion of a person'. Such legislation 'might express a moral or an ideological victory' (Rorty 1988: 8), yet plurality would remain our fact of life.[21] This cautions against the still magnetic notion of an ultimate, supra-regional form of person – be it self-directing individual or moral community – that would be the normative measure of all others, legal personality included.

Unlike the pluralism of personhood she endorses, for Rorty the urge to unity is a potential fanaticism. So it was when each of the rival early modern confessions sought to impose itself as the universal Church. Again it is the question of secularisation and the relations of Church and State. If Koselleck is right, the idea of progressive secularisation and definitive enlightenment is wrong. The religious mode of life has continued into modern times: critique is religion by other means. Hence our inquiry: to what extent do today's normative critics of law depend on the enduring power of an other-worldly ethic and its intellectual prestige – in a certain milieu – in their quest to reunify positive law and a moral ideal?

10

SECTS, LAWS AND RIGHTS

Even as Kant argued the special status of his faculty, the American Revolution was under way. Religious enthusiasms crossed the Atlantic. Longstanding sectarian loyalties that had fuelled religious conflicts in England touched entire American populations like nothing else, even taxation. In America, too, religion proved a 'crystallisation point around which other important social problems settled', as Schilling (1988: 277–8) observes concerning German circumstances where confessions 'formed the core of competing political programs'. In turning to the American scene, however, it is worth noting his distinction of 'confessions' and 'denominations':

> 'Confessionalisation' is a far less familiar term . . . especially to British and American audiences, who are better acquainted with 'denominations' as private religious associations than with state churches. The formation and development of 'confessional churches' (*Konfessionskirchen*) are, by contrast, central topics in German history between the sixteenth and the nineteenth centuries. They were exclusively established, or at least privileged, creeds and ecclesiastical organisations within a particular society . . . Each formed a highly organised system, which tended to monopolise the world view with respect to the individual, the state, and society, and which laid down strictly formulated norms in politics and morals.
>
> (Schilling 1986: 22)

Perhaps only the Anglican was near to a confessional Church in Schilling's sense. Yet the intertwining of religion and politics that marked confessionalisation was not lacking in the English-speaking countries.

Indeed, 'the New World increasingly became the stage upon which the rivalry between the European forces of Reformation and Counter-Reformation took place' (Zakai 1992: 61). A transatlantic Puritan historiography suggested that 'history and prophecy were inextricably bound to one another, with prophecy placed within the historical dimension, and history – as the realisation of prophecy – situated within the prophetic dimension' (Zakai 1992: 19). History became providential, serving the self-induced sense of crisis whereby early modern Protestants convinced themselves that the course of human history was nearly run and divine intervention was at hand. England was inscribed into this American history in two quite different ways. First, settlement in Virginia was seen as the divinely ordained act of genesis undertaken by England as God's chosen vehicle for the final struggle with the papal Antichrist whose Spanish and Portuguese followers were advancing into the Americas. Second, however, the Puritan settlement in New England was seen as the 'exodus' of the true 'Israelites' from an England now itself identified as the doomed Church of Laodicea whose destruction was prophesied in *Revelation.* This second view saw only England's apostasy, its utter failure to embrace the ideal of perfectionist Puritans: total cleansing of the Church of England to make way for the 'society of saints'.

With an England split by the Civil War, a Europe ravaged by the Thirty Years War,[1] and a threat of Turkish incursions into Central Europe, such sermons as Robert Cushman's – delivered at New Plymouth in 1621 – become intelligible:

> And if it should please God to punish his people in the Christian countries of *Europe* (for their coldnesse, carnality, wanton abuse of the Gospel, contention, &c.) either by Turkish slavery, or by Popish tyrannie, which God forbid, yet if the time be come, or shall come (as who knoweth) when Satan shall be let loose, to cast out his flouds against them, here [in New Plymouth] is a way opened for such as have wings to flie into this Wilderness.
>
> (in Zakai 1992: 124)

For Puritans in New England, return from that Land of Promise to a degenerating England was a return to 'Egypt' where 'you must worship the beast or the image of the beast' (in Zakai 1992: 66). For such believers, this was the England with which they had broken their bonds and, like Noahs early warned by God, set sail.

A political programme crystallised around the faith of a New England self-promoted as a 'sacred Christian society'. As Zakai (1992: 222–3) recalls, the Anglican apologist Richard Hooker rejected 'the Puritan quest for a theocratic universe, as exemplified in the Puritan claim that "Scripture ought to be the only rule of all our actions"'. In 1663 John Davenport, the New England divine, wrote that '*theocratic*, or to make the Lord God our Governour, is the best form of Government in a Christian Common-wealth, and which men that are free to chuse (as in new Plantations they are) ought to establish' (in Zakai 1992: 235). Concerning the settlement at New Haven, Davenport's *Discourse about Civil Government in a New Plantation Whose Design is Religion* proposed that Church and State should form a 'co-ordinate state, in the same place reaching forth help mutually each to other for the welfare of both, according to God' (Zakai 1992: 237). The aim was to avoid both the problem of separation with its conflict between spiritual and temporal orders and, on the other hand, the problem of unification where, as in papal rule, the civil sphere was dominated by the ecclesiastical power. Yet exclusivity arose here too. Only church members – '*Saints by calling*' – could hold office in this godly government that viewed all of life as one divine domain. Such exclusivist tenets were held by radical English Puritans also. Hooker depicted the spirit of exclusiveness that characterised the conduct of English Puritans as an inner group meeting in an upper room, a spirit that provoked Hobbes's warning in *Leviathan* (4: 44) against those who claimed their present Church was the true kingdom of God. In fact the pure theocracy of the New England saints waned when it came to actual government. But it endured as a potent habit of mind, an intellectual desire to ground all social provisions, legal and governmental, in a set of higher principles or fundamental values.

In the years before the 1776 Revolution, few historical bonds were stronger in the minds of the American colonists than that between Anglican Church and British monarchy. This identification gave no pleasure to those who were not loyalists, whether Enlighteners such as Thomas Jefferson seeking to have the Virginia legislature disestablish the Anglican Church and establish freedom of religion,[2] or the fervent adherents of Dissenting denominations eager to denounce Anglicanism as papism in disguise. These denominations are the key players on the colonial American scene as Jonathan Clark describes it. In *The Language of Liberty, 1660–1832*, Clark's revision of the established historiography of the Revolution, the prime cultural fact about early modern America was the 'conflict between denominations'.[3] This religious conflict, continued on from English history, was carried to a climax in the American setting:

> [T]he American Revolution displays, on a vast canvas, all these ancient British and ecclesiastical conflicts played out to a conclusion: militant imperial Anglicanism versus sectarian and ethnic diversity; heterodoxy and what we know as the international Enlightenment versus dour, tradition-conscious orthodoxy, both Anglican and Calvinist; religious exclusiveness versus demands for toleration and the separation of Church and State; the right of rebellion versus the duty of allegiance: all these momentous issues made the American Revolution (among its other aspects) the last great war of religion in the western world, and potentially offer a more accessible set of indices to the roles of religious ideologies than the reform movements of late-eighteenth-century England, belated and poorly supported as they were.
>
> (Clark 1994: 305)

The principal theses of Clark's polemic find expression here: the continuity of events in America with previous ecclesiastical strife in England; the primacy of sectarian motives – heterodoxy and Dissent above all – in early modern Anglo-American political relations; the American Revolution as a transatlantic civil war of religion. It is an invitation to face the fact that atavistic religious resentments rather than moral values and political principles played the 'revolutionary' role. To accept the invitation calls for caution. That religion has played a central role in American political history no one disputes. But not all Americans were religious, and not all the religious were fanatical sectarians. So there is reason not to leap from Revolution as pure moral virtue to Revolution as sectarian viciousness and nothing but.

The Language of Liberty also draws together Anglo-American law and Christian religion. Their 'point of contact' was provided by the events of 1776:

> A rebellion of natural law against common law and a rebellion of Dissent against hegemonic Anglicanism were the same rebellion, since their target was the unified sovereign created by England's unique constitutional and ecclesiastical development: King, Lords and Commons, indivisible and irresistible, credited (according to Blackstone) with absolute power by the common law, dignified with divine authority by the Church.
>
> (Clark 1994: 5)

Clark's revision of the American myth of origin insists on a particular identity of law and religion. As their target, the colonists took aim at the oppressive trinity of British monarchy, Anglican Church and English common law. Against this composite monster of king, bishop and judge they raised their rebel champion in the figure of the Republic, Dissenting Christianity and natural law. This is not the separating of religion from law we have been tracing. But in a key respect Clark's revision runs parallel to the present theme: the resilience of Christian habits of mind and sectarian modes of life. In positing a continuity between heterodox Dissent, rationalist deism and Enlightenment reason – what Reventlow (1985) identifies as the 'spiritualist-intellectualist' tendency – Clark displaces the comforting belief that enlightened secularisation has definitively marked off our civilised 'modernity' from the passional moral violence of a communitarian Christian past.

Depicting the American Revolution as an inter-denominational civil war undoes the amnesia that has masked its sectarian derivations:

> By the first centennial, the image of the Revolution as a holy war had expanded within the folk memories of the American sects to the point where the divisions and ambiguities within those denominations were forgotten . . . Yet, paradoxically, this retrospective homogenisation of the positions of colonial denominations acted to secularise the historical interpretation of the Revolution and to drain the role of the sects of its immense significance.
>
> (Clark 1994: 390)

By restoring visibility to the fact and consequences of sectarian diversity, Clark challenges progressivist studies premised on a notion of 'Enlightenment as a process of secularisation, embracing as a necessary unity aristocratic scepticism, bourgeois materialism and proletarian emancipation from patriarchal social relations' (Clark 1994: 14). As he goes on to say, 'each of these component parts has been challenged separately, and finally the ensemble itself is progressively challenged'. In place of heroic images of Commonwealthmen or fables of democratic-minded popular readers of Locke, respectful of one another's property rights and thus ideally community-minded, Clark argues the 'immense significance' of sectarian conflict and enduring 'denominational traditions', millenarian fervours and religious civil war.

Not everyone will accept the argument. To focus on the role of sectarianism in the American Revolution challenges a cultural historiography that has 'remained securely within a secular framework of interpretation' to recognise that 'early-modern societies were essentially sectarian in their dynamics' (Clark 1994: 41). Nor was it a question of doctrines alone. Although he does not labour the point, Clark traces the historical significance and practical effects of doctrines in their cultural settings. The sects' sometimes elaborate theological ideas had definite consequences for how adherents actually conducted themselves in the 'kingdom or empire' within which these doctrines took hold. The way doctrines were lived out in practice was as important as their ideology. Like the present essay, Clark's study concerns the history of an ethos. What, he asks, could heat Americans to the fever of rebellion and the passion of civil war? His answer minimises the role of philosophical ideas of freedom. 'Americans did not,' Clark (1994: 45) writes, 'in the 1760s, suddenly adopt the ideas of John Locke.'[4] Indeed, there was no public demand for Locke's works. His *Second Treatise of Government* waited until 1773 for a colonial reprinting, and '[e]ven this did not release a long-frustrated enthusiasm', the next American edition being in 1937 (Clark 1994: 26). By contrast, avalanches of devotional, theological and ecclesiological works were reprinted. The enthusiasm necessary for revolution came not from the philosophy of moral freedom but from habitual sectarian resentments. These religious routines were anything but abstract speculations: 'Far from being secularised, spiritual commitments, zeal and hatreds were transferred to the political arena in the 1770s to greater effect than at any time since 1688–9' (Clark 1994: 40). It was not Enlightened theses on democracy but the Dissenting sects' archaic spiritual 'zeal and hatreds' that furnished a 'dynamics' for mass revolutionary action, propelled by tales of martyrdom in the Boston 'massacre'.

Progressivist theses cannot account for what Clark terms the 'self-image' that allowed Americans of different denominations to bond together in an anti-Anglican civil war. Into the eighteenth century, Dissenters and Anglicans alike 'insisted on living in a mental world, an extension of the seventeenth century, in which theology still claimed to dictate conduct' (Clark 1994: 16). Not excluded from the civil sphere, radical theology furnished the appropriately extremist preparation for religious civil war, that is, for taking up arms 'in a context which denominational conflict made apocalyptic' (Clark 1994: 35). In such a context it was routine to demonise one's rival into the ultimate degree of moral degeneracy, and to spiritualise one's own denomination to the ultimate degree of moral perfection. Of such stuff the self-images of the diverse sects were made. And because dissent in religion went easily (if not inevitably) with rebellion in politics, '[t]he tyranny of sin was subtly transformed into the tyranny of kings and bishops' (Clark 1994: 39). In this way religious passion easily transformed everyday complaints against government into matters of ultimate right and moral principle.

Given our own self-image as modern, secular and critical intellectuals, we baulk at an account that takes so seriously conduct at once fanatical in its attachments to ancient religious enmities and utopian in its religious fantasies of America as the New Israel in which only Christ is King. But an intellectual commitment to secularisation and critique can itself become a redemptive ethical mode. To take this disposition on might mean we cease to count the evidence of historical reality, thus marginalising the religious dimension of our history. As Clark (1994: 43) argues, when it came to rousing passions to the highest pitch, it was the denominational ministers who 'were able to draw together popular audiences, sometimes of many thousands, and exhort them to a frenzy of collective commitment that secular politicians did not begin to approach until the Chartist mass movements of Victorian England'.[5] This power of attraction was a matter of traditional sectarian routines, now enhanced by a communications technology that distributed the 'true word':

> In the early-modern period it was religious sects which, more than any other social groups, possessed international networks of communication which both mobilised their supporters and kept them informed of the activities of friends and enemies on two continents; by letters industriously written and sought, published journals, evangelical newspapers and magazines, and unwearied itinerancy, the degree of cultural contact surpassed anything yet available in a secular context.
>
> (Clark 1994: 43)

If denominational conflict had this communal mobilising power, it is feasible to conclude with Clark (1994: 146) that 'the conflict among different persuasions of Christians is revealed as a chief determinant of the idioms of discourse within which all political conflicts were articulated'.

More could be said on the relative roles of heterodox Christology, ecclesiology and ecclesiastical polity in the American Revolution.[6] However, our present interest is the specific interaction of religion and law. While treating religion and law as the 'two dominant idioms of discourse' in early modern America, Clark (1994: 11) in practice has law playing very much second fiddle to religion. The common law is depicted as more or less assimilated by the colonists, the third element of the oppressive bloc, alongside the English monarch and the Anglican Church. This assimilation is made more complex by differences within the common law tradition, by the presence of rival jurisdictions in civil and canon law, and by the contemporary rise to favour of a particular kind of natural law. In this circumstance, legal history was not isolated from religious factors:

> Law did not exist in an intellectual vacuum. Not only its structure but the pattern of its evolution was profoundly influenced by the currents of thought around it and, especially, by the religious context in which it was located.
>
> (Clark 1994: 111)

Different hypotheses can be derived from this proposition. The present essay explores the historical demarcation of the religious from the legal. For Clark, it is one of their historical complicities that matters.

If the rebellion of Dissent against Anglicanism was also a rebellion of natural law against common law, the rebels nonetheless drew from the authorities of English common law whatever lessons seemed to support their cause. This was not easy with Blackstone's *Commentaries*, to the extent that he grounded the British monarchy and the Anglican Church in the law of nature and made the English constitution an organic support for Anglican hegemony in the colonies (Clark 1994: 88–9). Sir Edward Coke was a different matter. Given his famous dispute with James I and his opinion, in *Bonham's Case* (1609), that the common law could void an Act of Parliament, Coke struck quite another note. Hence Clark's (1994: 100) observation that, in the colonial setting, 'Coke's doctrine was to be far more powerful' than in England. Americans persisted in appeals to ancient common law liberties enshrined in Magna Carta as if these liberties were inalienable natural rights.[7]

A popular view of common law as in a papist bond with monarchy and Anglican Church exerted a contrary pressure. Pursuing an ancient quest for religious liberty against Anglicanism, Dissent sought for conflict between laws. The hated *Book of Common Prayer* – imposed by the Act of Uniformity (1662) and itself imposing the authorised liturgy, doctrine, church and civil polity – helped determine colonial dispositions to the common law by contributing to what Clark terms 'the polarisation of a common idiom', that is, 'natural law versus common law'. Clark argues that one of the 'novel and sensational features' of the American Revolution was the fact that its goals 'came increasingly to be expressed in the language of natural law and natural rights which was to have an equally explosive impact in the old order in Europe after 1789' (1994: 93). It was only 'late in the contest' that this new idiom emerged, but there was no mistaking the outcome: 'the shared legal tradition was polarised into an antithesis between a common law and a natural law understanding of sovereignty' (Clark 1994: 105).

However, the division installed between positive and natural law was itself in part a religious strategy. The appeal to natural law was less a relay of continental natural law theorists than the redeployment of an 'old term in denominational discourse' (Clark 1994: 113):

> The Revolution was not what it claimed to be in this key respect: Americans' use of natural law tropes as a critique of the common law sovereign had, after all, been only skin deep. American revolutionaries' use of natural rights was indeed devastating in its results; but it was temporary, for political argument in the new republic quickly reverted to controversy over the specific meaning of a written constitution, and it was to a large degree cosmetic, for it redescribed and derived its force from the idea of fundamental law within colonial denominational traditions.
>
> (Clark 1994: 136)

A regression from the language of natural law to traditional denominational discourse brings into view the role of deism and the 'international Enlightenment' which Clark associates with Christian heterodoxy. From the outset, Clark (1994: 6) leaves no doubt that '[s]ome principles traditionally ascribed to the natural law tradition might equally better be traced to the ecclesiastical polities of Protestant Dissenters'. Hence 'legal thought alone does not explain that process [of polarisation] which can only be understood in terms of the impact upon colonial law of adjacent developments in colonial religion' (Clark 1994: 94).

In fact natural law remained a 'minor theme' in the years before the Stamp Act Congress of 1765. From then, however, natural law thinking became of serious intellectual import, a timing consistent with Koselleck's chronology of Enlightenment networking. In 1766, speaking for his fellow Virginians, Richard Bland insisted that 'we must have recourse to the Law of Nature, and those Rights of Mankind which flow from it'. The canonical names of Grotius and Pufendorf, Locke and Domat were invoked in efforts to 'open the way for a natural law rejection of the common-law sovereign', as the first Continental Congress considered whether to have recourse 'to the law of nature, as well as to the British constitution' (Clark 1994: 103). Reviewing this course of events, Clark (1994: 108–10) concludes that '[t]he glories of the law of nature rapidly became a trope of colonial discourse'. But it was a familiar trope, a vehicle for the 'fundamental law' long known to Calvinist Dissenters as the divine law (Clark 1994: 96). The religiosity of these appeals to natural law was heightened by the practice of '[c]olonial polemicists [who] acquired the habit of parading strings of authorities, like Grotius, Pufendorf, Locke, Burlamaqui and Vattel; this compulsive name-dropping did not mean that those authors had been widely read or deeply understood' (Clark 1994: 112–13).[8]

But more was at stake. Clark (1994: 129) identifies a symptomatic shift in the lectures of James Wilson, Justice of the Supreme Court and Professor of Law at the College of Philadelphia. Between 1774 and 1790, Wilson moved from the usual appeal to natural law as the authority for limiting common law jurisdiction towards rejection of 'much of the natural law tradition in the name of the new American conception of liberty, and of the immediate access of the virtuous American citizen to the true content of the natural law as the will of God'. This is the voice of Enlightened deism as the chosen civil religion for America as the moral State. But, as Clark (1994: 386) argues, 'by 1800 Deism had been swamped in many states by a massive evangelical revival'. If the victory went to evangelicalism, this is in keeping with Clark's (1994: 304) 'model' of the Revolution in which it was sectarian heterodoxy, not secular rationalism, that furnished 'principled opposition to the established order'.[9]

There was heterodoxy among the signers of the Declaration of Independence, notwithstanding that a majority were Anglicans. As Clark (1994: 337) writes, 'the great mass of their American contemporaries was unaware of the contribution of religious doubt to the politics of the Founding Fathers'. On the one side, there were Enlightened deists such as Franklin and Jefferson; on the other side, the great bulk of 'late-eighteenth-century America was still conducting an old quarrel, strongly repetitive of the terms of debate in England between *c.*1670 and 1730, in its critique of what were identified as absolute monarch and arbitrary rule' (Clark 1994: 338). If the sects were still 'tending and ripening their seventeenth-century traditions, ideals and resentments', the Enlightened elite was already cultivating its superior moral ethos along deist lines.

In Virginia, Clark (1994: 341–6) speculates, such sentiments circulated among the Anglican gentry as a result of 'the penetration of fashionable ideas in seats of learning' such as Jefferson's alma mater, the College of William and Mary. Although he notes that Jefferson's religious views remained 'largely unknown to his contemporaries', Clark (1994: 347–8) makes no mention of Masonic networks to which Jefferson, like Franklin, had access while in France. In fact some clergy knew Jefferson as a 'confirmed infidel', an impression not contradicted by the future president's recommendation, in his *Notes on the State of Virginia*, of free inquiry to cleanse the 'present corruptions' of Christianity. Written in Paris in 1781, the *Notes* were published in an edition limited to 200 copies. They conclude with an appeal to freedom from any civil authority in matters of religious belief and worship. In contractarian style, Jefferson limits governmental authority over these 'natural rights' to those rights 'we have submitted' to our rulers:

> The rights of conscience we never submitted, we could not submit. We are answerable for them to our God. The legitimate powers of government extend to such acts only as are injurious to others. But it does me no injury for my neighbour to say there are twenty gods, or no god. It neither picks my pocket nor breaks my leg.
>
> (Jefferson 1964: 152)

Jefferson draws three deductions from this principle. First, for all the strife that Christians have suffered, 'we have not advanced one inch toward uniformity'. Second, therefore, a sceptical and relativising conclusion is justified: if 'a thousand millions of people' inhabit the earth and 'profess probably a thousand different systems of religion', then 'ours is but one of that thousand'. Third, however, the fact of plurality is positive, on condition that the State favours no one sect: given freedom, the 'several sects perform the office of a Censor morum over each other' (Jefferson 1964: 153). This confessional pluralism rests on an overarching Enlightenment faith in reason.

It is timely to recall a lesson from Bodin and Thomasius, a lesson that Jefferson either did not know or had a philosophical motive for forgetting. Religious freedom was not a human right retained by the sovereign individual and not transferred to the State. It was an attribute the State had granted to individuals when it expelled religion from a role in civil government. The liberal inversion of the real history of religious freedom was already in place with Jefferson's discourse of moral self-determination. This discourse inflated the natural law tradition to the point where the religious freedom granted by the State was translated into an innate freedom based in conscience and forever levied against the State.

In fact, if appeals to the natural rights of man could seem 'novel and sensational', for other commentators the novelty was more apparent than real. Thus, '[t]o dissect a natural right was to find a British right and it was natural because the British possessed it'. Hence, '[n]atural rights were the reflection, not the essence; they were the confirmation, not the source, of positive rights' (Reid 1987: 95). Natural rights, in other words, derived from historical privileges held as of right by the English estates, not from universal features of moral humanity that any State must respect. Yet the latter notion has so deeply taken root that '[c]onstitutional law can make no genuine advance until it isolates the problem of rights against the state and makes that problem part of its own agenda' (Dworkin 1977: 149). To pursue this agenda is to forget that the genius of the State was to solve disputes without recourse to ultimate moral rules and uncompromising religious principles. It is also to forget that what now count as rights have a historically mixed provenance rather than a unified source in private moral conscience or in natural law principle. These played their part, but only alongside quite other styles of right deriving from the ancient privileges and traditional freedoms that attached to certain social strata. The ubiquitous American conviction that the individual's moral conscience sets limits to government and law might itself derive from a specific political history, one marked by a colonial innocence of the experience of Absolutism (Oestreich 1968).

There is also the religious derivation. For Gierke (1934: 114), the notion of 'inherent' natural rights as distinguished from 'acquired' civil rights was implicit in 'all the doctrines in which, from the Middle Ages onwards, the law of nature is exalted above the State'. These doctrines were in large part Christian. In his polemic against the anachronistic reading of individual rights back into Roman law, Michel Villey, too, identifies the 'droit subjectif' as a Christian phenomenon, ever more expansive and now ever more nebulous.[10] For Villey, the genesis of subjective rights housed in the autonomous individual lies in William of Ockham's nominalist rupture with the realism that had held sway into the age of Aquinas. There is more to this point than Villey's (1964: 110) engaging irritation with 'the wild deployment of the individualistic urge [*le déploiement désordonné de l'initiative individuelle*]' to which this rupture led: from Ockham's move emerged the 'anti-juridical' disposition that now sustains the vision of endless individual rights existing independently of the means to exercise them in an actual system of law.

In a critical discussion of Villey's thesis, Tierney (1988), too, recognises the centrality of Christianity in the emergence of rights theories and, more generally, the function of rights as an instrument of Christianisation. The historical displacing of an objective nature by a subjective right rested on the dual ground of a theological doctrine and the historical life practice of which it was part. The doctrine was that of the supreme value of the immortal individual soul. The practice was that of the other-worldly cloistered life, centred on asceticism, transformative discipline and private mysticism. Franciscan ascesis was the highest form of spiritual or contemplative life to which fallen man could aspire. However, Tierney tracks the legal phenomenon of a subjective right not to Ockham but to the twelfth-century canon lawyers who developed mechanisms for 'individualising' contracts and agreements (Tierney 1988: 23).

In America, the rise of the 'rights of man' was itself inseparable from a particular life practice: not that of the cloister, perhaps, but certainly that of academic intellectuals, allies of the clergy. Natural law theory was 'school-learning', a particular historical pedagogy:

> Several important American colleges, following the Scottish and dissenting pattern . . . taught a natural law-based moral philosophy as part of the arts curriculum. Apart from general political talk of rights, the theory of rights outlined here was thus the first, and certainly the first systematic, exposition of the topic to which significant parts of the American intelligentsia were exposed while still boys in their teens.
>
> (Haakonssen 1991: 43)

The role of the academy was central. In the mid-seventeenth century, having famously prepared himself and the world for the universal events of Christ's imminent reign on earth, Jan Amos Comenius was invited by Governor Winthrop of the Massachusetts Colony to become president of Harvard College, 'where both Indians and colonists would be trained to attain universal knowledge' (Popkin 1992: 108). When Geneva became caught up in the turmoil of the French Revolution, Jefferson 'actively promoted the idea of importing the whole of the Geneva faculty, at George Washington's expense, and locating it "so far from the federal city as moral considerations would recommend and yet near enough to it to be viewed as an appendix of that, and that the splendor of the two objects would reflect usefully on each other"' (Haakonssen 1991: 58n). The universities of Geneva and Edinburgh constituted, in Jefferson's parlance, the 'two eyes of Europe'.

When Americans moved towards a doctrine of inalienable rights, this was in large part an outcome of the central place accorded to natural law theory in the arts curriculum. As a representative instance, Haakonssen (1991: 54) cites John Witherspoon's lectures on moral philosophy at the College of New Jersey at Princeton, 'one of the main centres for the education of the new American mind'. By comparison with Clark's sectarians, Witherspoon is a muted figure.[11] Yet his post in a prestigious institution of learning gave weight to his religiously based questioning of merely civil concepts of rights and duties. The reasoning is a variation on the familiar doctrinal theme of the limits of human understanding. In this fallen world, humanity cannot rely on its own moral powers, corrupted as these are by sensuousness. In the name of 'natural conscience', the Christian philosopher will thus call into question any claim by mere worldly agents to a moral absolute. No final value can be accorded to any actual arrangements for the civil good, because these will be contingent on the imperfect faculties of humanity in its present state.

But this was a curriculum for 'boys in their teens'. The point was not only philosophical truth but to train into the boys a prestigious purgative capacity: to doubt all worldly claims and to see beyond existing institutions to the higher (or deeper) truths of 'natural conscience'. Historically speaking, it is not difficult to appreciate the intellectual discipline of this exercise in the arts curriculum for students destined for the educated moral elite. To listen to our contemporary cultural critics, we might suppose this moral capacity had now quit the scene. In fact, with mutations appropriate to its mass dissemination in the critical academy, this capacity has persisted.

So too has 'rights talk'. Thomas Haskell (1987) explores the 'curious persistence of rights talk in the "Age of Interpretation"'. An intellectual scepticism about the grounds of knowledge coexists with an enthusiasm for humans' universal moral and political rights. Is this what Leo Strauss had in view when characterising modern rationality as scepticism in metaphysics but dogmatism in politics? Dogmatic political enthusiasm for unquestioned rights co-exists with the hermeneutic practice of calling any ostensible meaning into question. This self-reflective practice is now disseminated in the critical academy, that almost compulsory church for intellectuals of our times.

11

THE LAW TRANSFORMED; THE LAWYER LOST

As a technique for drawing out signification and truths concealed below the surface of the text, hermeneutics was a part of biblical exegesis. In the distinctive Protestant mode of reading Scripture as hiding a meaning meant for you, the distinction between public surface and private depth installed a tension between immediate objective experience and deferred revelation of subjective meaning. Calling any apparent meaning into question threw the reader back on to themself, casting doubt on any existing interpretation and focusing attention inwardly on the self. Hermeneutics was a novel instrument for transforming the day's events into the scene of one's possible salvation.

It is in keeping with this remarkable Christian technique of literate self-reflection that we now find a major legal historian publicly confronting the moment where 'one's belief in one's own objectivity is drawn into question'. At the start of *The Transformation of American Law, 1870–1960: The Crisis of Legal Orthodoxy* Morton Horwitz confesses his uncertainty about himself:

> As one sees both theories and causes as more contingent, one's belief in one's own objectivity is also drawn into question. Is it just my own story, with all the connotations of skepticism and subjectivity that the word 'story' implies? No; I still aspire to give the best possible explanation, but without the wish to suppress all the difficulties by intoning pieties about what a terrible place the world would be without an objective account.
>
> (Horwitz 1992: viii)

It is fascinating to see a specialised mode of calling oneself into question, practised and perfected in the disciplines of Christian hermeneutics and more recently literary studies, taking hold in the legal sphere. We observe the struggle when, as a result of Horwitz's new capacity for anxiety about his own objectivity, 'the book constantly wavers between, on the one hand, conventional efforts at historical explanation that continue to derive from nineteenth-century models of objectivity, and, on the other hand, the recognition that modernism has challenged the objectivity of these forms in many ways' (Horwitz 1992: ix).

The historian does not wholly succumb. However, the critical pressure to abandon the old way of doing history – travestied as empty 'pieties' – has gripped him. There is no suspicion that new and even emptier pieties might lie in store. Much more anxiety is to come. It seems impossible to hold the line at a problem of epistemology. Elsewhere Horwitz might perform the 'reality test', setting a legal procedure against the prevailing social circumstances in order to assess the adequacy of the match.[1] But, as with his worry about his own 'story', the problem of representation slips irresistibly into the deeper form of a moral crisis of self. This is not to charge Horwitz with engaging in the 'self-absorption' of the Romantics who so enraged Carl Schmitt by transforming every circumstance into an occasion for endless dialogue with and about themselves. Yet, with each twist toward 'interpretive and deconstructive intellectual movements' (Horwitz 1992: viii), the historian of law is turning a question of objectivism into a questioning of himself. As Weber (1968: 506) observed, '[i]t is the intellectual who conceives of the world as a problem of meaning'.

It is as much a matter of intellectual comportment as of true (or false) ideas. Two centuries ago, as has been noted, a German Enlightener devised an intellectual exercise for resisting Kant's one-sided emphasis on intellectual objectivity and pure abstraction:

> Even as it is certain that all individuals taken together would never, with the powers of vision granted them by Nature alone, have managed to detect a satellite of Jupiter which the telescope reveals to the astronomer, so it is beyond question that human powers of reflection would never have produced an analysis of the Infinite or a Critique of Pure Reason, unless, in the individuals called to perform such feats, Reason had separated itself off, disentangled itself, as it were, from all matter, and by the most intense effort of abstraction armed their eyes with a glass for peering into the Absolute. But will such a mind, dissolved as it were into pure intellect and pure contemplation, ever be capable of exchanging the rigorous bonds of logic for the free movement of the poetic faculty, or of grasping the concrete individuality of things with a sense innocent of preconceptions and faithful to the object?
>
> (Schiller 1967: 41, 43)

It would be excessive to suggest that Horwitz swings from the hard fixity of intellectual objectivism to the soft fluidity of 'the poetic faculty'. But his mode of worrying about legal meanings is a sign that the practice of aesthetic critique and moral problematising developed in the 1790s by Friedrich Schiller has migrated into today's American jurisprudence. This self-styling exercise was designed not for lawyers but to let German men of letters loosen themselves from a comportment that, for Schiller, was too dominated by the Kantian cult of abstraction. Of itself, Horwitz's frisson of risk at putting himself into question is not the equal of the intense inwardness achieved by Puritan specialists or by Schiller's aesthetes. But it is of that family. It is the process of conscience-formation at work, now inside the law school, supported by a critical programme resting on what Horwitz (1992: 270) terms his 'hermeneutic understanding of reality'.

A reason for grounding this essay in Koselleck's (1988) thesis on critique as a relay of religion is the currency of 'crisis' in discussions of the contemporary law school. At the outset I recorded Kronman's (1993: 2) dismal diagnosis of the 'crisis that now threatens the collective soul of American lawyers', a crisis brought about in part by the success of critical theory. Conversely, in Horwitz's (1992) *The Transformation of American Law, 1870–1960: The Crisis of Legal Orthodoxy*, 'crisis' is welcomed as the achievement of legal critique. Horwitz and Kronman trace a similar track – from Legal Realism to Critical Legal Studies – but to very different outcomes. Horwitz embraces the 'crisis of legal orthodoxy' occasioned by the Realists' critique of the idea that legal reasoning was self-executing and neutral. This crisis provides the focal point for his prototypical attack on the notion of law's neutrality. To take a representative instance, Horwitz recalls Herbert Weschler's famous confession that, since value choices were admissible only if justified as 'neutral principles', he could find no principle neutral enough validly to condemn State-enforced racial segregation. In support, Weschler (1959: 19) offered an exemplary Kantian definition: 'A principled decision . . . is one that rests on reasons with respect to all the issues in the case, reasons that in their generality and their neutrality transcend any immediate result that is obtained.' He then argued against seeing segregation in terms of discrimination, but found in freedom of association the transcendental 'neutral principle' that justified the US Supreme Court's decision on the segregation cases. This is Horwitz's response:

> [T]he neutral principles school sought to avoid ever having to decide whether one group was victimising another, since that inevitably involved substantive evaluation of the justice of their respective claims. The emphasis on generality foreclosed any intervention to reform unjust social practices in precisely those cases in which the dominant groups had the greatest stake in justifying the status quo. By abstracting the question of segregation from its concrete historical meaning in order to avoid being accused of having a result orientation, Weschler achieved neutrality through formalism – that is, by simple [sic] assuming the equal legitimacy of both groups' desire to choose freely with whom to associate. In its unhistorical abstractness, neutral principles analysis combined with ethical positivism to produce a new conservative formulation in orthodox legal thought.
>
> (Horwitz 1992: 268)

Here we have a gallery of Horwitz's themes (which are those of legal critique more generally). First, the rejection of 'formalism' and the advocacy of 'substantive evaluation'. This differentiation of 'formal' from 'substantive' rationality is, of course, a standard neo-Kantian theme taken up by Weber, who identifies substantive with arbitrary rationality, a conduct of life in which the whims of a ruler or the priestly oracles of theocratic cultures dominate any concern with establishing neutral procedures and autonomous rules of the game. Horwitz, however, associates substantive valuation with the moral and political achievement of social justice for subordinated communities. Second, Weschler's recourse to neutral principles of law is condemned as 'unhistorical abstractness'. By contrast with such abstraction, Horwitz will lock legal rules into their 'concrete historical meaning', with 'history' and 'meaning' neatly taking up their assigned role as one pole of the dialectic, the other being 'abstraction' and 'form'. Third, by rejecting formalism and neutral principles, Horwitz lays claim to a morally and politically progressive jurisprudence. This he contrasts with the conservatism of 'orthodox legal thought'.

Horwitz's history of the 'crisis of legal orthodoxy' in the period from 1870 to 1960 is made vital by its attack on a mode of legal thought 'outmoded' both by material circumstances such as the epochal rise of 'organisational society' and by ideal values such as respect for 'social justice' (Horwitz 1992: 105). Just how 'concrete' is this history, so nicely structured as a dialectical reconciliation of real history and ideal morality? This device allows Horwitz (1992: 267) to criticise a Weschler left behind by history's advance and morality's growth: 'From the perspective of a generation later, Weschler's difficulties in holding racially discriminatory statutes unconstitutional have that inaccessible quality of ancient structures of understanding derived from a time when a fundamentally different moral order seemed to prevail.' *The Transformation of American Law* is also made vital by its author's moral claim to be a scholar for whom – as Frankfurter wrote in dedicating to Brandeis his treatise on the labour injunction – 'law is not a system of artificial reason, but the application of ethical ideas, with freedom at the core'. The separation of law from morality is dismissed as delusory:

> The 1950s search for 'neutral principles' was just one more effort to separate law and politics in American culture, one more expression of the persistent yearning to find an olympian position from which to objectively cushion the terrors of social choice. The search for neutral principles has always been the secular alternative in religiously pluralistic American society to a direct resort to religious authority. Yet it has served similar dogmatic and legitimating functions. One of its most important influences has been to encourage the production of abstract jurisprudential debate divorced from more particular (and inevitably controversial) political and moral visions.
>
> (Horwitz 1992: 271)

Neutral modes of thought are reduced from positive achievement to psychical compensation for a now unavailable religious exercise. The historical separation of law and morality is being closed down. The neutral administrative

State as historical bulwark against the depradations of religious enthusiasm is being displaced by a new moral enthusiasm.[2]

Horwitz does not understand his project in these historical terms at all. On the contrary, attacking the nineteenth-century notion of law as 'an internally self-consistent and autonomous system of legal ideals, free from the corrupting influence of politics', he associates his Progressive Legal Critique of this Classical Legal Thought with 'a deep sea change in American consciousness that one might broadly describe as a fundamental break with theological and doctrinal modes of thought' (Horwitz 1992: 142). This critical jurisprudence is neo-Kantian, defining itself against religion but in favour of morality. Imagining himself fully secular, Horwitz turns to psychology to debunk legal formalism and judicial neutrality as surrogate forms of theological certainty. He wonders whether 'the fate of the first generation of basically secular intellectuals', that is, those of the late nineteenth century, was 'to cushion the terrors of unbelief by constructing a system of categories sufficiently rigid to alleviate their fear that only the threat of the here-after can keep people from turning into beasts' (Horwitz 1992: 199). Once this psychical connection is asserted, legal neutrality is easily discredited by association:

> There seems to be an important relationship between the psychological inspiration for religious fundamentalism and similar underlying sources of legal fundamentalism. For the recently irreligious person, profession or nation, does the secure rigidity of secularised categories substitute for those earlier stern substantive prescriptions grounded in religious truths?
> (Horwitz 1992: 199)

In fact, this psychological device absorbs the historical density and technical particularity of both legal and religious systems of life, as if these were somehow contained in advance in the structure of human subjectivity and anxiety. But the device also lets Horwitz frighten his readers by treating State and law in that particular intellectual manner which likes to threaten by presenting an intolerable alternative: either a universal order or the nightmare of ungrounded being. Taking up Jerome Frank's 'fear of a standardless universe that religious and legal fundamentalism shared', Horwitz (1992: 177), in effect, rejects anything like Koselleck's historical account of the de-theologised political State.

The Transformation of American Law is an encomium to Legal Realism as the 'culmination of the Progressive challenge to legal orthodoxy' (Horwitz 1992: 5). Centred in the 1920s and 1930s, this movement extended the late nineteenth-century critique of conservative jurisprudence into our own times through Law and Economics and Critical Legal Studies. Its achievement was to de-legitimise Classical Legal Thought as 'neither neutral, natural nor necessary, but . . . instead a historically contingent and socially created system of thought' (Horwitz 1992: 6). The Legal Realists' lesson – that the formal rules of law do not determine the actual outcomes of cases – is not always viewed so generously. More radical critics debunk law altogether, not merely its claim to autonomy, demanding total transformation of individual consciousness and social being. Yet there is reason to agree with Horwitz that legal development cannot be understood independently of historical and political circumstances. The question is whether those circumstances are understood in their own terms or clamped into a unifying dialectical history of the sort that Koselleck (1988) identifies as the instrument of post-Enlightenment critique.

The essential pre-history of Legal Realism lies in the Progressive attack on 'modes of categorical thinking by portraying them as formalistic and artificial' (Horwitz 1992: 18). The formal theory of contract as a neutral meeting of free and equal wills was the prime target. But the search for a neutral jurisprudence had lost its mooring in social reality with the rise of massive corporate power. In consequence, the search became an abstraction that idealised the image of contractual freedom as operating regardless of the circumstances. It was the destiny of Progressive Legal Thought to swing things back from this disembodied ideal towards historical reality.[3] The laudatory history drawn in *The Transformation of American Law* depicts the Realists' project from 'our post-Realist perspective' (Horwitz 1992: 62). Everything is done to prevent us associating this project with an orthodoxy. Unlike a 'coherent intellectual movement' or a 'systematic jurisprudence', Legal Realism in its intellectual dimension 'expressed more a set of sometimes contradictory tendencies than a rigorous set of methodologies or propositions about legal theory' (Horwitz 1992: 169). The claim to stand outside existing institutions often prefaces a claim to have a fuller overview of them. So Horwitz's preparedness to leave Legal Realism in a state of indefinition is not necessarily a prelude to modesty. In fact he represents the 'contradictions within Realism' as what allow this particular intellectual movement – unlike other jurisprudential traditions – to 'connect with real political struggles' (Horwitz 1992: 170). That being said, Horwitz has no hesitation in seeing Realism as continuing the Progressive project to displace a Classical Legal Thought that had erred in basing itself on the demarcation of the legal from the moral and political. Nor does he hesitate in identifying the Realist non-movement's 'lasting contribution' as 'its critique of the claims of orthodox legal reasoning to be able to provide neutral and apolitical answers to legal questions' (Horwitz 1992: 206).

Despite the promotion of 'real political struggles', it is finally for a conceptual achievement that Legal Realism is most applauded, being 'perhaps the earliest expression in America of cultural modernism or what Peter Novick calls "cognitive relativism"'.[4] By this term Horwitz (1992: 181–2) refers to the Realist argument for 'the socially constructed character of frames of reference, categories of thought, and legitimating concepts', an argument that was 'linked to their passionate desire to challenge the claimed objectivity of deductive and analogical reasoning'. The challenge was to right a wrong by reconnecting law to 'social reality' and to moral politics in response to the 'perception that law and life were out of sync'. As we are told, Legal Realism 'continued to be an intellectual force in the postwar period' (Horwitz 1992: 187). If it finally retreated, 'it did so primarily because its heirs had lost all connection to the Progressive politics that originally gave it meaning and inspiration' (Horwitz 1992: 7).

There are some problems in Horwitz's history of Legal Realism as that moral and political culmination of earlier Progressive Legal Critique which succeeded in bringing Classical Legal Thought into crisis. At the outset, Horwitz (1992: viii) proclaims his freedom from 'those philosophical dualisms that have stereotyped all forms of theoretical debate over the last two (or is it four?) centuries', adding that '[w]hether it is the "fact–value" or "mind–body" or "theory–practice" or "subjective–objective" or "idealism–materialism" or "freedom–coercion" dualities, almost all these efforts at mutually exclusive categorical formations have come to seem less and less satisfying'. Without doubting Horwitz's wish to be free of the 'dualities' standard in critical social theory, we can ask why the distinction between a progressive politics and a conservative jurisprudence is endorsed as if self-evident. But in particular we can ask whether his history – philosophically orchestrated as a reconciliation of opposites – is not itself completely dependent on the dialectical mode of thought which the academy now counts as being critical.

In Horwitz's account of modern American law, the dialectic balances the transcendental principle of objective reason by swinging towards the contingent flux of historical reality. This intellectual back and forth is taken to establish a forward-moving process that guides 'Progressives' to moral postures and political positions that are unsurpassably right. In reading *The Transformation of American Law* and finding the duality of 'thought' and 'social reality' almost throughout, we begin to suspect that 'critique cannot escape the orbit of the binary concepts that it seeks to problematise because critique is itself nothing more than a theoretical oscillation between these concepts' (Hunter 1993: 125–6).[5] 'History' becomes just one pole. The priority goes now to thought or consciousness, now to history or social reality, as the following examples show. On the one hand, the idea of 'private law was forced to come to terms with the emergence of organisational society and the decline of decentralised markets'; on the other, 'developments in thought' occasion change in legal institutions (Horwitz 1992: 5, 11). Or again, on the one hand, 'standardisation of commercial transactions began to overwhelm the desire to conceive of contract law as expressing the subjective desires of individuals'; on the other, '[t]he emergence of a distinction between public and private law is one important example of the effort to create a private realm immune to the dangers of redistribution' (Horwitz 1992: 37, 26–7). In underscoring this oscillation between a 'pressure to bring the law into closer touch with society' (Horwitz 1992: 5) and the counter-pressure to bring social institutions, including law, into line with moral and political norms of social justice, my aim is not to pick a fault in Horwitz's logical consistency. On the contrary, it is to show how faithful an exponent he is of the dialectical mode of critique that recasts historical circumstances into exemplary polarities before reconciling them into a higher synthesis.

Along with the hermeneutic turn to self-reflection for legal historians, there is then also this pious fidelity to the dialectic. It is deployed as the means to liberation from existing institutions (antithesis) and to reunification of 'law and life' such that these will be no longer 'out of sync' (synthesis). The critical manoeuvre that Koselleck describes is on display. Unbound, Legal Realism takes on the attributes of the ideally free and self-determining human subject, able to move this way or that, between 'ideal' and 'real', never fixed to one or other pole. It is a powerful gesture of intellectual status and moral superiority. But it is also yet another relay of the reorchestration of the empirical historical record into a 'history' that is more philosophical than descriptive.

To the extent that it historicises his work by locating it as a particular intellectual practice, Horwitz might not welcome this praise. However, there is an option here that he does not take: to cease treating the legal conduct of life in terms of dialectically orchestrated antonyms. This would break the habit of discussing law either as a reified institutional practice lacking a normative moral-political ideal or, alternatively, as a real-world practice that drags metaphysically abstract ideas back to earth. This habitual move is how dialectical historicism reunifies the separate spheres of life into a single process of development. The legal system is reduced to an incomplete manifestation of a more fundamental moral process. This is the problem of historicist critique.[6] Whether denouncing the present as morally incomplete or promising the future reconciliation of law and morality, critique routinely joins history and consciousness in the philosophical figure of the human subject.[7] The dialectical turn functions to recover a unity supposedly lost with the divided being that, so they say, came with the rise of the modern State. It would therefore be interesting to explore a Christian genealogy for this figure.[8]

When Horwitz 'elevates' a crisis in American law to an advance in 'thought', he assumes an intellectual persona that sees the pattern of 'thought' across all fields without itself being limited to the vision of one. A descendant of Kant's moral philosopher, this persona knows the direction of humanity's advance to justice, thanks to a transhistorical self-consciousness that speaks across the centuries. Or, more psychoanalytically inspired, it speaks to us of hidden psychical cravings that an as yet incomplete humanity can only sublimate by various institutional subterfuges which critique will, of course, unmask. In Horwitz we glimpse traces of these flights, perhaps limited by the fact that he ends his history of the 'crisis of legal orthodoxy' at 1960, before the current high tide of critical theory.

It is this same crisis that Anthony Kronman (1993: 1), in *The Lost Lawyer: Failing Ideals of the Legal Profession*, diagnoses as a situation in which the American legal profession 'now stands in danger of losing its soul'. His concern is with a lawyer who is lost and a lawyer we have lost, although the emphasis lies with the former: the 'crisis' now threatens the 'capacity of a lawyer's life to offer fulfilment to the person who takes it up' (Kronman 1993: 2). At issue is a traditional 'character-virtue', a belief in 'prudence' and 'practical wisdom', that has been lost. Citing Lincoln and Earl Warren as exemplars, Kronman personifies this character-virtue in the figure of the 'lawyer-statesman'. The demise of this persona is 'a catastrophe for lawyers' and 'a disaster for the country as well' (Kronman 1993: 3).

Responding to the situation, Kronman (1993: 4) makes two moves. First, he offers a moral apologia and a philosophical specification for the persona of the lawyer-statesman. Turning to moral philosophy, Kronman locates a continuing tradition of prudential principles running from Aristotle to us. Second, he explores 'the intellectual and institutional forces that are now arrayed against the ideal of the lawyer-statesman and that together have caused its decline'. Turning to the sociology of knowledge, he locates social conditions that supposedly determine these ideals and principles. Three damaging 'forces' are held responsible for 'a sea change in the profession as a whole' (Kronman 1993: 165): the commercialisation of law in the practice of the leading law firms, the bureaucratisation of the courts, and the 'currently dominant movements in American legal thought, which share a powerful antiprudentialist bias' (Kronman 1993: 4).[9] His account of these movements – again Law and Economics and Critical Legal Studies – depicts the penetration of the law school by a critique that generates a crisis in the profession and drives Kronman (1993: 7) to his 'gloomy conclusion'.

Kronman ties Law and Economics and Critical Legal Studies into a 'legal science' approach to law. In part it is a matter of their common target: the craft practice of the common law tradition. In part it is a matter of a counter-tradition of critique that he, like Horwitz, traces to an earlier movement in American jurisprudence, Legal Realism. Here, however, there was a dual tendency: one branch of Legal Realism was 'scientific', the other 'prudentialist' (Kronman 1993: 168). In their claim to see through the empirical surface disorder of the law and in their antiprudentialism, Law and Economics and Critical Legal Studies are related to the former tendency. Analysing Legal Realism the better to understand certain intellectual practices in today's law school, Kronman settles on Christopher Columbus Langdell's late nineteenth-century redesign of the Harvard law curriculum in terms of a 'geometry of law' as the key error of modern American jurisprudence:

> Langdell was firmly convinced that the study of law must be made rigorously scientific if law schools were ever to become as intellectually respectable as other university departments. Previously lawyers had been educated, for the most part, in law offices under the supervision of practising attorneys. This older regime – as old as the common law itself – Langdell thought haphazard and inexact; his ambition was to replace it with a new system of legal education, one in which the primary forum of instruction would be not the law office but the academic classroom

and library, and whose masters would be professors rather than practitioners.

(Kronman 1993: 170)

Kronman takes the claims of science at face value, as independent of circumstance, such that a 'rigorous science of law may be built upon a very thin fund of experience, like the discipline of geometry itself' (Kronman 1993: 172). This does little to encourage a view of the geometry class too as experience, albeit experience of a specialised sort.

Yet the elements of a less de-contextualised account are here. There is Langdell's concern with intellectual status and an approach to law as a field of knowledge that was prestigious because 'peculiarly within the province of university intellectuals rather than that of seasoned practitioners' (Kronman 1993: 173). A reflective philosophical practice is proposed to displace the existing craft approach to law as practical know-how. For all its science, this was a battle for dominance between two cultural milieux and their different forms of conduct, the academic classroom with its elevated discipline and the law office with its worldly commerce. The disinterested project to detach law from commerce and reground it in science was not unrelated to a particular interest. Thus, 'to emphasise the elevated status of the professionals trained at Harvard, Dean Langdell's school increased the admission requirements to admit only college graduates' (Carrington 1991: 134–5).

Langdell and the scientific project had their opponents from the start, among them Oliver Wendell Holmes. Kronman selects the Legal Realists as the main antagonists. The scene is the Yale Law School in the decades following 1920. Of the scholars he discusses, Kronman's account of Karl Llewellyn is instructive by virtue of depicting two Llewellyns, the earlier proponent and the later opponent of a science of law. In his earlier mode, Llewellyn merely qualified the purity of Langdell's geometer by shifting the object of scientific investigation from rule-systems to judicial behaviour and its underlying causes, thus seeing through law's ostensible disorder to its hidden regularities. This science of judicial behaviour was the first Llewellyn's instrument for raising legal scholarship to the level of a social science. However, Kronman underscores Llewellyn's reluctance to extend the domain of scientific description to the normative domain of speculation on what law ought to be. This was a path that others did not fear to tread.[10]

In *The Common Law Tradition*, a study emerging from lectures at Yale in 1940, the second Llewellyn authored the 'best account of common-law adjudication that any American has ever offered' (Kronman 1993: 211). Llewellyn is responding to a crisis occasioned by a critique: the crisis of confidence in appellate judgments that affects both litigants and judiciary. *The Common Law Tradition* is an attempt to arm the victims of critique by confirming appellate judging as meeting its purposes because of and not despite its independence from theoretical or scientific foundations:

> [B]asic to most of both the misconceptions and the cross-purposings of the realist controversy, was an absence everywhere of the concept of craft, of craft-tradition, of craft-responsibility, and of craftsmanship not as meaning merely the high artistry of God's gifted, but as including the uninspired but reliable work of the plain and ordinary citizens of the craft. The existence of a craft means the existence of some significant body of work knowhow, centred on the doing of some perceptible kind of job. This working knowhow is in some material degree transmissible and transmitted to the incomer, it is in some material degree conscious, it is to some degree articulate in principles and rules of art or of thumb, in practices and dodges or contrivances which can be noticed and learned for the easing and the furtherance of the work. A healthy craft, moreover, elicits ideals, pride, and responsibility in its craftsmen. And every live craft has much more to it than any rules describe; the rules not only fail to tell the full tale, taken literally they tell much of it wrong; and while words can set forth such facts and needs as ideals, craft-conscience, and morale, these things are bodied forth, they live and work, primarily in ways and attitudes which are much more and better felt and done than they are said. Now appellate judging is a distinct and (along with spokesmanship) a central craft of the law side of the great institution of Law-Government.
>
> (Llewellyn 1960: 214)

The craft of appellate judging as Llewellyn describes it is mundane in its dodges. It has a definite but limited distribution and duration. Inseparable from the purposes of 'Law-Government' and thus informed by actual problems, it cannot be wholly formalised into rules. It combines mental and bodily abilities not as a perfect synthesis ready for the next world but in order to perform a job in this one. This cheerful miscegenation of ideals and behaviours, theories and practices simply pays no heed to intellectuals' habitual subordination of the second term of each pair.[11] Referring to this passage, Kronman (1993: 214) observes that 'a judge whose task is to apply the law will be guided in his deliberations by what might be called the *ethos* of his office', that is, by the habits of judicial craftsmanship instilled by practice.

Llewellyn was countering the critical view of appellate judging as pre-theoretical and lacking the reflexive theoretical grounds that alone guaranteed predictability. His tactic was not to seek some grounding theory to give adjudication a normative direction. On the contrary, for Llewellyn as for Hale three centuries earlier, coherence came from regular procedure and habitual practice. Something more flexible than the usual antinomy of theory or conceptual chaos is envisaged, something akin to a capacity for improvisation. Faced with a new case, Llewellyn's judge goes 'questing for a *legal* way to see and to pose the issue, and for a *legal* line along which to puzzle' (Llewellyn 1960: 119). The coherence of adjudication depended on this craft capacity. It did not derive from a theoretical illumination. Llewellyn (1960: 17–18) estimated that legal adjudication involved a 'reckonability equivalent to that of a good business risk'. He then dispenses with the notion of a fundamental rational ground or ultimate moral horizon as the critical standard against which the actual practices of lawyers can be assessed. The persona appropriate to the judicial context is one that has the 'kind of experience, sense and intuition which was characteristic of an old-fashioned skilled horse trader in his dealings either with horses or with other horse traders' (Llewellyn 1960: 201).

Empowered but not elevated by this practical ethos, Kronman depicts the quite different disposition of today's critical legal scholars:

> All offer . . . abstraction as a key to understanding the hidden order of the law, whose deep uniformity is concealed (they maintain) by the superficial variety of its doctrines and principles. In their insistence on the need to look beneath the surface of the law to the structures that underlie it, in their emphasis on the simplicity and ubiquity of these structures, and in their belief that only a theory of the highest possible abstraction can describe them, the leading theoreticians of the critical studies movement have encouraged an outlook hostile to the prudentialism on which the lawyer-statesman ideal is based.
>
> (Kronman 1993: 168)

'Abstraction' is not just a problem of ideas. When Kronman links it to a 'hostile outlook', we move from ideas to the particular intellectual comportment of critical 'theoreticians' who have their own craft practice in the academic milieu: to unmask a previously 'hidden order' from the 'superficial variety' of actual legal phenomena, an order invisible to others but which the theorists count as the reality of law. What is this intellectual comportment that raises its exponents above the practitioners by seeing invisible structures – geometrical, linguistic, ideological or moral – as the real condition of law's possibility?

This question is encouraged by Kronman's account of classic critical texts: Duncan Kennedy's (1977) 'Form and substance in private law adjudication' and Roberto Unger's (1986) *The Critical Legal Studies Movement.* All law, for Kennedy, folds back into an exemplary antithesis taken to mark the present stage of human development: action for self (or, in history of ideas terms, individualism) versus action for others (altruism and communitarianism). Deploying this antithesis to embrace whatever empirical law might come up with, the critic envisions life as a permanently generative tension. The 'conflict among our own values and ways of understanding the world is here to stay' (Kennedy 1977: 1712). This critical craft is pre-eminently dialectical. Kronman uses the term in relation to Kennedy, but to characterise an idea not to describe a particular intellectual technique. In the academic setting, the critic's capacity to allow no exit from the tension through 'metaprinciples' functions both as a discipline of self and as a model of conduct for students to imitate. Kennedy talks of a transformative 'change in attitude'. In our present circumstances – predictably depicted as one-sidedly individualistic and insufficiently communal – the dialectical critic leans towards the pole of community and altruism as the way towards a fuller mode of being. As for the mass of uncritical lawyers, they are depicted as operating within these deep polarities they do not suspect but which the reflexive philosopher will bring to consciousness:

> The opposed rhetorical modes lawyers use reflect a deeper level of contradiction. At this deeper level, we are divided among ourselves and also within ourselves, between irreconcilable visions of humanity and society, and between radically different aspirations for our common future.
>
> (Kennedy 1977: 1685)

In Kronman's paraphrase, Kennedy draws the intellectual threshold that sets the philosopher and his 'visions' above those lawyers who have not yet seen beyond their actual arguments and existing institutions:

> If we are to grasp the hidden order in these arguments, we must look through them to the organising conceptions of political morality that lie beneath their surface. This requires that we break . . . with the discourse of the practising lawyers and judges. For the 'visions of the universe' that give their arguments a hidden structure cannot be systematically elaborated in the practical and particularistic terms lawyers and judges themselves employ. These visions make their way into legal discourse only in an incomplete and broken form. To see them whole – to grasp the simple inner unity of each and to understand the depth of difference between them – we must substitute the methods and vocabulary of philosophy for those of law.
>
> (Kronman 1993: 245)

This is the usual neo-Kantian subordination of empirical practice to reflexive philosophy, execution to conception. But it is also the unfinished 'conflict of the faculties' attempting to displace one ethos by another inside the law school.

How does Roberto Unger look in this dialectical light? Kronman identifies the antiprudential nature of Unger's project: to tie critical legal studies backward to the project of scientific realism, yet also forward to a future transformation of society and existing systems of power in a way that would see the end of the present legal profession. This is a current analogue of Koselleck's spiritual Enlighteners whose 'sense of self' was so great they believed they could 'eliminate the State altogether'. Unger's critique conforms to the three-step post-Kantian dialectic. First, like Horwitz, he rejects the 'formalism' that held legal reasoning to be ideally independent of moral prejudices or political interests. Second and symmetrically, Unger rejects the existing 'real', that is, the 'objectivism' of believing that any existing polity could express individual freedom or without constraint embody our full subjectivity. This dual rejection of formalism and objectivism, of course, anticipates the third and decisive step up to a higher reflexive consciousness of the historical situation: Unger's revelation that a 'guiding vision', hidden until brought to light by critique, has in fact determined the polity and imposed its contingent interpretation of the law we now happen to have. The legal sphere is unmasked as having been open all the time to the tainted interests of existing politics. The issue of critique as the instrument of the interests of religion is not raised.

This whole movement of thought depends on a particular moral anthropology: a 'being whose most remarkable quality is precisely the power to overcome and revise, with time, every social or mental structure in which he moves'. This 'context-transcending agent', in the world but not 'entirely of it' (Unger 1986: 22–3), has as its special feature a 'negative capability' that Unger (1986: 93–5) views as a 'radicalised version' of an idea created by the 'great secular doctrines of emancipation of the recent past – liberalism, socialism and communism – and by the social theories that supported them'. Absolutism and the State that actually granted religious freedom rate no mention.

With this moral anthropology and persona comes a special exercise of mind for partially withdrawing from the present State and imaging up the new moral-political society. By way of setting for this exercise Unger (1986: 106) proposes 'formative contexts' which ensure that '[a]t any given time, related sets of preconceptions and institutional arrangements shape a large part of the routine practical and conceptual activities that take place while remaining themselves unaffected by the ordinary disturbances that these activities produce'. These contexts are more normative and dialectical than actual institutional settings. They are in fact techniques of mind for critical academics engaged in an exercise of moral self-shaping that both rejects the historical real and counters the otherwise undirected vigour of the movement of transcendence. The discipline of this extraordinary critical ethos installs in its practitioners a capacity to organise their moral being within this contrapuntal play.

Then comes the third stage, the synthesis that brings this counterpoint to consciousness. To do this is to enter the new moral community of those freed by critique. Unger observes that some contexts are more open and self-transforming than others. Most closed and least self-transforming are those contexts whose members unreflectively take them as simply given in the nature of things. Conversely, the critic sees them as the historical constructs of human agency. But who is actually possessed of a competence so special that it allows them to conduct themselves as if they saw through all 'the social and mental forms . . . that have ever been produced'? In what setting is such a competence actually exercised?

Defending common law prudentialism, Kronman represents Unger in terms of an 'extraordinarily abstract ideal'. The problem of abstraction as detachment from actuality returns. However, redescribed as a particular conduct of moral life, abstraction is a perfectly concrete phenomenon with its specific intellectual techniques and institutional channels of dissemination. For Kant, the critical philosophy was precisely not one among other conditioned conducts of life. For Unger, the critical philosopher remains the persona that abstracts itself from the given circumstances of a law that it inspects from an unconditional vantage point – a consciousness dialectically organised by mutually destabilising oppositions. Rights become the scene of a perpetual counter-politics:

> The ideal aim of the system of rights, taken as a whole and in each of its branches, is to serve as a counterprogram to the maintenance or re-emergence of any scheme of social roles and ranks that can become effectively insulated against the ordinarily available forms of challenge. (Unger 1986: 41)

This 'system of rights' is existing law and society transformed by a virtuoso exercise of dialectical critique into a future vision of moral community. The categories of right that Unger envisions go far beyond the liberal dispensation of rights for exercise in areas of life immune to governmental regulation. 'Destabilisation rights' would give individuals 'a claim upon governmental power obliging government to disrupt those forms of division and hierarchy that, contrary to the spirit of the [Unger's "superliberal"] constitution, manage to achieve stability only by distancing themselves from the transformative conflicts that might disturb them' (Unger 1986: 53). As a vision of ends, the 'system of rights' does less to specify the means that the new disposition of roles and ranks presumably entails than to excite us with the moral persona modelled to this ultimate degree.

Such a persona is too rare to be universal. Yet its dissemination through the critical academy has seen it penetrate habitats once the preserve of quite other personae, among them Kronman's prudential common lawyer. Faced with the academic canonisation of this critical persona, we might recall the history lesson: in early modern Germany, the task faced by a post-confessional civil jurist such as Thomasius was not only to bring stability to the role and regularity to the tasks of the secular lawyer. The primary and immediate imperative was to safeguard the secular lawyer from the then 'ordinarily available forms of challenge', namely Calvinist, Lutheran and Catholic zealots seeking to use the secular law for their own religious ends.

For Unger, in our own luxurious times and peaceful circumstances, the task has become aesthetic: to reconcile institutional divisions into the higher synthesis and unity of a favoured moral-political vision:

> [I]f the institutional plan that decrees the existence of a distinct judiciary alongside only one or two other branches of government is reconstructed, and if long before this reconstruction the belief in a logic of inherent institutional roles is abandoned, legal expertise can survive

> only as a loose collection of different types of insight and responsibility. Each type would combine elements of current legal professionalism with allegedly non-legal forms of special knowledge and experience as well as with varieties of political representation. This disintegration of the bar might serve as a model for what would happen, in a more democratic and less superstitious society, to all claims to monopolise in the name of expert knowledge an instrument of power.
>
> (Unger 1986: 111)

Kronman resists this prophetic imagery of a profession transformed – 'disintegrated' – for a future spiritual politics. Indeed, as law is reabsorbed into morality – Kronman (1993: 261) speaks of an 'Archimedean moral theory external to the law' imported by critique into the law school – a quite anti-professional image of the future emerges. The new lawyering will be the 'defence of individual or group interests by methods that reveal the specificity of the underlying institutional and imaginative order, that subject it to a series of petty disturbances capable of escalating at any moment, and that suggest alternative ways of defining collective interests, collective identities, and assumptions about the possible' (Unger 1986: 111). 'Underlying institutional and imaginative order' or 'the basic imaginative structure of social existence' are not descriptions of historical fact. They are cognitive elements of a moral exercise in dialectical self-questioning. In this way the critical intellectual reinforces the self-discipline required to call this world endlessly into question.

Kronman adopts precisely the vocabulary – character, disposition, ethos, persona – to recognise what is going on. Yet he remains so committed to denouncing scientific realism as a false idea that he does not address Critical Legal Studies as a style of missionary behaviour now at home in a 'heathen' law school that it is engaged in converting. Because he, too, frames the relation between common law and legal science within an exemplary opposition of moderated prudence and all-embracing rationality, Kronman does not approach that conflict as an overlap between two relatively autonomous histories. He thus reserves the terms ethos and disposition, character and persona for the prudentialism of which he approves and for its embodiment: the lawyer-statesman. Conversely, scientific realism is treated as a pure abstraction, a horribly wrong idea. The alternative is to treat scientific realism, too, as ethos and disposition, character and persona. To redescribe legal critique not in terms of true (or false) ideas but in terms of a specialised ethical persona would raise the historical question of that persona's moral status and political prestige. Tracing it to a theological genealogy might suggest why this persona could now penetrate the law school as it has the humanities academy.

Kronman diagnoses a crisis in the relation between legal teaching and legal scholarship. Where the critical legal theorist occupies the seminar room, the pedagogy becomes continuous with the scholarship. For students this is a 'disaster' (Kronman 1993: 269). The trouble lies in the mismatch of levels: between a critical theory that pursues rational abstraction or dialectical syntheses of law and moral theory, and a practical training in the case by case knowhow needed for routine professional work. Kronman describes this mismatch between critical legal theory and prudential legal training as a 'pathological division'. The subtitle of Koselleck's *Critique and Crisis* is *Enlightenment and the Pathogenesis of Modern Society*. For both writers, the pathologising agent is the critic. However, there are the perennial divergences between philosopher and historian. Kronman adopts a general critique of modernity as soul-destroying rationalisation and assumes that religion is dead. Koselleck does neither.

That modern Western existence has been rationalised to the point of losing contact with the life-world is a familiar critical and aesthetic litany. As confirmation, Kronman turns to Max Weber, under the subhead 'Honesty'. Weber epitomised unsentimental honesty. He wrote to a correspondent, 'My decisive inner requirement is "intellectual honesty": I say what is' (in Mommsen 1984: 43). Or, as he told his listeners in the German Federation of Free Students: '[W]hat is decisive is the trained relentlessness in viewing the realities of life, and the ability to face such realities and to measure up to them inwardly' (Weber 1946: 126–7). Weber's topic was: what sort of persona goes with the science taught in the university today? By 'science' (*Wissenschaft*), he understood all methodically organised fields of knowledge, among them the discipline of jurisprudence. It was not a case of opposing science to art. The key distinction lay between knowledge and morality. Weber confronted his listeners with this proposition: the moral norm that justifies pursuit of a discipline in the eyes of its practitioners goes no further than the instituted limits of that discipline. Is it possible to build an ethic on this capacity to face the facts and 'say what is'? Or fashion an ethical persona appropriate to the 'world as it really is in its everyday routine' (Weber 1946: 128)? Or see as an ethical achievement of the first order a career which is 'utterly prosaic', 'devoid of all religious or philosophical significance' and does not claim to know the 'answers to the ultimate questions of life'?

In his lament for the common law, Kronman targets science and abstract theory, not religion and critical philosophy. To sustain his argument that Critical Legal Studies lie in the direct lineage of Hobbes, Kronman cannot present them as religion. Indeed, at the end of *The Lost Lawyer*, the displacement of religion by science becomes the reason why the once prudential American legal profession 'now stands in danger of losing its soul'. But what if it is the residual prestige of a religious ethos that gives the critics their force inside the law school? This is the question that Koselleck (1988: 1) would have us ask, given his account of '[t]he moral doctrines as the real heirs of religion'. Yet Kronman (1993: 315) does point to an answer: nearly all teachers of law 'work in universities [and] are directly exposed to the special attitudes that flourish in university communities'. He adds that 'universities are by their nature unworldly places'. Does the law school now house the two conducts of life – the legal-administrative and the religious – that the early modern State took such pains to separate? In contemplating this overlapping of two great conducts of living, we might learn if this is just a passing scuffle or a far more longstanding conflict whose effects remain to be seen.

12

NOW THAT THE SAINTS ARE MARCHING IN

Hell is the destination of the strict jurist. For Nikolaus Hieronymus Gundling, at first a follower but later a philosophical critic of Christian Thomasius in those crucial early 1700s, it was entirely possible 'to be just and yet not virtuous (*honestus*)'. *Justum* was subordinated to *honestum* and the result was stark: he 'who lives merely as a strict jurist will go to hell' (in Rüping 1968: 106). Could there be a more direct reconnection of law to religion? Such opinions as Gundling's had been the certainties of confessional religion; they have become the truths of philosophical morality. Gundling will serve as icon for those waging continuing critical war on the early modern attempt to separate moral salvation from civil law and government. His heirs are with us. If Koselleck is right, with ever more students trained by critical intellectuals, those zealously 'virtuous' heirs of Gundling, there will be a persisting religious revenge on existing institutions.

The moral inadequacy of positive law is an old critical refrain. 'Statutes and formulas,' said Kant (1963: 86) in the late 1700s, 'those mechanical tools of the rational employment of [man's] natural gifts, are the fetters of an everlasting tutelage.' Too tightly bound to worldly interests to carry humanity forward to its truly moral future, positive law is at best a provisional substitute for inner morality and self-determination. Kant's successors have the scent of moral victory. When law is reunited with morality, the Absolutist separation of religion from law and religion is reversed. Other voices, remembering the history of this separation, have been less eager to reunify the spheres. Instead of unity, Carl Schmitt recalls the smoke of battle that has continued since European jurisprudence first emerged:

> In vehement struggles with the Church and theology during the thirteenth and fourteenth centuries, jurisprudence established itself as a 'faculty' and maintained it in the tumultuous circumstances of a feudalism that was reaching its end. The sixteenth century, which experienced the blossoming of a humanistic jurisprudence, was also a time of bloody confessional civil wars. Great jurists of this epoch became the victims

> of an intolerant fanaticism, whereby both sides of the law had their martyrs'.
>
> (Schmitt, in Ulmen 1985: 7)

Following Schmitt, Koselleck built his thesis of 'critique and crisis' on the historical fact that, to end religious civil war, the State had released religion from any role in government. Less historical jurists have forgotten or never knew why Christian conscience was separated from the legal regulation of civil life.

It would be naive to expect thanks to flow to those few – we should include Max Weber and Amelie Rorty – who argue for an anti-theocratic plurality of 'orderings of life' and recall today's critics to their religious genealogy. Whether Koselleck's account of the French Revolution as a religious civil war or Jonathan Clark's account of the American War of Independence as something less than a moral progress for humanity, such projects risk rejection in a humanities academy more theological than it knows. Few critical intellectuals actually want to be called holy. In the field of academic law, Roberto Unger's explicit self-identification with Christianity can embarrass those who pride themselves on being critical and secular. Yet it does not embarrass enough to stop a flock of followers endorsing his conviction that the existing order of this world requires moral transformation. The separation of law and morality is anathema in an academic milieu where moral rules and political principles are taken as the proper basis for law and government.

A predictable objection will be heard. Without moral principles, conduct cannot be ethical. Yet recall the chilling footnote to Koselleck's history: the Enlighteners' moral critique of the State was continuous not only with prior religious modes of thought but with a subsequent 'German National Socialism whose loss of reality and Utopian self-exaltation had resulted in hitherto unprecedented crimes' (Koselleck 1988: 1). Again there is a standard objection: Nazism is what eventuates when formal law and bureaucratic government go unchecked by moral principle. In fact the history paints a contrary picture. The Nazi political regime viciously attacked the professional neutrality of German State lawyers and bureaucrats for following 'an enterprise . . . empty of moral worth' and a 'merely external and formalistic concept of duty' (Caplan 1988: 194). This State administration and its juristic-civic culture continued the Prussian tradition to which Thomasius and his students at Halle had contributed a founding initiative in the early eighteenth century. With the Nazi seizure of power, however, an overwhelming moral and political fervour 'superseded the conventional dualism of state and society, as well as the separation of powers and the positivist tradition in private and public law' (Caplan 1988: 197). Far from clinching the case against non-principled government and the formal positive law of a 'strict jurist', the Nazi 'loss of reality' marked a 'period of profound assault on the personnel and principles of the German administration' (Caplan 1988: 322).

The religious explanation of contemporary critical intellectualism will not soon become canonical even in the humanities academy. What of the law school? Of course, outside the legal academy only certain kinds of lawyers have any professional concern with critique. Even inside, critique is not a dominant practice. Nor is it all necessarily wrong. The great exponents of Critical Legal Studies – Kennedy and Unger – possess an elaborate legal knowledge. Nor in signalling a religious disposition in the law school are we unmasking something hitherto entirely hidden. Academic lawyers with the prestige of Roberto Unger and Ronald Dworkin publicise the religious impulse in their moral and political programmes for the transformation of law and legal education.

The following example of critical jurisprudence is indicative of a currently dominant mode.[1] In a volume advertising itself as 'the first work of contemporary jurisprudence systematically to apply critical philosophy to the common law', Douzinas, Goodrich and Hachamovitch (1994) make the 'contingency of law' central to a critique purporting to uncover the 'political and cultural significance' of the 'substantive institutions of law'. For Goodrich and his co-authors – let us call them 'the critics' – the objective is 'the breakdown of traditional conceptions of legal reason' when confronted by 'conceptions of the contingency of law and the plurality of legal experience'. Playing with words, they offer a manifesto for their new conception: 'the legality of the contingent'. The proposition is this: 'Contingency is the condition of legal judgement and the limit of its reason' (Douzinas *et al.* 1994: 1). There is no recognition that the common law has proved durable in the face of novel circumstances, an institution broadly capable of what Llewellyn called 'reliable work'. Instead, there is the predictable pair of asymmetrical counterconcepts: 'While contingency may be subject to laws it must also always escape legality'.

Does the suggestion of a future life beyond mere legality reimplant a religious disposition in the sphere of law? Perhaps. But if we ask how the critical movement operates in this instance, there is no doubt: it is faithfully dialectical. First, a thesis of fixity is imputed to the common lawyers who are said to lay claim to formal and objective reason. Second, 'contingency' is made the antithesis of this fixity, confronting reified law with the flux of historical reality: 'The demise of the various sciences of law and of their accompanying substrate of systemic concepts throws legal theory back into the life-world or the experience of the legal institution' (Douzinas *et al.* 1994: 1). The third panel of the triptych brings the moral synthesis. Reinformed by contact with 'history' and 'the life-world', a once-fixed law transmutes into morality:

> To respond to the legality of the contingent is to formulate an account of the amorphous, incidental, fluid and indefinable realms of justice and judgement, carriage and miscarriage, politic and ethic of common law. This project is predicated upon a theoretical and political radicalism that returns to the specific histories and disciplines of common law and interrogates them in the strange-sounding name of justice.
>
> (Douzinas *et al.* 1994: 1–2)

The dialectic lets the critic vault the given. In this instance, the given is both the untheorised positivism of the common law profession and the high academic theory of formal structuralism embraced until recently as a crucial critical resource. But favour is now swinging back towards informal categories such as 'life-world' and 'experience' that structuralists once rejected as hopelessly mortgaged to moral humanism. The new 'radicalism' is to reabsorb law into morality. In fact, the critics' clericalism is scarcely hidden from view. Defining themselves as 'heretics', an oppositional role now prestigious within the critical academy, they reject the 'church' of a common law doctrine that 'has increasingly assumed rather than proved or practised the relation of God, justice or truth to legal acts' (Douzinas *et al.* 1994: 7). They preach in the name of 'the politics of reason' that lies beyond the common law but 'has always been a dimension of governance of ecclesiastical and civil law' (Douzinas *et al.* 1994: 2).

We recognise this intellectual comportment. Moving between the poles of formalism and flux, the dialectical pendulum is here swinging back from formalism towards individual feeling and moral subjectivity (be it the judge re-equipped with a private conscience or the inevitably honest woman who at last has her day in court). Given this arc, even Dworkin's insertion of moral philosophy into the process of judicial interpretation is rejected as contributing to the 'law's perpetuity' and thus failing to establish 'a set of subjective and relative values [or] a critical standard against which acts of legal and judicial power can be judged' (Douzinas *et al.* 1994: 19). The critics take Dworkin's proposition of moral principles that furnish a 'right answer' in every case as impeding a full return to conscience and the moral self since 'judges are never left to their own devices'. Thus '[t]he dreaded supplement of judicial discretion (in other words the individual morality of the judge) . . . is firmly kept outside the system' (Douzinas *et al.* 1994: 19). Justice, intone the critics, is 'either a critical concept or it is totally redundant if not positively harmful for jurisprudence in that it encourages an unquestioning attitude to law'. As usual the dialectical display precedes a unifying moral claim: 'In this unceasing conjunction and disjunction, this alternating current between the most general and calculating and the most concrete and incalculable, or between the legality of form and legal subjectivity, lies the ethics of a critical legal response to the material legal person, law's morality of the contingent' (Douzinas *et al.* 1994: 24).

Having debunked 'modernist legality' as a 'wholly positivised conception of juridical phenomena . . . predicated upon the exclusion of ethics, morality, value and indeed substance from questions of law, legality, validity and form', the critics come to the familiar assertion that law's 'procedures are technical and its personnel neutral' (Douzinas *et al.* 1994: 16, 17) This is their exorcism of a strict legality whose neutrality they construe as an absence of sensuous feeling and morality. It could be Schiller speaking. The critics define their own morality and politics against 'a purely formal set of normative constraints without any deeper justification than the validity of its law-applying institutions'. They further denigrate these institutions as locked into 'a blind justice, a geometry of rules (*more geometrico*) without the sensibility of proportion, perception of place or understanding of harmony or even principle that the critical tradition had required of the practice of law' (Douzinas *et al.* 1994: 17).

An inflated expression of distress with the present accompanies this gesture. The critics ask 'whether any residue of transcendence and alterity remains or whether all society has become immanent to the operations of a totalitarian discourse that allows nothing to escape' (Douzinas *et al.* 1994: 23). This pessimism turns out to be momentary. It is belied by the finally triumphant tone of their moral apostrophe to themselves: '[c]aught between the call to justice and a lack of any determinate criteria for ethical action, critical legal studies is left with responsibility – indeed, one might say it is left with the responsibility for responsibility' (Douzinas *et al.* 1994: 22).

As with eighteenth-century Lutheran clergy agonising over their new status as State officials of public morality, the critics confront the fact that by 'becoming a school, by dint of its academic registration and place, as well as its substantive applications to the teaching of law, [Critical Legal Studies] takes on a new political responsibility' (Douzinas *et al.* 1994: 8). Indeed, 'it would be irresponsible in the extreme not to admit to the political commitments of institutional attachment'. But this circumstance is immediately elevated into the phantasmic image of a future communal moral 'politics' that operates in the 'interstitial institutions of law'. Here the critics make the shift from an 'espousal of creeds' to a 'politics of contingency and a need of (gregarious) uncertainty' (Douzinas *et al.* 1994: 9). To take up Critical Legal Studies now is to enter an intellectual conduct of life that 'adverts to the conflictual coupling of belonging and the desire for escape'. Of course from this dialectical union emerges a proper moral progeny:

> The history of a closure is always dual and duplicitous: our language, institutional practice and scholarship inevitably belong to the tradition while at the same time seeking its decomposition. The desire for escape, for a transcendence which would go beyond the institution or the positivised system of governance is an impossibility. The recognition of this impossibility, the double bind of belonging and estrangement, the unhappy consciousness of this boundary or limit opens the domains of ethics and justice as the distinguishing feature of the contemporary politics of critical legal scholarship.
>
> (Douzinas *et al.* 1994: 13)

So nicely structured, the 'return to the institution and its histories' becomes a liberating 'recovery of those silenced and repressed voices of lawyers, visionaries, outsiders and rebels that inhabit the boundaries of an institution' (Goodrich 1994: 15).

The critical programme pursues its de-repressive gestures, stigmatising existing law before proclaiming the recovery of the morality and religion which was repressed. In *Oedipus Lex*, Goodrich (1995: 240) proposes a psychoanalytic critique of legal history as repression, a 'critique . . . attentive precisely to the differences or others enfolded in law'. With bravura, the critic-analyst recovers from the 'unconscious' of the common law the various memories it has repressed: predictably the feminine, the ethnic and the theoretical all return, but so too does the spiritual. The 'unity' of the common law, we are told, was 'built upon the sacrifice, the devouring of other laws, not least those of conscience, of spirituality, and of the soul' (Goodrich 1995: 242). Or again, having referred to the 'history of the negation of spiritual power . . . within the temporal law', Goodrich (1995: 247) confirms that '[t]he concern of critique is here to recollect the spiritual power of law'. No doubt there is an element of play in this manoeuvre. The negation of the spiritual had to fail in some respect, otherwise there would be no repressed memory of 'conscience' or 'soul' for the critic to recover.

Such a project – in which '[t]he relation of conscience to positive law . . . is central to the understanding of the history and critique of law' – is quite different from the present undertaking. It seeks to return secular law to 'sacral' conscience. The critical project, it seems, is closed to the possibility that the historical disengagement of a secular legal regulation of public life from the violence of spiritual community was a positive or even useful achievement. On the contrary, the whole impetus of this critique is to reunite law and religion, albeit a 'civil' religion now in the guise of a dialectical aesthetics that supports the moral and political formation of the human subject: 'the reference to conscience should be understood . . . [as being] to the substance of subjectivity, to an unconscious discipline or juristic soul' (Goodrich 1995: 236). The reference is to subjectivity, not to a specifically Christian mode of regulation. Yet the 'order of progression or enfolding of exterior law and interior progression' is surely a relay for the dialectic of inner and outer, soul and body, whose origins and present exercise are profoundly religious.

How might we respond to these gestures? In the first instance, we can tie them to their history. The term 'critique' cannot be used indifferently across different historical and cultural contexts. Koselleck, for instance, refers it specifically to that mode of transcendental moral questioning of existing institutions and mundane forms of life which was elaborated by Enlightenment intellectuals marginalised by the new State system. By contrast, Douzinas *et al.* link up a current critical stance with all past criticisms of common law:

> The pervading postmodern sentiment that 'things are not going well', that justice has miscarried or law has separated itself from ethics, has accompanied innumerable distinct cultural movements and styles from asceticism to pursuit of the millennium, gnosticism to iconoclasm, romanticism to the baroque.
>
> (Douzinas *et al.* 1994: 3)

Noble forebears and progressive allies are anointed to fashion before our eyes a transhistorical movement of resistance. American Legal Realists 'and their latter-day inheritors . . . find swift empathy among radicals in profaning the law review, satirising legal language or simply further exposing the distance and subjection that passes as law in an age where all other cultural phenomena speak to a restless uncertainty' (Douzinas *et al.* 1994: 3). A 'specific tradition of critique within English law' is posited.[2] Retrospectively made precursors of present-day critical realists are those English Renaissance civil lawyers who 'refused to accept the irrational particularism, the haphazard comparisons or kadi justice of a spuriously nationalistic common law' (Goodrich 1994: 6). Then as now, it seems, the target was a 'formalism' which sustained a 'judicial prerogative, namely the arbitrium, dictate or fiat of the judge'. All this is less historical than philosophical.

If Koselleck is right, such philosophical critique is a specialised intellectual technique of antithesising and synthesising practised by a certain social stratum. Its practitioners demonise the present, preaching an Endtime message: unless the divisive institutions of this world are transformed in their underlying structure, the unity of a moral society will not eventuate. Once the tension was all too real: in the seventeenth century between present existence and future salvation (or damnation) the choice was truly terrifying. Fewer academic intellectuals now regulate their conduct in anticipation of the Last Judgement or the imminent ending of historical time. In this sense critical dialectical projects such as that for the 'legality of the contingent' represent a pale persistence of Christian 'expectings'. The best-known critical legal scholar, Roberto Unger, embraces the Christian vision, dialectically. A presently dominant perception, he argues, wrongly separates morality and politics from law as antithetical spheres of value and fact. Unger refuses any such separation, proposing instead a reconciliation of the spheres. There is brilliant synthesising imagery of future social relations that will be neither merely legal nor merely moral-political once a mutual modification of law and moral politics reconciles the fact of values and the value of facts. Thus transformed, society will become what Unger terms 'superliberal'. It will be free from State interventions as we have known them, yet also pass beyond the constraining individualism of present liberal politics. It is, indeed, an exemplarily dialectical vision of 'an institutional structure, itself self-revision . . . [that] would provide constant occasions to disrupt any fixed structure of power and coordination in social life'. From this oscillation between stability and conflict will emerge the long-delayed human polity whose completeness lies in it being endlessly 'open to self-revision and more capable of dismantling any established or emergent structure of social division and hierarchy' (Unger 1983: 592, 607). It is the new moral community.

This is another point at which to recall Carl Schmitt's (1986: 74–5) account of 'subjectivised occasionalism', the name he gave to that cultivated romantic capacity to 'move between the compressed ego and expansion into the cosmos' and to make '[e]very historical moment . . . an elastic point in the vast fantasy of the philosophy of history'. Schmitt, for one, had no doubt that this capacity was historically related to a Christian metaphysics, one in which God constantly transforms mundane circumstances into occasions for spontaneous and unconstrained creation.

But what relation can this have to the training in law that has produced and must produce technicians who will staff the many legal and administrative offices, public and private? To regret this training as merely technical would be like treating the daily journey to work as a failure to climb the stairway to heaven. Do these men and women require a step up to a higher mode of moral being or an ethos that allows them 'to measure up inwardly' to the routines of their day to day offices? Does their conduct of living represent a shortfall in human moral development, a lesser form of life than the moral personality revealed in religion, philosophy or art? In fact these men and women demonstrate a comportment that is historically rare and ethically distinctive in a Christian culture: a measure of ability to keep one's religious principles and moral convictions separate from the technical norms demanded by legal and administrative office. Without imagining that academic legal training was ever purely technical and wholly prudential in Kronman's (1993) sense, the fact remains: there is an unsurpassably brute side to a legal training that works not through critical or theoretical reflection but through direct inculcation. This cannot be replaced by a reflexive critical exercise. But then, by and large, students training in law are not the future saints of moral redemption or political critique.

In this post-critical essay, the challenge is to grant ethical prestige to mundane forms of life. Schilling and Koselleck throw secular government and worldly law into a better than usual ethical light by recalling the historical circumstances to which they were the early modern State's response. Something might also be gained from common law historiography. For instance, Milsom records that the common law's 'first achievement, that of having come into existence at all', was 'not an exploit of juristic thought but of administration':

> Most of the important justices in eyre in the twelfth century, the chief justiciars including Henry II's justiciar Glanvill himself, no doubt the shadowy figure who wrote the book we know by Glanvill's name, most of those who figure in thirteenth-century records mainly as judges, the mysterious Bracton – all these were what we should call civil servants.
> (Milsom 1981: 38)

Critical intellectuals will complacently expect no surprises from an 'administrative' history. In reality, this legal history brings us face to face with extraordinary possibilities. Recall when common law cut its ties to theology and ultimate truth:

> [T]he spirit which made the Reformation possible saw divine justice as

> belonging to another world than this; and in this world it was never again possible to believe whole-heartedly in the existence of a right answer to every dispute.
>
> (Milsom 1981: 91)

This startling claim is uttered as an aside. How might it be used today, when moral philosophers are returning to the law school confident that there is a right answer 'if one cares to dig'?

It is rare to find legal historians responding directly to moral philosophers or critical theoreticians of law. Two representative examples must suffice. In the course of his essay on the rise and fall of the legal treatise, Brian Simpson (1987: 274) takes on a moral philosopher, Ronald Dworkin. He distinguishes two options for dealing with 'the disorderly and unmethodical appearance of the common law system'. The first option was to take a 'practical approach to the disorderly condition of the law, to tidy it up, to systematise it'. Importantly, 'no particular theoretical view of the nature of the common law was involved'. The second option meant working at a higher level altogether: 'An alternative and essentially theoretical approach was to maintain that the law was already systematic, however improbable this claim might appear to the uninitiated' (Simpson 1987: 282). To deal with this second approach, Simpson explains that he 'must digress into jurisprudence'.

The fact of digression is important. Given the present pattern of intellectual prestige in the academy, it is probably impossible for legal history to confront moral philosophy and critical theory head on and be heard. The historian promises no momentous breakthrough to a higher level of being and offers no flamboyant moral critique of existing law and society. Indeed, Simpson (1987: 282) declines to engage with the philosophical discourse: 'It is not my concern . . . to discuss the theory analytically, but to relate it to the history of legal literature.' This is truly how to hold one's intellectual nerve. The form of the digression is important, too: a target is first defined, then given a history. Simpson identifies a particular mode of legal thinking – the 'essentially theoretical approach' – not in order to engage with its truth (or falsity) but to show it has its own limited historical circumstances. This mode of thinking is then tied to the fortune of one particular kind of legal writing: the attempted recasting of common law into maxims or fundamental principles.

Rather than elevating the historical practice of maxim writing to the level of universal principle, Simpson lowers the principle to the level of a specific intellectual practice. Hence the disclaimer: 'I do not intend to discuss whether the [common] law "really" did rest on principles, but to investigate the relationship between the belief in their existence and the forms of legal literature' (Simpson 1987: 284). Such beliefs are contingent on the historical kinds of legal writing, including maxims, that determine 'the appropriate way for jurists to behave' (Simpson 1987: 274). What is more, in the common law system maxim writing proved a dead end. It is 'extinct'.

Having established the historical demise of this literature, the historian 'digresses' into jurisprudence. Here he identifies a living fossil – Ronald Dworkin's recasting of the law in terms of underlying moral principles:

> In *The Model of Rules* and subsequent writings and revisions Dworkin boldly – and somewhat improbably – disinterred the belief in the existence and central significance of principles of law, lurking behind and making rational the apparently disorderly and arbitrary process of adjudication. Dworkin's more recent and flamboyant exposition of this view has claimed that there is always, or almost always, a right answer if one cares to dig, and there is now an elaborate literature on the subject, which pays virtually no attention to the historical pedigree of the theory involved – and the theory, like most things in jurisprudence, is of extreme antiquity.
>
> (Simpson 1987: 282).

The mortuary metaphors are unmistakable. Only the dead letters of a failed literary tradition are 'disinterred' if you dig here. Yet the attack is oblique, as it must be for a historian confronted by the now 'elaborate literature'. The historian does not deny the fact of wishful thinking, since 'life might be much simpler if the common law consisted of a code of rules, identifiable by reference to source rules'. However, 'the only way to make the common law conform to the ideal would be to codify the system, which would then cease to be the common law at all' (Simpson 1987: 368). To characterise attempts to reunite the law with moral principles, Simpson (1987: 381) draws a useful distinction. Such attempts, he writes, are 'surely a programme, or an ideal, and not a description of the *status quo*'.

Perhaps it is easier to say no to social theorists than to moral philosophers. Alan Watson rests his case against social theorists on the historical evidence of law's immunity to societal determinations and thus to treatment in terms drawn from the discipline of social theory. Taking the example of the French *Code civil*, Watson illustrates a proposition 'of the highest importance':

> The proposition is that in any country, approaches to lawmaking (whether by legislators, judges or jurists), the applicability of law to social institutions, the structure of the legal system, the formulation and scope of legal rules are all in very large measure the result of past history and overwhelmingly the result of past legal history, and that the input of other even contemporary societal forces is correspondingly slight.
>
> (Watson 1988: 20)

Because judicial decisions and legislation are pursued within a particular legal system and because legal systems rest on 'legal borrowing and the ancient roots of law', the extent to which law is explicable in terms of social theory is limited. On the contrary, the historical evidence is that law 'has to a very considerable degree a life of its own' (Watson 1988: 22).

Evidence that law has a 'life of its own' is provided, surprisingly perhaps, by law's 'failures' to be transparent to societal forces. These forces change but, for the most part, the law 'remains, not because of any particular message, but simply because it is there' (Watson 1988: 55). This points to a sense of contingency not possessed by Goodrich. It is a matter of 'law being out of step with society' (Watson 1988: 87). Watson (1988: 133) simply denies that 'law mirrors life' (or should do so), or that it 'typically stands in a fixed relationship to the economic and political circumstances of the times'. In this way he shows as historically inconsequential the urge to elevate (or debunk) law by relating it to great moral principles or grand political visions. The separation of law and society or social theory is neither blamed nor praised. It is faced as a historical reality: 'the dynamic causal relationship between law and society which is often thought to keep the former in close harmony with the latter simply does not exist'. Some legal rules are changed to accord with social norms but, Watson insists, 'it is a non sequitur to argue from that to the conclusion that law reflects the needs and desires of society or its ruling elite'. For their part, however, social theorists of law 'cannot admit that important legal rules may be largely dysfunctional' and continue to pursue their theoretical programmes. They must impute some functional relation between law and society, typically reading law as the condensation of dominant social forces and then criticising it as such. For Watson, this is to neglect 'the historical element: a precise study through centuries of the possibility of persistence of defects in legal rules, principles, and systematics, when curable defects were known and not remedied'. To illustrate this neglect, Watson cites his exchange with Ric Abel, a leading figure of the Law and Society movement. Abel had admitted that despite a lack of 'expertise in the historical data themselves, the object of [his] Essay will be to clarify that theory and criticise it from the perspective of contemporary scholarship in law and social science' (Watson 1991: 84–5). Watson (1991: 86) observes, 'For Abel, the perspective of modern sociology of law so obviously leads one to the correct result that an examination of the data of comparative legal history is not needed.'

Even in the recondite field of early common law historiography we now find critical programmes aimed at returning positive law to its 'original' relation with religion and morality. One such programme is Harold Berman's (1983: iii–vii) 'integrative jurisprudence' that – in faithfully dialectical fashion – aims to be neither 'exclusively political and analytical ("positivism")' nor 'exclusively philosophical and moral ("natural law theory")'. From a broad historical sweep that takes us back to eleventh-century ecclesiastical government by canon law instruments designed to meet the Church's purposes, Berman draws the slogan: 'Law must be treated as an essential part of both the material structure of Western society . . . and its spiritual life' (Berman 1983: 296). To take our distance from this dialectical programme to reunify law and spirituality is not to deny a historical fact long since asserted by Maitland: any acceptable definition of the State must refer to the administrative organisation of the medieval Church.

Conversely, for Hale in England and Thomasius in Germany, what mattered was to separate the spheres of religion-morality (*honestum*), law (*justum*) and civil manners (*decorum*), not to unify them. The English judge maintained the rule of law through the excesses of the 'late ill times'. The Prussian jurist prepared future officers for a secular State administration responding to the carnage of confessional civil war. Each held to the conviction that the legal best provided for public peace and the 'morate' for peaceful sociability. Independent of religion and philosophy, as different departments of existence, law and manners had their own forms of agency. But they were not perfectible. Like conscience, perfection was for the spirit only, a purely inward matter. As their historical experience and Christian convictions told Hale and Thomasius, spiritual imperatives and moral principles were not effective regulators of fallen man, especially in the circumstance of religious civil war. For this task, law and manners were better.

Moral philosophers and critical theorists have been very busy but, three centuries later, we still don't know for sure if Gundling was speaking true or false in asserting that 'who lives merely as a strict jurist will go to hell'. Gundling treats the jurist as a subtraction from a fuller moral mode of being. His brisk statement exemplifies the still standard subordination of law as mere instrument to religion and morality as ultimate ends. However, we do know what had happened when the confessional State bonded government to the evangelical ends of a moral community:

> The consequence was a linkage of the fate of an individual State to that of a particular confession, only partially controllable by the statesmen and politicians of the time, a linkage that especially in the sixteenth century repeatedly threatened to put the existence of State and society in question.
>
> (Schilling 1981: 26)

In fact, if Koselleck's genealogy is correct and post-Enlightenment criticism is a relay of the religious form of life, the relation in question is one of competition between religion and law, departments of existence that the State had separated in order to save peace. In seeing today's moral critics of law and government as heirs of religion, the point has not been to debunk but to redescribe the critical mode of thought in its historical role. A longrunning contest thus continues.

NOTES

1 RELIGION BY OTHER MEANS

1 On the importance of institutions that allow political opponents to coexist despite their disagreements of principle, see Berlin (1991). Berlin records the shock of his own intellectual discovery, through Vico, that cultures or 'life-styles' are 'incommensurable with one another: each must be understood in its own terms—understood, not necessarily evaluated'. From this he concludes, 'So we must engage in what are called trade-offs—rules, values, principles must yield to each other in varying degrees in specific situations' (Berlin 1991: 9, 17).

2 The topic being Hobbes, contrary views proliferate. In Caton (1988: 142) we find a Hobbes who 'destroyed the independent authority of the Bible and indicated to the sovereign that the Bible can be used to support whatever doctrine one pleases'. To illustrate this traditional view of an atheistic Hobbes which, he admits, was the opinion of most of Hobbes's contemporaries, Reventlow (1985: 526n) cites Gooch's assessment: 'Though [Hobbes] professed to be an orthodox Christian, he was entirely destitute of religious sentiment'. But the religious accounts continue to appear. For instance, on Hobbes as a post-lapsarian Calvinist, see Martinich (1992). For recent views on Hobbes and religion, see Tuck (1989) and Burgess (1990).

3 Hobbes's Leviathan State is denounced as totalitarian (Arendt 1958: 139) or praised as liberal (Coleman 1977). Against the Absolutist-totalitarian position a liberal might thus cite *Leviathan*, chapter 27: '[S]uch a common power, as may be able to defend them from the invasion of foreigners, and the injuries of one another, and thereby secure to them in such sort, as that by their own industry . . . they may nourish themselves and live contentedly'. Perhaps it is a case of calling enlightened absolutism 'liberal'.

4 Koselleck does not refer to the role of sexual asceticism in the Christian's preparation for the new age. On this, and the manner in which for early Christians the notion of sexual renunciation 'threw a switch' into the new age, see Brown (1988).

5 Roberto Unger's vision of liquidating the existing legal profession in its present state is an example of this projection. See Chapters 11 and 12 below.

6 I have limited myself to Koselleck's historical thesis concerning the rise of the early modern Absolutist State and the compensatory emergence of Enlightenment critique that led to the crisis of that State. The present essay does not work through Koselleck's exegesis of the texts of the critical tradition, from Masonic manuals to the philosophical writings of Voltaire, Rousseau, Diderot, Raynal, Turgot, Lessing and Schiller to name a small selection from the gallery of *Critique and Crisis*. However, I return to the case of Schiller, in order to consider the role of the aesthetic persona in the critique of law.

7 Koselleck is not alone in arguing this general thesis. On how 'the Heavenly City thus shifted to earthly foundations', see Becker (1932: 42).

2 INVISIBLE AND SPIRITUAL: VISIBLE AND EXTERNAL

1 In Koselleck's Preface to the English edition of *Kritik und Krise*, written thirty years after the original edition, we read: 'Since 1688 at the latest Britain, by contrast, underwent a different development [from the Continent]. She never experienced the tension between State and society which so shaped the nations of the European continent. Both spheres remained sufficiently interlinked through Parliament and the judicial constitution to appreciate that all moral questions represented at the same time political problems. The Utopian ideas of the continental Enlightenment therefore never gained a foothold across the Channel. There it was the Scottish moral philosophers with their sober theories rooted in social history who set the tone and who began to respond to the economic lead gained by Britain. At first the Scots moved in the wake of Britain's progress which was soon also to affect the whole of the European continent. This was an important point to which my book gives no more than marginal attention' (Koselleck 1988: 2–3). Perhaps this rosy view of British realism would itself look quite utopian when set against the current inroads of critique into the humanities and other fields, including law.

2 For a contrary view, see Becker (1994).

3 Hooker has been compared to St German in that, with his *Doctor and Student* as a 'systematic theory of law within an English context . . . St German did for English common law what, a generation or so later, . . . Richard Hooker did for the Anglican church' (Guy 1985: 19). On St German, see Chapter 3 below.

4 'A-moral' because, in the University of Halle Thomasius's struggle was waged on two fronts: against the Pietists, but also against the new philosophers of moral reason, Wolff in particular, whose line led to Kant. See Chapter 9 below.

5 Care is needed in making anything like a general characterisation of Puritanism, now that it has been deconstructed into myriad streams of thought and courses of action. Even contrasting a contestatory Calvinism and a defensive English Arminianism has been called into question by Lake (1982), White (1983) and Tyacke (1987). For a qualifying view, see Lamont (1993). Despite this ever more ramified treatment, David Little's (1970) study of Puritanism as a definite ordering of life retains the merit of exploring the relations of law and religion in a Weberian perspective (albeit the Weber of the 1970s: the social theorist and builder of abstract categories of social structure – Little's research was guided by Talcott Parsons). It is no surprise, then, if Little deals in very general types of social order, of which the Anglican and the Puritan conveniently form two. That said, it is helpful to be reminded that, while 'fascinated by the problem of order', Weber 'was unwilling to dissociate normative patterns of belief and action from the actual elaboration of institutional arrangements' (Little 1970: 218). Unfortunately, Little does not pursue this line of thought, even though he mentions Weber's historical studies of religious beliefs and practices. In reading Little, I therefore keep in mind the new Weber that Wilhelm Hennis (1988) has proposed. See Chapter 9 below.

6 Traditionally, 'most divines taught that conscience was the application to a particular case of a person's knowledge of right or wrong. That knowledge was made up of two ingredients: the natural law of reason, or law of nature, which was universal to all human beings, and knowledge of the word of God, which required appropriate religious education. Many Calvinists, convinced of the depravity of man, tended to be sceptical about the value of the universal law of nature; they placed their emphasis not on this "natural conscience", but on the "renewed conscience", divinely enlightened in those born again' (Thomas 1993: 30).

7 We do not forget, however, that Calvin believed that even a tyrannical sovereign should be obeyed, since any order is better than none, that is, better than a state of nature in which men would 'live like dogs and cats'.

3 CONSCIENCE AND LAW

1 Lord Nottingham's son, Daniel, was responsible for the parliamentary handling of the toleration issue that led, in 1689, to the passing of the Toleration Act. There is little agreement as to the merit of this legislation where religious freedom as a fundamental principle is concerned.
2 On the political functions of anti-Catholic sentiment, see Miller (1978).
3 For Yale (1957: xlvii), 'Lord Nottingham's choice of words [in *Cook v. Fountain*] suggests he was not unacquainted with this background.'
4 The following paragraphs rely on Yale (1957).
5 Chancery's interventions into the business of the courts of law did not please those 'common lawyers who regarded the Chancellor's activities as an arbitrary interference with the due course of the law and the constitutional rights of Englishmen' (Plucknett and Barton 1974: xlvii). Hence, later, the famous conflict between Sir Edward Coke and Lord Ellesmere as to the relative authorities of the courts of law and the Chancery.
6 Likewise, in relation to the requirement that even in the most difficult cases a decision be reached in the Court of Chancery, without the possibility of sending a case to the Parliament (although a Chancery decree might be reversed on appeal to the Lords), we find Lord Nottingham declaring in 1681 in *Charles Howard v. Henry, Duke of Norfolk, et al.*, 'I know I am very likely to err, for I pretend not to be infallible; but that is a thing I cannot help. Upon the whole matter I am under a constraint and under an obligation which I cannot resist. A man behaves himself very ill in such a place as this [the Court of Chancery] that he needs make apologies for what he does; I will not do it' (in Yale 1957: lxxxix).
7 A century after Lord Nottingham, Blackstone proposed just this view of equity and common law in the *Commentaries on the Laws of England* (I, 61–2).
8 '[I]n Lord Nottingham's own reports the paucity of reliable precedent in equity is evident from the relative amount of citation when both legal and equitable questions arise' (Yale 1957: li). The logic that traditionally denied the need for precedents in equity, where each individual case is decided – casuistically – on its particular merit, is self-evident.
9 Anne Conway's 'rakish husband', Lord Conway, is the Restoration viscount notorious for his observation on the mores of his stratum: 'we eat and drink and rise up to play and this is to live like a gentleman, for what is a gentleman but his pleasure' (in Shapin 1994: 52).
10 Popkin (1992: 117n) indicates that a new Latin/English edition of Conway's work, by Peter Lopston, has been published in 1982 at The Hague. On Anne Conway, see Merchant (1980: 253–68). Conway's conception of the universe as one living spirit was designed in part to refute Hobbes's conception of the universe as God's body and the human soul as material.
11 We are not wrong to infer, with Popkin (1992: 116n) that something of this pan-spiritualism returns with today's ecological theorising.

4 THE COMMON LAW'S CRITICS

1 This is not to deny all congruity of interests between common lawyers and Puritans. At the most general level there was common cause in setting limits to the claims of royal prerogative and arbitrary exercise of power (Eusden 1958). More specific was the joint interest of Puritans and common lawyers in curtailing the procedure known as *ex officio mero* in the prerogative courts (Porter 1958: 158–60).
2 In practice this contrast was always less than pure. For instance, the 'spiritual' civilians of Doctors Commons vigorously pursued a monopoly in the profitable jurisdiction over international commerce (Coquillette 1988).
3 Along with the exclusion of 'scholarly examination', Goodrich attaints the common law

with excluding not only its own history, but 'the impurities of desire, the body and sexual love . . . all those features of human relation that will always threaten to escape normativity or the constraint of the legal machine . . . The figure of the feminine is in many respects the exemplary other of the legal form, the coincident archetype of both its exile and repression' (Goodrich 1992: 221–2). This leads to a familiar eulogy of the moral-political promise of a deconstructive hermeneutics of law. But, we might ask, what is it reasonable to expect of a legal system?

4 In fact, as Goodrich (1990: 30) shows by the following citation, Fraunce's criticism could be directed at both the university and the Inns of Court: 'as in the universities as in the Inns of Court, the greedy desire of a superficial show in unnecessary trifles makes us want the true substance: they for haste to get prebend by a degree, make light work and run over two or three epitomes; and we by a moote book and a Brookes abridgment climb to the bar and bar ourselves utterly of the substance of the common law'. Fraunce's self-diagnosis prefaces *The Lawiers Logicke*: 'for myself, I must needs confess I was an university man eight years together, and for every day of those eight years, I do not repent that I was an university man' (in Goodrich 1990: 21). After studying and teaching rhetoric and literature at Cambridge University, Fraunce studied law at Lincoln's Inn in London. He never practised.

5 The tag 'conditions of possibility' immediately identifies the neo-Kantian habit of mind that sustains this mode of critique. The theory-based critical intellectual thinks to break with the empirical or the given by uncovering the real determinations of the existing forms of life. Thus: 'The critical project may indeed be reformulated as a history of the repressed event of judgment, a reconstruction of the conditions of possibility of judgment' (Goodrich 1992: 221). The same proposition is articulated as a critical program in Goodrich (1990: 2): 'Critical legal theory might well come eventually to be defined as the theory of particular laws, its concern being to read and re-read what Foucault (following Kant) termed the "conditions of possibility" of particular texts, legal texts, and here the texts of common law. In this form, theory is not concerned with the classical but uninteresting questions of what law in general is, or with how one can acquire an objective knowledge of law, but rather with the historical and ontological issue of how law is lived, what are its habitual forms, what is the deep structure that allows its repetition in ever different forms.'

Two points must be made here. First, we can question the shift in levels of analysis between the actual forms of law and, on the other hand, the abstract yet enabling 'deep structure'. This is simply the shift to a higher level of meta-empirical insight – theory – that the critical (Kantian) intellectual always claims to make in order to lift himself clear of the empirical given. Second, we should note that for Michel Foucault at least, unlike Goodrich, there was no lasting commitment to the (Kantian) notion of language as the antecedent formal condition of all possible particular statements. Thus the ill-fated project of *The Archaeology of Knowledge* had no progeny, Foucault breaking with it to explore instead in his last works the historical ethics of the Classical age. Here there is none of the intellectual pretension to break from the particular to the 'conditions of possibility' of the particular.

6 The unconcern with historical circumstance is confirmed by a note that imports Nietzsche to characterise the 'anti-intellectualism' of the common lawyers in Tudor and Stuart times (Goodrich 1992: 207n). This is cultural history in true idealist style.

7 I return to the cultural phenomenon of critical legal studies in Chapters 11 and 12.

8 Chapter 27 of *Leviathan*, 'Of Civil Laws', covers issues that receive fuller exposition in the *Dialogue*. In both works the common lawyers are treated as a faction whose independence threatened the social order that only a unified sovereign authority could maintain.

9 The project of reforming the laws of England was a mere fragment in Bacon's larger programme for renovating all thought and knowledge. In the proem to *The Great Instauration*, Bacon proposed 'to commence a total reconstruction of the sciences, arts, and all human knowledge, raised upon proper foundations'.

10 Cropsey does not discuss the tract that Holdsworth published as *Reflections by the Lrd.*

Cheife Justice Hale on Mr. Hobbes his Dialogue of the Lawe (see below, Chapter 5). Hale died in 1675, so the unpublished manuscript must have been circulating among the judiciary for some time before that date. As for its wider circulation, according to Haley (1968: 217–19), Aubrey wrote to John Locke in 1672 about Hobbes's *Dialogue*: 'I have a conceit that if your Lord [Shaftesbury] saw it he would like it.' Cropsey does not reference this incident either. At lower levels in the legal profession Hobbes's works received cruder treatment. In his study of the role played in English constitutional history by the topos of fundamental law and rights, Gough (1955) cites a barrister of the Inner Temple, John Whitehall, in his *Leviathan Found Out* (1679). In what Gough terms this 'absurd travesty' of Hobbes, Whitehall attributed to *Leviathan* the argument that 'customs are not laws by virtue of prescription of time, but by constitutions of their present sovereigns' and concluded: 'Mr. Hobbes principally aimed at the supplanting of our Common Law, and thereby make the readier way to bring all men's properties into uncertainty and confusion.' In Whitehall's 'wild accusation', Hobbes's view was 'the readiest means, and most plausible, to vest all [property] in the army'. Gough judges Whitehall's next point 'even more puerile': 'But Mr. Hobbes in the same paragraph makes a little amends for this; for though he had given the Common Law a box on the ear to make it stagger, he hits it a clap on the other to set it upright again; for he saith that when an unwritten law shall be generally observed, and no iniquity appear in the use of it, then it can be nothing but a Law of Nature, and obliges all mankind. Well said, Mr. Hobbes, for now he makes every custom (which an unwritten law implies) unalterable by Act of Parliament; for an Act of Parliament against the Law of Nature is void.' As Gough then comments: 'Hobbes certainly meant no such thing, and Whitehall has simply misunderstood what Hobbes meant by the "obligation" of a law of nature; but it is of interest to note in passing yet another assertion of the idea that in certain circumstances acts of parliament could be held to be void' (Gough 1955: 144).

11 There is no simple equation of Puritanism with millenarianism. On this, Caton (1988: 178n) offers a helpful qualification of the opinion advanced in William Haller's (1938) *The Rise of Puritanism* that '*Clavis Apocalyptica*, a high-flying millenarian tract full of prophecies, was the epitome of Puritan pietism. This view is not supported by Daniel Neal, writing in the 1720s (see his *History of the Puritans*, vol. 5). He stated that millenarianism was a heresy among them, attributed to the Anabaptists. Puritans were above all concerned with church regiment, which meant the divine right of the presbytery; strict observance of the Sabbath, and strict conformity to catechisms and directories; elaborate casuistry about the abolition of Christmas, the use of the Apocrypha in service, the exchange of wedding rings.'

12 The title page of one of the two 1681 editions specifies a dialogue between a Philosopher and a Student of the Common Law, whereas the text calls this speaker simply Lawyer. However, '[t]he seeming distinction between Lawyer and Student of the Law, drawing attention to a disparity between a qualified person and an apprentice, proves in the context of the *Dialogue* to indicate an identity: Hobbes considers the members of the legal profession to be studiers of something they do not make but in which it is their duty simply to become versed: lawyers are never rightly more than students of the law, a point that must be pressed emphatically in respect of the common law, which is thought by its hierophants to be generated by themselves out of their enriched reason' (Cropsey, in Hobbes 1971: 10).

13 Cropsey's hypothesis of a shift in Hobbesian politics from absolute to constitutional rule is totally rejected by Stoner (1992: 128): 'If the shift from *Leviathan* to the *Dialogue* involves a move from a public doctrine of sovereign right to a legal order built on public opinion, the ground of Hobbes's political science is itself shaken, and [Cropsey's] mere "difference of emphasis" in fact demands revision of his whole project.' Stoner will not entertain any such discontinuity in Hobbesian thought.

14 See the exposition of this doctrine of Bracton in Kantorowicz (1975: 168–73).

15 For those wishing to confirm Reventlow's (1985) thesis of a theological ground to Hobbes's

political scheme, it is notable that in the *Dialogue* Hobbes has the Philosopher propose reversion to the old practice, abandoned by Henry VIII, of appointing bishops to the place of chancellor: 'The Bishops commonly are the most able and rational Men, and obliged by their profession to Study Equity, because it is the Law of God, and are therefore capable of being Judges in a Court of Equity. They are the Men that teach the People what is sin; that is to say, they are the Doctors of Cases of Conscience. What reason then can you shew me, why it is unfit, and hurtful to the Commonwealth, that a Bishop should be a Chancellor, as they were most often before the time of *Hen.* 8. and since that time once in the Raign of King *James*?' (Hobbes 1971: 99).

16 Appendix III in Holdsworth (1945: 499-500) outlines the editorial history of Hale's 'Reflections'. As already mentioned, they represent a characteristic instance of the contemporary practice of manuscript circulation and debate, Hobbes's *Dialogue* being unprinted until six years after Hale's death in 1675. As for the 'Reflections', they were first printed in 1921. It is possible that Hobbes's manuscript was passed to Hale as Chief Justice of the King's Bench by Vaughan, Chief Justice of the Common Pleas. See Yale (1972: 122n). Tuck (1993: 342) speculates that Hale and his fellow judge, John Vaughan, read Hobbes's *Dialogue* on the occasion of the 1668 parliamentary debate on the Atheism Bill.

5 THE COMMON LAW'S DEFENDERS

1 In fact, Hale displayed a 'singular attitude to publication', refusing to publish his legal writings yet going into print on matters pertaining to religion and science. As Baker (1979: 165–6) notes, Hale's major legal works were posthumous publications: the *History of the Common Law* in 1713, the *History of the Pleas of the Crown* in 1736, and the *Prerogatives of the King* only with Yale's 1976 edition for the Selden Society. Yale (in Hale 1976: xxvi) writes, 'Hale was not a publishing author in the sense that he was evidently far from disposed to put his legal writings before the public.' So he wrote to analyse his own thinking, and for a limited manuscript circulation. A matter such as the nature of royal prerogative was not the stuff of casual publication in Hale's times.

2 Coke's famous passage (in *C. Litt.* 97b) on the common law as artificial reason has been glossed as follows: '[L]aw is a work of reason in this sense, that it is the nature of law to be reasonable; and the test of its reasonableness, [Coke] thinks, is its ability to withstand the test of time' (Lewis 1968: 339). If this gloss is right, Hobbes's assault on common law as a casuistical outrage based in the case law of judicial precedents not in reason is at least in part wide of the mark.

3 Hobbes's *Dialogue* has the Philosopher deny any interest in 'art' or 'rhetoric'. We begin to see how high minded is this rejection of worldly skills in favour of pure understanding and universal reason.

4 For Hexter (1980: 486), '[n]o earlier philosopher . . . had more systematically and successfully denied temporality a significance in the essential order of things than Hobbes did'. But Hobbesian temporality went with a reductive political science: 'Since all men live under sovereigns, their civil history marks only the stupid slide of one polity or another away from peace and sovereignty toward civil war and the state of nature.' See also 'Time, history and eschatology in the thought of Thomas Hobbes', in Pocock (1971).

5 Far from being 'closed' to other systems of law, Hale ends his chapter on 'Trials by jury' with a reasoned comparison of the relative advantages of common law and civil law procedures. He concludes, it is true, in favour of the former: 'And thus stands this excellent Order of Trial by Jury, which is far beyond the Trial by Witnesses according to the Proceedings of the Civil Law, and of the Courts of Equity, both for the Certainty, the Dispatch, and the Cheapness thereof: It has all the Helps to investigate the Truth that the Civil Law has, and many more . . . And as this [common law] Method is more certain, so

it is much more expeditious and cheap; for oftentimes the Session of one Commission for the Examination of Witnesses for one Cause in the Ecclesiastical Courts, or Courts of Equity, lasts as long as a whole Session of *Nisi prius*, where a Hundred Causes are examined and tried' (Hale 1971: 166–7).

6 A normative proposition of this sort has to confront the empirical evidence that, in the absence of Absolutist rule, 'civil war has not constantly broken out in England after the Restoration' (Kriele 1969: 218)

7 Bobbio (1993: 117n) cites chapters 14 and 15 of *Leviathan* among Hobbes's 'countless passages' on natural law.

8 Milton and Locke, the greatest English theorists of tolerance, both opposed granting freedom of confession to Catholics. This was their part in mass hysteria of the sort that generated the Popish Plot. Indeed, in his 1641 tract *Of Reformation touching Church Discipline in England, and the Cawses that hitherto have hindered it*, Milton found that if 'religion attained not a perfect reducement' in Elizabeth I's reign, this was because of 'the great places and offices executed by papists, the judges, the lawyers . . . for the most part popish' (in Prest 1972: 174).

9 '[T]he *Dialogue* is a windy, inept and unpersuasive attack on the common law and its practitioners – the barristers at the bar, and the judges on the bench. In this long diatribe, Hobbes makes assertions about the laws of England that are singularly irrelevant to the actuality. He claims, for example, that Chancery rightfully has appellate jurisdiction in error over all the common law courts, that royal proclamations have the binding force of statute, that it is proper for the King personally to sit as judge on the bench of any of his courts' (Hexter 1980: 472). This negative assessment is not universal. Thus, for Yale (1972: 137), '[i]n the *Dialogue* . . . Hobbes speaks more surely and logically' on sovereign power than he does in *Leviathan*.

10 It seems that nothing had changed since the earlier seventeenth century when, as Burgess (1988: 4) describes them, Englishmen were 'typically, if to varying degress, possessors of common law minds'.

11 To this view attaches the standing of Hexter's appointment as Charles S. Still Professor of History at Yale University and his studies on the discipline of history. Indeed, 'in the second half of the twentieth century no historian in the United States has accomplished more in the way of sustained reflection on the practice of historiography than Jack Hexter' (Mink 1980: 5). *The History Primer* provides a guide to historians who want to define their disposition towards philosophy. In particular, Hexter's target is the 'analytical philosophy of history', a theory-driven and science-emulating enterprise to which he opposes his own view of historical study as a specific professional craft (Hexter 1971: 65). No wonder Hale's reflections on Hobbes's anti-historical critique of common law reason and his account of judicial action as a trained exercise in deciding particular cases struck a chord in this historian.

12 Pocock (1971) discusses the sense in which Hobbes was not a historical thinker. More recently (1990), he has characterised Hobbes as bivalently 'atheistic' in religion but 'enthusiast' in philosophy.

6 RELIGION, LAW AND CIVIL MANNERS

1 Hale's father was a barrister 'who abandoned the law because he had scruples as to the morality of the practice of "giving colour" in pleading' and who educated his son 'in Puritan principles' (Holdsworth 1937: 574).

2 In a manuscript note, Hale recorded how in keeping the Sabbath he put his faith to practical use: 'The more closely I applied myself to the duties of the Lords day the more happy and successful were my businesses and imployments of the week following. So that I could

from the strict or loose observation of this day take a just prospect and true calculation of my temporall success in the ensuing week' (Hale, in Prest 1972: 210). A plan for one's own 'temporall success in the ensuing week' is not a millenarian vision of a humanity's spiritual transformation. This is in keeping with Hale's sense of proportion.

3 We recall Hobbes's argument that religious conscience was not a binding power, because it required 'nothing but endeavour'. See Chapter 1.

4 Baxter, author of *Additional Notes on the Life and Death of Sir Matthew Hale*, was 'intimately acquainted with Hale, and though his account has little to do with Hale as lawyer or legal scholar, it is very revealing of Hale as philosopher and friend' (Yale, in Hale 1976: xxxiin).

5 Those clergy who accepted appointment to clerical office during the Commonwealth were later referred to as latitudinarians. Hale accepted appointment to judicial office under Cromwell.

6 Gilbert Geis (1978) discusses the 1662 trial in psycho-historical terms of Hale's and the common law's 'misogynistic bias' regarding witchcraft and rape. The relation of law and religion is not discussed. To discuss witchcraft without referring to religion is like discussing rape without referring to men. Equally, if witchcraft was de-criminalised in Absolutist Germany, is this a sign of a less misogynistic culture or of different relations between politics and religion? For the 1662 trial report, see *Cobbett's Complete Collection of State Trials*, VI, 687–702.

7 Tuck (1979) shows that Selden was one of the few English writers approved of and cited by Hobbes.

8 Failure to take the oath meant exclusion from access to the Commonwealth courts.

9 For discussion, see Gough (1955).

10 On this, with specific reference to Hobbes's response, see Skinner (1972). It was in the Engagement Controversy that the Cromwellian regime cited Hobbes's account of civil obligation in *De Cive* as legitimating its position.

11 On the Jewish element in seventeenth-century religious and political thinking, see the wonderful essay on Spinoza and the Quakers in Popkin (1992).

12 This is not to claim an English monopoly on the historical approach to law. On the contrary, it is a chance to cite Donald Kelley's (1967) study of Guillaume Budé as the sixteenth-century French lawyer-turned-philologist whose work was the 'real basis for the first historical school of law'. However, if Budé 'did for Roman law what . . . Erasmus' New Testament was to do for Biblical studies' (Kelley 1967: 812), this was a matter of reforming a university discipline. Infiltrating university law faculties with the new cause of philological discipline was not part of Hale's agenda. Nor did the single-minded task of minute restoration of classical purity to Justinian's *Digest*, freeing the text from the glossatorial excesses of *Accursianitas*, find an equivalent in Hale's common law milieu. On the other hand, in a manner that parallels Hale's approach, Budé's disciple François Baudoin would argue that 'the real key to jurisprudence was history, by which one could determine both the original meaning and the chronological development of laws' (Kelley 1967: 830).

13 For recent discussion of the Elizabethan Society of Antiquarians and its 'centrality to seventeenth century political discourse', not least because '[m]ost members had professional connections to the court', see Peck (1993: 95–8). She notes an absence of consensus among today's historians as to the 'political implications of English antiquarianism'.

14 For all its originality, Maitland does not find Hale's *History* an unqualified success. On the contrary, in his 'Materials for English legal history', Maitland writes of Hale: 'Unfortunately he was induced to spend his strength upon problems which in his day could not permanently be solved, such as the relation of English to Norman law, and the vexed question of the Scottish homage; and just when one expects the book to become interesting, it finishes off with protracted panegyrics upon our law of inheritance and trial by jury' (Maitland 1911: 5).

15 'Taking "legislation" to mean "law changing" – in contradiction to the restorative, declaratory, explicative, and implementary roles that Acts of Parliament can play or be seen as playing – Hale's bias was prolegislative, as Coke's was antilegislative. For one thing, Hale was a law reformer himself. His essay "The Amendment of the Laws" is a masterpiece of conservative liberalism. Its final tendency is to support legislative alteration of the common law' (Gray, in Hale 1971: xxix). It is worth illustrating Hale's 'grass-roots' reformist disposition. Thus 'one of Lord Chief Justice Hale's motives for proposing (in the 1660s or 1670s) the establishment of a network of county courts to replace the existing moribund jurisdictions [of manorial and borough courts] was that "by this means the students and professors of the law, who are now generally driven or drawn up to London, so that there are scarce any left in the country, will have some encouragement to reside in the country, and the country not left to the management of attorneys and solicitors' (Lemmings 1990: 169).

16 Tuck (1979: 84, 132) identifies a source of this image in Selden's account of natural laws that have been 'limited for the conveniency of civil society', then 'increased, altered, interpreted, and brought to what now they are; although perhaps, saving the merely immutable part of nature, now, in regard of their first being, they are not otherwise than the ship, that by often mending had no piece of the first materials, or as the house that's so often repaired *ut nihil ex pristina materia superit*'.

17 Hale's *History*, with its gestures of enthusiasm commending the interest of his topic, might have been composed with the function of a student guide in mind. His pedagogic concerns, after all, are noted even by his critic, Roger North: 'I have known the Court of King's Bench sitting every day from 8 to 12, the Lord Chief Justice Hale managing matters of law to all imaginable advantage to the students, and in that he took pleasure, or rather pride. He encouraged, arguing when it was to the purpose, and used to debate with counsel, so that the court might have been taken for an academy of sciences, as well as a set of justice' (in Heward 1972: 110–11). See too Hale's Preface to Rolle's *Abridgment*, published in 1668 on the advice of the other judges at Westminster and with the express purpose of furnishing a student text.

18 Of course, as Shapiro (1983: 183) points out, 'a sophisticated and consistent treatment of the law of evidence could not develop until the jury had ceased to be witnesses as well as judges of matters of fact'. In Hale's time this division of functions was still in the process of emergence.

19 Cromartie (1995: 195) notes but does not pursue the ethical dimension implied in Hale's description of his natural philosophy as a means to 'carry the mind up to God'. For all that Hale seems to treat philosophising as a form of spiritual exercise, we see here an ethos opposed to that of the common lawyer, resting as it does in the tradition of contemplative metaphysical speculation that will later give us Kant.

20 Concerned to avoid generalising Elias's sociological model, Koenigsberger (1986: xii) still prefaces his inquiry by asking a general question: why did 'monarchies fail to become absolute in the Netherlands and in Britain', unlike in France and in Brandenberg-Prussia?

21 In his historical account of lawyers as a profession, Prest suggests that 'it is likely that the most common and straightforward way of identifying lawyers in early modern England was by their appearance and dress. Thus when John Smyth (1567–1641), barrister of the Middle Temple and Steward to the Berkeleys of Gloucestershire, sought in his chronicle of that family to disparage Anthony Huntley, one of his unlearned predecessors, he mentioned that Huntley was accustomed to preside over his master's manorial courts wearing "a white feather in his hat". Such a sartorial lapse was evidently conclusive proof of Huntley's amateur status and low standing, "a man fitter for fairs and markets of cattle . . . than to grapple in the combats of Littleton". Lawyers (except judges and serjeants) wore black or dark colours; in the late sixteenth and early seventeenth centuries they were notorious for affecting ruffs and well-trimmed beards, "cut as close as a stubble field" and might carry a pen

case at the waist, but not a sword' (Prest 1987: 68). The pen is mightier than the sword when it is backed by the force of the law.

22 On the procedure of readings, see Prest (1972: 120–4). On post-Restoration readings, see Lemmings (1990: 78–89).

23 For the more complete history of the Inns of Court, see Prest (1972) and Lemmings (1990).

24 Unlike the universities where, as Stone (1964) shows, less than half the students were of gentle birth and the proportion of peers-esquires was minuscule. See Prest (1972: 31).

25 Prest (1972: 46) observes that the Inns maintained their prestige in part because the emerging division of the legal profession into higher (barrister) and lower (solicitor) branches allowed an ethos of 'disinterested advocate, serving the public good by pursuing his own and his clients' private ends' to be claimed by the former branch, an ethos regulated by 'a complex code of etiquette'.

26 '[B]etween Wyatt and Surrey and the appearance of Spenser and Sidney, all the poets, in fact almost all writers of any value, were connected with the inns of court . . . they were the literary center of England' (Finkelpearl, in Prest 1972: 155n). Literary scholars of the 'new historicism' movement have argued that Renaissance drama was inseparable from the staging of the political power-plays of the time. See, for instance, Greenblatt (1980). However, we should note Prest's (1972: 205) comment that the most godly and Puritan of the Inns, Lincoln's Inn, 'did not employ troupes of professional actors to stage their "lewd ungodly entertainments" during the Grand Weeks'. Indeed, 'from 1627 onwards no gaming was permitted in the hall on Saturday nights, "for the better preparing to keepe holy the Saboth Day"'.

27 'Augustine Baker, who gave up a flourishing practice at Gray's Inn to become a Benedictine monk, pointed out that law was "a most terrene study, as whose subject is worldliness . . . apt to cause answerable quality of spirit in the student . . . very remote from desires or thinking of celestiall or everlasting goodnesse"' (Prest 1972: 217).

28 Prest (1972: 217) records that '[c]ontemporary comment on the religious attitude of common lawyers most frequently emphasised their secularism and indifference to spiritual matters'. Rather than a failing, can we see this disposition as a cultural accomplishment of a de-theologising kind?

7 SEPARATION OF POWERS

1 For a comparative study of the political thought of Bodin and Hobbes, see King (1974).

2 For Bonney (1991: 316), 'Bodin's commonweal was an harmonious ordering of the body politic in conformity with the laws of God, not an abstract state subject to natural law.' Bonney associates the latter position with Hobbes's doctrine of the sovereign state.

3 The Spanish Ambassador to France witnessed the massacre at first hand and reported: 'As I write, they are killing [the Huguenots], ripping their clothes from them, dragging them through the streets, pillaging their homes, not even sparing a child. This morning, before noon, they had killed 3000 people . . . Praise be to God!' (King 1974: 51).

4 For an overview and basic bibliography of the nine French wars of religion, the last and longest of which continued for twelve years, see Bonney (1991: 163-79). As he comments, having recalled that in 1562 the Bishop of Nîmes – albeit unsuccessfully – appealed to Catholic children to murder Protestants, 'Perhaps the single most important factor was the belief that the end of the world was at hand and that the second coming of Christ was imminent' (Bonney 1991: 500). As to the scale of mass action, he notes that '[p]rinted prophecies induced panic, and panic in turn unleashed collective violence during the French wars of religion'. This usefully reminds us not only of the prevalence of the printed word but of the fact that the print did not necessarily operate as a rationalising force.

5 In a note, Holmes (1988: 40n) aptly summarises Bodin's anti-perfectionist politics: 'He was more concerned to avoid murderous disorder than to achieve divinely anointed perfection.'
6 This year can be taken as normal, at least by comparison with 1572, the time of the St Bartholomew Massacre. As Bonney (1991: 171) puts it: 'The massacres were seen by Catholics as a miraculous escape from Protestant tutelage . . . Even by the standard of atrocities in the French wars of religion, the manner and extent of the violence in the following two months was grotesque.'

8 THE CONFESSIONAL STATE

1 For instance, in this confessional climate, the excitement generated by undirected Bible reading, that is, by private reading of 'Luther's book' without the guiding hand of clergy, was so feared by the Church of Rome that, in 1559, Pope Paul IV included all vernacular Bibles among the books banned in the first Index. See *The New Cambridge Modern History, vol. 2* (1967: 63–4).
2 There is an economic history lesson here for today's enthusiasts of global marketing of administrative skills. The monopoly of the market does not outlast the local production of skills. The focus on monopoly formation parallels Norbert Elias's historical argument on State formation. The administrative brilliance of the medieval Church has been recognised by scholars ranging from legal historians such as Harold J. Berman to social historians such as C. Stephen Jaeger. In *Law and Revolution: The Formation of the Western Legal Tradition*, Berman (1983: 42) shows 'the deep roots of Western institutions and values in the pre-Protestant, prehumanist, prenationalist, preindustrialist and precapitalist era'. Among these 'institutions and values', the Western legal tradition is traced back to the Papal 'Revolution' of the eleventh century, under Gregory VII, and to the centralising and standardising administrative genius of the medieval Church as 'a *Rechtsstaat*, a state based on [canon] law' (Berman 1983: 215). In *The Origins of Courtliness: Civilising Trends and the Formation of Courtly Ideals*, Jaeger (1985) draws attention to the persona of the 'courtier-bishop' whose poetic-administrative role included generating chivalric romances aimed at taming and 'courtising' – to borrow Elias's term – a warrior aristocracy into good Christians. Mastery of ceremonial etiquette, a crucial attribute of this remarkable persona, was being taught in German cathedral schools by the 1100s.
3 The fields of technical knowledge needed for expert administration of the territory and its population were thus termed *Polizeiwissenschaften* or policy sciences. On Cameralism, see the unsurpassed but still neglected study by Small (1909).
4 Hobbes raged against the reforming Separatists, but without asking to what extent a capacity for conscientious 'innerliness' and freely rendered obedience was one on whose widespread distribution effective government depended. Nor is it clear that Hobbes appreciated the need for States, however rational their political theory, to find a communitarian power equal to the mass bonding power of Christian enthusiasm.
5 In concluding his study of Cameralism, Small (1909: 587) offered the following summary statement: 'In spite of the necessary inaccuracy of a brief theorem, especially when it is antithetic in form, the contrast between German and American conceptions of civic experience may be stated approximately as follows: *From the beginning the Germans have regarded the state as primarily a unit, and only secondarily an aggregate. From the beginning Americans have regarded the state as primarily an aggregate, and only secondarily a unit.* This contrast is the necessary starting-point for American interpretation of German polity.'
6 For the English translation of *De constantia*, see Lipsius (1939).
7 Book Five, for instance, treats military training. According to Oestreich (1982: 6), it was this book which 'first stimulated' the reforms that were to make the Dutch army a model for other European States.

8 This neo-Stoic persona has been the object of critique from a feminist historiography that views Oestreich's thesis in the light of modern gender organisation (Outram 1989).
9 In the next chapter, we consider Kant's claim to redeem 'official' theology by recourse to the universal and disinterested reason of critical philosophy.

9 CONFLICT OF CONFESSIONS; CONFLICT OF FACULTIES

1 See, for instance, Collins (1995).
2 I wish to thank Ian Hunter for his generous guidance on Thomasius. The following paragraphs draw on his research, see Hunter (forthcoming). For a survey in English of Thomasius's contributions to theoretical and applied philosophy, see Haakonssen (forthcoming).
3 On Thomasius's use of Osse's *Testament*, see Small (1909: 23–39).
4 In England, however, the proportion of law students of noble birth was much lower than in Thomasius's new faculty of jurisprudence at Halle, the 'gentry' from which the Inns recruited having no precise equivalent in the German *Bürgertum*. Only a small minority of students at the Inns of Court were sons of the upper nobility, and there were even fewer younger sons of rural gentry than had been thought. See Prest (1972: 87–9).
5 There is some parallel with Hale's remarks on the historical role of the English clergy. See Chapter 6.
6 On the question of *adiaphora*, of the authority to specify what things – particularly in the outward show of ceremonies and public conduct – could be declared indifferent and what essential for God's purposes, see Verkamp (1977). Typical among English authorities is Thomas Starkey's formulation: 'Thinges indifferent I call all suche things by which goddis worde are neither prohibited nor commanded' (in Verkamp 1977: 29). As we recall, Hobbes had shrunk Christian doctrine to one principle which he took to be unexceptionable for all Christians: that Jesus is the Christ. Beyond that, all other matters of faith are private matters, and therefore indifferent.
7 There is a broad correspondence between the differentiated roles of prince, man and Christian and the categories of *iustum*, *decorum* and *honestum* elaborated in the *Fundamenta iuris naturae ac gentium*.
8 As Tuck (1987: 117) goes on to say, the minimalist core of universal moral principles – as recovered by the modern natural law theorists – 'could also be used for the same reason to describe relations between different civil societies, the first use to which it was in fact put, in the writings of Grotius'.
9 A sense of the circumstances against which such a law emerged can be gained from Bartlett's (1994: 208) discussion of the 'jural autonomy' that went with the endless ethnic conflicts between pre-modern populations in Europe.
10 McClelland (1980: 43–5) contrasts developments at Göttingen, the new university in Hannover, with arrangements at Halle. In relation to plans for a faculty of jurisprudence at the former, he cites a contemporary comment to the effect that Thomasius's line on Statist territorialism was so strong that it left Göttingen with a chance to recruit strongly among the Catholic and imperial nobility and teach a law curriculum that was 'more in line with the laws of the Empire'. At Göttingen, too, the courtly arts were central.
11 Thomasius's adversaries even complained that he was offering lectures free of charge in order to draw students from theology to law.
12 In this philosophical usage, the terms 'theoretical' and 'practical' refer respectively to knowledge of nature and precepts of action.
13 As Kant (1979: 29) explains, the faculty of philosophy is called the 'lower' faculty because, unlike theology, law and medicince, it does not give commands: 'for a man who can give commands, even though he is someone else's humble servant, is considered more distinguished than a free man who has no one under his command'.

14 Arguably, the critical approach hides the work that has gone into its own exercise as a remarkable achievement in Western culture. Instead, the emphasis is on the figure of the sudden 'breakthrough' to a higher level of moral or theoretical consciousness.

15 On this juridico-discursive conception of power in 'Two lectures' and 'Truth and power', see Foucault (1980: 78–108; 109–33).

16 Commentators have objected to this polarity. See, for instance, Cousins and Hussain (1984: 237), for whom Foucault's writings on power proceed by setting up a spurious opposition between 'legal regulation' and 'normalisation'. They find that the *rapprochement* of law and norm in the first volume of *The History of Sexuality* then 'casts aspersions on the propriety of the two sets of oppositions: law and norm and legal regulation and normalisation that structure so much of Foucauldian analysis of power'.

17 Describing the legal scene in eighteenth-century France, van Caenegem (1992: 25) observes a 'variety and fragmentation of the organisation of justice (if it may be called organisation) [that] lasted to the end of the *ancien régime*'. See also Collins (1995).

18 Mainstream sociology reaches the limit of its imagination in this area with general schemes for a unified history of subjectivity and a grand narrative that moves from social fixity and external ordering of conduct to individualisation and internal responsibility, and then to fragmentation and modern anxiety.

19 The complexity of Weber's wrestling with this issue lies in the fact that he did not denigrate the unified personality in itself, refusing to accept that it was a possible ethical reality in the conditions of everyday life in the specialised life-orders of capitalism. To believe otherwise was to risk losing touch with the actual circumstances and to refuse to face up to the facts, a habitual practice of the literati with whom – insofar as they claim to know about modernity – Weber always runs out of patience. See Hennis (1988: 92–3).

20 Hennis (1988: 102) thus cites Weber's uneasiness – when looking at the world from the optic of religion – 'with a culture becoming ever more senseless in its further differentiation and development'. But the question remains: how do we live in this circumstance, not how do we detach ourselves from it?

21 An individual may – and usually will – have a number of personae. But the several personae cannot usefully be summed up into a whole. Indeed, the sum is impossible, as the English sociologist T.H. Marshall whimsically recorded in 'A note on "status"': 'I find it impossible to do the required sum. How do you add together, for instance, doctor, father, councillor, wicket-keeper, church warden and husband to get a unitary result?' (Marshall 1977: 226–7). On the argument that 'the fragments of legal personality [are not] capable of being summed into a fully recognised person', see Cousins (1980).

10 SECTS, LAWS AND RIGHTS

1 Zakai (1992: 174–6) cites Thomas Hooker's 1631 account of the devastation of Protestant communities in Bohemia, the Palatinate and Denmark: 'You cannot go three steps but you shall see the head of a dead man. And go a little further and you shall see the heart picked out by the fowls of the air, or some other sad spectacle.' This, suggested Hooker, was the imminent fate of England now: 'As sure as God is God, God is going from England.'

2 As well as in Virginia, Anglicanism was the established Church in five other American States.

3 In *Revolution and Rebellion: State and Society in England in the Seventeenth and Eighteenth Centuries*, Clark (1986) offered an alternative to the habitual search for signs of support for religious freedom among early modern radicals, turning instead to the political work of Anglicans.

4 As Clark (1994: 235–6) observes, we are now learning that Locke 'did not construct his political theory around a democratic objection to monarchy. The guiding themes in Locke's intellectual development were theological. Shaftesbury confessed to a fellow conspirator,

while in exile, that he owed his Socinian opinions in religion to Locke's influence; it was such views which identified even an Anglican episcopal, not merely a papist, regime as tyrannical. Anglicans sought not merely to impose a theology, but a theology which Socinianism identified as anathema.'

5 Clark does not invite us to consider the further possibility: Chartism too might better be seen as a religious movement, rather than as evidence of a secular break with the past.

6 On these important issues, see Clark (1994: 303–81).

7 By the late eighteenth century, however, the professor of jurisprudence at the College of Phildalephia, James Wilson, was marking out Americans' distance from these traditional English remedies. Whereas English 'rights' at common law were merely what the State had chosen to grant to individuals, it was the American State's role 'to secure and to enlarge the exercise of the natural rights of its members' (Haakonssen 1991: 19–20).

8 In fact the same practice – albeit with different ends – can be observed at the very highest levels of the English courts under Lord Mansfield.

9 Accounts written from the perspective of historical philosophy can take a different line on the relative contributions of philosophy and evangelical or millenarian religion. See, for instance, Haakonssen (1991) on the role of Scottish moral philosophy and natural law theory.

10 See Villey (1961, 1964, 1983).

11 By way of reminder that 'America had many Millenarians who saw the emergence of an independent government as a sign of the unfolding of the Providential Plan', Popkin (1992: 312n) cites the instance of David Austin, a clergyman – denomination unspecified – who 'in 1794 announced that "the kingdom of the mountain, began on the Fourth of July, 1776, when the *birth* of the Man-Child – the hero of civil and religious liberty – took place in the United States". The Man-Child is then going to slay the beast and overthrow Babylon.' As Popkin observes, Austin 'was also preparing to ship Jews to Palestine for the Millennium'.

11 THE LAW TRANSFORMED; THE LAWYER LOST

1 'The process of generalisation and abstraction in late-nineteenth-century law . . . had the effect of freeing legal rules from the reality testing that regular encounters with the concrete particularities of social life might entail' (Horwitz 1992: 15).

2 Horwitz (1992: 9) recognises that in America, '[t]hroughout the revolutionary period and for a time thereafter, the problem of the tyranny of the majority expressed as much the fear of religious as of cultural, political, or economic domination'. Moreover, Horwitz (1992: vii) prefaces *The Transformation of American Law* by signalling 'the profound significance of the Civil War in American legal history'. Yet the historical relations of State neutrality and civil war go unexplored. Other than the mention of a 'trauma' that might have favoured a 'state that could stand above all factions and interests', there is only a tentative comment on Saul Touster's discussion of Holmes's shift to anti-abolitionism, having come in the course of that terrible war to see abolitionism as a fanaticism 'associated not with young men of deep sympathies and generous sentiments but with communists, Christian Science, the Catholics on Calvin, Calvin on the Catholics' (Touster 1965: 449). For Horwitz (1992: 116), '[t]he lesson Holmes seems to have derived from his own Civil War experiences is that all passionate appeals to conscience and morality inevitably resulted in the destruction of a fragile social order'. Given the degree to which Horwitz's argument itself rests on an appeal to morality, it is no surprise if Holmes's view is not endorsed. The idea of State neutrality is simply deemed conservative, and the possible relations between such neutrality and the experience of civil war are blotted out by an intensely moral critique of legal objectivism, of the positivist demarcation of law from normative morality and politics, and a dismissive psychologisation of the detachment of lawyers from 'social reality'.

3 As Horwitz (1992: 175) reminds us, the term 'Legal Realism' was first used in Jerome Frank's (1930) *Law and the Modern Mind*, a work that Horwitz nicely terms 'radioactive'.

4 In his study of the 'objectivity question' as it has arisen for American professional historians, Novick (1988: 144) shows 'cognitive relativism' in relation to systems of meaning and modes of thinking emerging from 'interwar social science' and its 'combination of ethical relativism and objectivist empricism'. He explicitly ties Legal Realism in with other problematisations of 'objectivity and detachment', noting the co-presence in it of a social scientistic and a critical-reformist side (Novick 1988: 145–50). More recently, cognitive relativism has come 'to trouble the [historical] profession because, for complex reasons, ethnographic attention came increasingly to focus on systems of belief, meaning and symbol' (Novick 1988: 549). Clifford Geertz is identified as the key figure in this further disturbance of the idea of objectivity.

5 Hunter (1993: 125–6) continues: 'the result of this theoretical movement is that neither side of the binarism . . . is decisively criticised or permanently renounced. To the contrary, the problematisation of a concept in dialectical critique is always a prelude to its reaffirmation as, with the reversal in the axis of critique, the dubious concept takes its turn as the self-evident ground for another round of problematisation. Radical doubt and programmematic adherence are thus curiously interdependent in this style of critique.' The scepticism in metaphysics and the dogmatism in politics that Leo Strauss took to be contradictory drives of the contemporary psyche might therefore be dual postures between which the virtuoso dialectical critic knows how to play.

6 Perhaps the term 'transcendental historicism' is incoherent, as is 'historical *a priori*' (Foucault 1972: 126–31), another version of this same intellectual fancy. For a suitably sceptical discussion, see Hudson (1993).

7 I make this point elsewhere in exploring the tenacious 'figure of thought that organises a particular kind of historical and theoretical commerce between the objects of law and literature . . . What is the figure that both acts in obedience to history, bearing in its consciousness the imprint of economic interest, yet simultaneously gives history the law or goal that brings this economic interest to being and consciousness? It is of course the two-faced figure of the subject' (Saunders and Hunter 1991: 492).

8 Against this, of course, is Horwitz's embracing of 'cognitive relativism'. He is at pains to distinguish this from 'ethical relativism', so the door back to a theological unity might not be entirely closed. Horwitz himself does not hesitate to attribute an intellectual movement such as legal formalism to a sense of spiritual loss. A religious anthropology is thus at work at least in some parts of his argument.

9 Carrington (1991) offers a similar diagnosis, exploring the historical models of American legal education as evidence of the rise and fall of the 'law teacher as public person', that is, as one who instructs students in republican values.

10 As exemplars of a normative scientific realism that was not satisfied with mere description, Kronman signals the work of Lasswell and McDougal (1943).

11 Arguing likewise that a cultural practice does not reduce to a statement of the rules or theory of that practice, a more recent French anthropologist, Pierre Bourdieu (1977), formulates the relation of practical craft and theoretical rule or code in just this way. His elaboration of the notion of habitus provides a useful descriptive tool that dispenses with a general relation between the practical and the intellectual, the institutional and the theoretical.

12 NOW THAT THE SAINTS ARE MARCHING IN

1 There are also neo-Kantian approaches that call existing law into question by reference to theoretically derived principles, epistemological, moral or political. Ronald Dworkin's work is located here. Also in a rationalistic vein is Gunther Teubner's reconceptualising of

law as 'autopoietic', that is, as a 'rule-governed set of systems, directives and processes undergoing constant [but] rule-governed change' (Teubner 1993: 22). At first glance, autopoiesis theory seems to align with an epistemological separation of the legal sphere from the sphere of morality (or of any extra-legal communicative system). As an autopoietic or 'self-referential' system, law defines its own limits, recognising extra-legal phenomena only by rearticulating them into legal terms: 'The law itself determines which presuppositions must be present before one can speak of a legally relevant event, a valid norm, and so forth . . . The degree to which law becomes autonomous is determined by the extent to which it constitutes self-referential relationships, ranging from minor normative cross-referencing to the circular closure of a hypercyclically constituted law' (Teubner 1993: 33–4). The legal apparatus draws on all sorts of metaphysical, moral and even aesthetic assumptions about human beings. However, it deals with these assumptions only insofar as they are legally constructable, that is, as attributes whose form and scope are specified by their role in a specifically legal ordering of conduct.

This seems in tune with the historical plurality of social spheres in complex, non-theocratic States, especially as Teubner excludes the possibility of a single overarching logic, adopting instead the notion of autonomous communicative realms or independent technical sub-systems. However, to the extent that it remains a theory of law's formal possibility, autopoiesis theory abandons nothing of the Kantian discontinuity or gap between empirical practice and a theoretical knowledge that reveals the formal conditions making that practice possible. Teubner (1993), following Luhmann (1982, 1985), traces the specificity of law from the legal system's formal conditions of existence, rather than from conditions that are historical and contingent. The latter establish porous yet real borders to a positive sphere that only slowly and imperfectly comes to be autonomous from religion, morality and natural law. But to follow the logic of autopoiesis usefully sharpens the point: there could be no natural law understood as a body of purely moral principles or norms that critique would import into the legal system by way of rectification.

2 This is despite the stated aim of understanding law as a 'series of deeply historical phenomena' (Douzinas *et al.* 1994: 6). Perhaps the 'deeply' signals that critique attaches itself not to a positive or descriptive history but to the normative philosophy of history described by Koselleck (1988). True to the manner of the philosophy of history, the past phenomena cited by our critics serve primarily as contributions to a future completing of presently incomplete ways of life.

BIBLIOGRAPHY

Arendt, H. (1958) *The Origins of Totalitarianism*, New York: Harcourt Brace and World.

Barbour, W. (1918) 'Some aspects of fifteenth century Chancery', *Harvard Law Review* 31: 834–59.

Bartlett, R. (1994) *The Making of Europe: Conquest, Colonisation, and Cultural Change, 950–1350*, London: Penguin Books.

Becker, C.L. (1932) *The Heavenly City of the Eighteenth-century Philosophers*, New Haven: Yale University Press.

Becker, M.B. (1994) *The Emergence of Civil Society in the Eighteenth Century. A Privileged Moment in the History of England, Scotland and France*, Bloomington: Indiana University Press.

Berlin, I. (1991) 'The pursuit of the ideal', in H. Hardy (ed.) *The Crooked Timber of Humanity*, New York: Knopf.

Berman, H.J. (1983) *Law and Revolution: The Formation of the Western Legal Tradition*, Cambridge, MA: Harvard University Press.

Bobbio, N. (1993) *Thomas Hobbes and the Natural Law Tradition*, Chicago: University of Chicago Press.

Bodin, J. (1962) *The Six Bookes of a Commonweal*, Cambridge, MA: Harvard University Press.

Bonney, R. (1991) *The European Dynastic States*, Oxford: Oxford University Press.

Bourdieu, P. (1977) *Outline of a Theory of Practice*, Cambridge: Cambridge University Press.

Brockliss, L.W.B. (1987) *French Higher Education in the Seventeenth and Eighteenth Centuries. A Cultural History*, Oxford: Clarendon Press.

Brown, P. (1988) *The Body and Society: Men, Women and Sexual Renunciation in Early Christianity*, London: Faber.

Burgess, G. (1988) 'Common law and political theory in early Stuart England', *Political Science* 40: 4–17.

—— (1990) 'Contexts for the writing and publication of Hobbes's *Leviathan*', *History of Political Thought* 11: 675–702.

Caenegem, R.C. van (1992) *An Historical Introduction to Private Law*, Cambridge: Cambridge University Press.

Caplan, J. (1988) *Government without Administration. State and Civil Service in Weimar and the Third Reich*, Oxford: Clarendon Press.

Carrington, P.D. (1991) 'Aftermath', in P. Cane and J. Stapleton (eds) *Essays for Patrick Attiyah*, Oxford: Clarendon Press.

Caton, H. (1988) *The Politics of Progress. The Origins and Development of the Commercial Republic, 1600–1835*, Gainesville: University of Florida Press.

Clark, J.C.D. (1986) *Revolution and Rebellion: State and Society in England in the Seventeenth and Eighteenth Centuries*, Cambridge: Cambridge University Press.

—— (1994) *The Language of Liberty, 1660–1832. Politcal Discourse and Social Dynamics in the Anglo-American World*, Cambridge: Cambridge University Press.
Coleman, F.M. (1977) *Hobbes and America. Exploring the Constitutional Foundations*, Toronto: Toronto University Press.
Collins, J.B. (1995) *The State in Early Modern France*, Cambridge: Cambridge University Press.
Coquillette, D. (1988) *The Civilian Writers of Doctors' Commons: Three Centuries of Juristic Innovation in Comparative, Commercial and International Law*, Berlin: Duncker & Humblot.
Cousins, M. (1980) '*Men's rea*: a note on sexual difference, criminology and the law', in P. Carlen and M. Collinson (eds) *Radical Issues in Criminology*, Oxford: Martin Robertson.
Cousins, M. and Hussain, A. (1984) *Michel Foucault*, London: Macmillan.
Cromartie, A. (1995) *Sir Matthew Hale (1606–1676). Law, Religion and Natural Philosophy*, Cambridge: Cambridge University Press.
Davis, N.Z. (1972) *Society and Culture in Early Modern France: Eight Essays*, Stanford, CA: Stanford University Press.
Delumeau, J. (1989) 'Prescription and reality', in E. Leites (ed.) *Conscience and Casuistry in Early Modern Europe*, Cambridge: Cambridge University Press.
Douzinas, C., Goodrich, P. and Hachamovitch, Y. (1994) 'Introduction: politics, ethics and the legality of the contingent', in C. Douzinas, P. Goodrich and Y. Hachamovitch (eds) *Politics, Postmodernity and Critical Legal Studies: The Legality of the Contingent*, London and New York: Routledge.
Dreitzel, H. (1996) 'Christliche Aufklärung durch fürstlichen Absolutismus. Thomasius und die Destruktion des frühneuzeitlichen Konfessionsstaates', in F. Vollardt (ed.) *Christian Thomasius*, Tubingen: Niemayer.
Dworkin, R. (1977) *Taking Rights Seriously*, Cambridge, MA: Harvard University Press.
Edie, C.A. (1985) 'Tactics and strategies: Parliament's attack on the royal dispensing power', *American Journal of Legal History* 29: 197–234.
Elias, N. (1978) *The Civilising Process, Volume One: The History of Manners*, Oxford: Basil Blackwell.
—— (1982) *The Civilising Process, Volume Two: Power and Civility*, Oxford: Basil Blackwell.
—— (1983) *The Court Society*, Oxford: Basil Blackwell.
Elton, G.R. (ed.) (1967) *Cambridge New Modern History, vol. 2. The Reformation 1520–1559*, Cambridge: Cambridge University Press.
Eskridge, W. (1990) 'Gadamer/statutory interpretation', *Columbia Law Review* 90: 609–81.
Eusden, J.D. (1958) *Puritans, Lawyers and Politics*, New Haven: Yale University Press.
Foucault, M. (1972) *The Archaeology of Knowledge*, London: Tavistock.
—— (1977a) *Discipline and Punish. The Birth of the Prison*, New York: Pantheon.
—— (1977b) *Language, Counter-memory, Practice. Selected Essays and Interviews*, Oxford: Basil Blackwell.
—— (1979) *The History of Sexuality, Volume One. An Introduction*, London: Allen Lane.
—— (1980) *Power/Knowledge: Selected Interviews and Other Writings, 1972–1977*, C. Gordon (ed.), New York: Pantheon.
—— (1985) 'What is Enlightenment?', in P. Rabinow (ed.) *The Foucault Reader*, New York: Pantheon.
—— (1989) *Foucault Live: Interviews 1966–1984*, S. Lotringer (ed.), New York: Semiotext(e).
—— (1991) 'Governmentality', in G. Burchell, C. Gordon and P. Miller (eds) *The Foucault Effect: Studies in Governmentality*, Chicago: University of Chicago Press.
Geis, G. (1978) 'Lord Hale, witches and rape', *British Journal of Law and Society* 5: 26–44.
Gierke, O. von (1934) *Natural Law and the Theory of Society*, Cambridge: Cambridge University Press.
Goldie, M. (1991) 'The theory of religious intolerance in Restoration England', in O.P. Grell,

J.I. Israel and N. Tyacke (eds) *From Persecution to Toleration. The Glorious Revolution and Religion in England*, Oxford: Clarendon Press.

Goodrich, P. (1986) *Reading the Law. A Critical Introduction to Legal Method and Tecnhiques*, Oxford: Basil Blackwell.

—— (1987) 'Literacy and the languages of the early common law', *Journal of Law and Society* 18: 422–44.

—— (1990) *Languages of Law: From Logics of Memory to Nomadic Masks*, London: Weidenfeld and Nicolson.

—— (1992) 'Critical legal studies in England: prospective histories', *Oxford Journal of Legal Studies* 12, 2: 195–236.

—— (1994) 'Salem and Bizance: a short history of the two laws', *Renaissance and Modern Studies* 37: 13–30.

—— (1995) *Oedipus Lex. Psychoanalysis, History, Law*, Berkeley: University of California Press.

Gough, J.W. (1955) *Fundamental Law in English Constitutional History*, Oxford: Clarendon Press.

Greenblatt, S. (1980) *Renaissance Self-fashioning from More to Shakespeare*, Chicago: Chicago University Press.

Guy, J.A. (1985) *Christopher St German on Chancery and Statute*, London: Selden Society.

—— (1993) 'The Henrician age', in J.G.A. Pocock (ed.) *The Varieties of British Political Thought, 1500–1800*, Cambridge: Cambridge University Press.

Haakonssen, K. (1991) 'From natural law to the rights of man: a European perspective on American debates', in M.J. Lacey, and K. Haakonssen (eds) *A Culture of Rights. The Bill of Rights in Philosophy, Politics, and Law*, Cambridge: Cambridge University Press.

Haakonssen, K. (forthcoming) 'Thomasius [or Thomas], Christian', in *Routledge Encyclopedia of Philosophy*, Routledge: London.

Hadot, P. (1990) 'Forms of life and discourse in ancient philosophy', *Critical Inquiry* 16, 3: 483–505.

Hale, M. (1971) *The History of the Common Law of England*, Chicago, University of Chicago Press.

—— (1976) *Hale's Prerogatives of the King*, London: Selden Society.

Haley, K.H.D. (1968) *The First Earl of Shaftesbury*, Oxford: Clarendon Press.

Haskell, T. (1987) 'The curious persistence of rights talk in the "Age of Interpretation"', *Journal of American History* 74: 984–1012.

Hennis, W. (1988) *Max Weber: Essays in Reconstruction*, London: Allen and Unwin.

Heward, E. (1972) *Matthew Hale*, London: Robert Hale.

Hexter, J.H. (1971) *The History Primer*, New York: Basic Books.

—— (1980) 'Thomas Hobbes and the law', *Cornell Law Review* 65: 471–90.

Hinrichs, C. (1971) *Preußentum und Pietismus: Der Pietismus in Brandeburg-Preußen als religiös-soziale Reformbewegung*, Göttingen: Vandenhoeck and Ruprecht.

Hobbes, T. (1960) *Leviathan, or the Matter, Forme and Power of a Commonwealth Ecclesiasticall and Civil*, Oxford: Blackwell.

—— (1971) *A Dialogue between a Philosopher and a Student of the Common Laws of England*, Chicago: University of Chicago Press.

Holdsworth, S.W. (1937) *A History of English Law*, vol. 6, London: Methuen; Sweet and Maxwell.

—— (1945) *A History of English Law*, vol. 5, London: Methuen; Sweet and Maxwell.

Holmes, S. (1988) 'Jean Bodin: the paradox of sovereignty and the privatisation of religion', in J.R. Pennock and J.W. Chapman (eds) *Religion, Morality and the Law, Nomos XXX*, New York: New York University Press.

Hooker, R. (1977) *Of the Laws of Ecclesiastical Polity*, vol. 1, Cambridge, MA: Harvard University Press.

Horwitz, M.J. (1992) *The Transformation of American Law, 1870–1960: The Crisis of Legal Orthodoxy*, New York: Oxford University Press.

Hudson, W. (1993) 'After Blumenberg: historicism and philosophical anthropology', *History of the Human Sciences* 6, 4: 109–16.
Hunter, I. (1993) 'Subjectivity and government', *Economy and Society* 22, 1: 123–34.
—— (forthcoming) *Rival Enlightenments: Civics and Metaphysics in Early Modern Germany.*
Jaeger, C.S. (1985) *The Origins of Courtliness: Civilising Trends and the Formation of Courtly Ideals*, Philadelphia: University of Philadelphia Press.
Jay, S. (1994) 'Servants of monarchs and lords: the advisory role of early English judges', *American Journal of Legal History* 38: 117–96.
Jefferson, T. (1964) *Notes on the State of Virginia*, New York: Harper Torchbooks.
Kant, I. (1963) 'What is Enlightenment?' in L.W. Beck (ed.) *Kant; On History*, Indianapolis: Bobbs-Merrill.
—— (1965) *The Metaphysical Elements of Justice*, Indianapolis: Bobbs-Merrill.
—— (1970) 'Idea for a universal history with a cosmopolitan purpose', in H. Reiss (ed.) *Kant's Political Writings*, Cambridge: Cambridge University Press.
—— (1979) *The Conflict of the Faculties*, Lincoln: University of Nebraska Press.
Kantorowicz, E. (1975) *The King's Two Bodies. A Study in Medieval Political Theology*, Princeton, NJ: Princeton University Press.
Kelley, D.R. (1967) 'Guillaume Budé and the first historical school of law', *American Historical Review* 72: 807–34.
—— (1993) 'Elizabethan political thought', in J.G.A. Pocock (ed.) *The Varieties of British Political Thought, 1500–1800*, Cambridge: Cambridge University Press.
Kennedy, D. (1977) 'Form and substance in private law adjudication', *Harvard Law Review* 89: 1685–778.
King, P. (1974) *The Ideology of Order. A Comparative Analysis of Jean Bodin and Thomas Hobbes*, London: George Allen and Unwin.
Koenigsberger, H.K. (1986) *Politicians and Virtuosi. Essays in Early Modern History*, London: The Hambledon Press.
Koselleck, R. (1985) *Futures Past. On the Semantics of Historical Time*, Cambridge, MA: MIT Press.
—— (1988) *Critique and Crisis: Enlightenment and the Pathogenesis of Modern Society*, Oxford: Berg.
Kriele, M. (1969) 'Notes on the controversy between Hobbes and the English jurists', in R. Koselleck and R. Schur (eds) *Hobbes-Forschungen*, Berlin: Duncker and Humboldt.
Kronman, A.T. (1993) *The Lost Lawyer: Failing Ideals of the Legal Profession*, Cambridge, MA: Harvard University Press.
Lacey, M.J. and Haakonssen, K. (1991) 'History, historicism, and the culture of rights', in M.J. Lacey, and K. Haakonssen, (eds) *A Culture of Rights. The Bill of Rights in Philosophy, Politics, and Law*, Cambridge: Cambridge University Press.
Lake, P. (1982) *Moderate Puritans and the Elizabethan Church*, Cambridge: Cambridge University Press.
Lamont, W.A. (1993) 'The Puritan revolution: a historiographical essay', in J.G.A. Pocock (ed.) *The Varieties of British Political Thought, 1500–1800*, Cambridge: Cambridge University Press.
Lasswell, H.D. and McDougal, M.S. (1943) 'Legal science and public policy: professional training in the public interest', *Yale Law Journal* 52: 203–95.
Lemmings, D. (1990) *Gentlemen and Barristers. The Inns of Court and the English Bar, 1680–1730*, Oxford: Clarendon Press.
Lewis, J.U. (1968) 'Sir Edward Coke: his theory of "Artifical Reason" as a context for modern basic legal theory', *Law Quarterly Review* 84: 330–42.
Lipsius, J. (1939) *Of Constancie*, New Brunswick, NJ: Rutgers University Press.
Little, D. (1970) *Religion, Order, and Law. A Study in Pre-Revolutionary England*, Oxford: Basil Blackwell.

Llewellyn, K. (1960) *The Common Law Tradition. Deciding Appeals*, Boston: Little, Brown.
Luhmann, N. (1982) *The Differentiation of Society*, New York: Columbia University Press.
—— (1985) 'The self-reproduction of law and its limits', in G. Teubner (ed.) *Dilemmas of Law in the Welfare State*, Berlin: De Gruyter.
McClelland, C.E. (1980) *State, Society and University in Germany, 1700–1914*, Cambridge: Cambridge University Press.
Maitland, F.W. (1911) *Collected Papers of Frederic William Maitland*, vol. 2, Cambridge: Cambridge University Press.
Marshall, T.H. (1977) *Class, Citizenship and Social Development*, Chicago: Chicago University Press.
Martinich, A.P. (1992) *The Two Gods of Leviathan: Thomas Hobbes on Religion and Politics*, Cambridge: Cambridge University Press.
Merchant, C. (1980) *The Death of Nature: Women, Ecology and the Scientific Revolution*, San Francisco: Harper.
Miller, J. (1978) *Popery and Politics in England, 1660-1688*, Cambridge: Cambridge University Press.
Milsom, S.F.C. (1981) *Historical Foundations of the Common Law*, London: Butterworth.
Mink, L.O. (1980) 'The theory of practice: Hexter's historiography', in B.C. Malament (ed.) *After the Reformation. Essays in Honor of J.H. Hexter*, Manchester: Manchester University Press.
Mintz, S.I. (1962) *The Hunting of Leviathan: Seventeenth-century Reaction to the Materialism and Moral Philosophy of Thomas Hobbes*, Cambridge: Cambridge University Press.
Mommsen, W.J. (1984) *Max Weber and German Politics, 1890–1920*, Chicago: Chicago University Press.
Novick, P. (1988) *That Noble Dream. The 'Objectivity Question' and the American Historical Profession*, Cambridge: Cambridge University Press.
Oestreich, G. (1968) *Geschichte der Menschenrechte und Grundfreiheiten im Umriß*, Berlin: Duncker & Humblot.
—— (1982) *Neostoicism and the Early Modern State*, Cambridge: Cambridge University Press.
Outram, D. (1989) *The Body and the French Revolution. Sex, Class, and Political Culture*, New Haven: Yale University Press.
Paulsen, F. (1908) *The German Universities and University Study*, London: Longmans, Green and Co.
Peck, L. (1993) 'Kingship, counsel and law in early Stuart Britain', in J.G.A. Pocock (ed.) *The Varieties of British Political Thought*, Cambridge: Cambridge University Press.
Plucknett, T.F.T. and Barton, J.L. (eds) (1974) *St German's 'Doctor and Student'*, London: Selden Society.
Pocock, J. G. A. (1957) *The Ancient Constitution and the Feudal Law*, Cambridge: Cambridge University Press.
—— (1971) *Politics, Language and Time: Essays in Political Thought and History*, London: Methuen.
—— (1990) 'Thomas Hobbes atheist or enthusiast? His place in a Restoration debate', *History of Political Thought* 11: 737–49.
Popkin, R.H. (1992) *The Third Force in Seventeenth-century Thought*, Leiden: E.J. Brill.
Porter, H.C. (1958) *Reformation and Reaction*, Cambridge: Cambridge University Press.
Postema, G.J. (1986) *Bentham and the Common Law Tradition*, Oxford: Clarendon Press.
Prest, W.R. (1972) *The Inns of Court under Elizabth I and the Early Stuarts, 1590–1640*, London: Longman.
—— (1986). *The Rise of the Barristers. A Social History of the English Bar, 1590–1640*, Oxford, Clarendon Press.
—— (1987) 'Lawyers', in W.R. Prest (ed.) *The Professions in Early Modern England*, London: Croom Helm.

Radin, M. (1932) 'The conscience of the court', *Law Quarterly Review* 48: 506–20.
Reid, J.P. (1987) *Constitutional History of the American Revolution: The Authority of Rights*, Madison: University of Wisconsin Press.
Reventlow, H.G. (1985) *The Authority of the Bible and the Rise of the Modern World*, Philadelphia: Fortress Press.
Rorty, A.O. (1988) *Mind in Action: Essays in the Philosophy of Mind*, Boston: Beacon Press.
Rüping, H. (1968) *Die Naturrechtslehre des Christian Thomasius und ihre Fortbildung in des Thomasius-Schule*, Bonn: Ludwig Röhrscheid.
Saunders, D. and Hunter, I. (1991) 'Lessons from the "Literatory": how to historicise authorship', *Critical Inquiry* 17: 479–509.
Schiller, F. (1967) *On the Aesthetic Education of Man*, Oxford: Clarendon Press.
Schilling, H. (1981) *Konfessionskonflikt und Staatsbildung: Eine Fallstudie über der Verhältnis von religiösem und sozialem Wandel in der Frühneuzeit am Beispiel der Grafschaft Lippe*, Gütersloh: Gerd Mohn.
—— (1986) 'The Reformation and the rise of the early modern State', in J.D. Lacey (ed.) *Luther and the Modern State in Germany*, Kirksville, MO: Sixteenth Century Publishers.
—— (1988) 'Between the territorial state and urban liberty: Lutheranism and Calvinism in the county of Lippe', in R.P.-C. Hsia (ed.) *The German People and the Reformation*, Ithaca: Cornell University Press.
Schmitt, C. (1986) *Political Romanticism*, Cambridge, MA: MIT Press.
Selden, J. (1927) *Table-talk*, London: Bernard Quaritch.
Shapin, S. (1994) *A Social History of Truth. Civility and Science in Seventeenth-century England*, Chicago: University of Chicago Press.
Shapiro, B.J. (1983) *Probability and Certainty in Seventeenth Century England. A Study of the Relations between Natural Science, Religion, History, Law and Literature*, Princeton, NJ: Princeton University Press.
Simpson, A.W.B. (1987) *Legal Theory and Legal History. Essays on the Common Law*, London: Hambledon Press.
Skinner, Q. (1972) 'Conquest and consent: Thomas Hobbes and the Engagement controversy', in G.E. Aylmer (ed.) *The Interregnum: The Quest for Settlement, 1646–1660*, London: Macmillan.
Small, A. (1909) *The Cameralists: The Pioneers of German Social Polity*, Chicago: University of Chicago Press.
Stone, L. (1964) 'The educational revolution in England, 1560–1640', *Past and Present* 28: 41–80.
Stoner, J.R. (1992) *Common Law and Liberal Theory. Coke, Hobbes, and the Origins of American Constitutionalism*, Lawrence: University of Kansas Press.
Stromholm, S. (1989) *Five Essays in Historical Jurisprudence*, Stockholm: Almqvist and Wiksell International.
Stroup, J. (1984) *The Struggle for Identity in the Clerical Estate. Northwest German Protestant Opposition to Absolutist Policy in the Eighteenth Century*, Leiden: Brill.
Teubner, G. (1993) *Law as an Autopoietic System*, Oxford: Blackwell.
Thomas, K. (1993) 'Cases of conscience in seventeenth-century England', in J. Morrill, P. Slack and D. Woolf (eds) *Public Duty and Private Conscience in Seventeenth Century England: Essays Presented to G.E. Aylmer*, Oxford: Clarendon Press.
Tierney, B. (1988) 'Villey, Ockham and the origin of individual rights', in J. Witte and F.S. Alexander (eds) *The Weightier Matters of the Law. Essays on Law and Religion. A Tribute to Harold J. Berman*, Atlanta: Scholars Press.
Touster, S. (1965) 'In search of Holmes from within', *Vanderbilt Law Review* 18: 437–72.
Tuck, R. (1979) *Natural Rights Theories. Their Origin and Development*, Cambridge: Cambridge University Press.

Tuck, R. (1987) 'The "modern" theory of natural law', in A. Pagden (ed.) *The Languages of Political Theory in Early-modern Europe*, Cambridge: Cambridge University Press.
—— (1989) *Hobbes*, Oxford: Oxford University Press.
—— (1993) *Philosophy and Government, 1571–1651*, Cambridge: Cambridge University Press.
Tyacke, N. (1987) *Anti-Calvinists: the Rise of English Arminianism, c. 1590–1645*, Oxford: Oxford University Press.
Ulmen, G.L. (1985), 'The sociology of the state: Carl Schmitt and Max Weber', *State, Culture and Society* 1: 3–57.
Unger, R. (1983) 'The critical legal studies movement', *Harvard Law Review* 96: 561–675.
—— (1986) *The Critical Legal Studies Movement*, Cambridge, MA: Harvard University Press.
Verkamp, B. (1977) *The Indifferent Mean. Adiaphorism in the English Reformation to 1554*, Columbus: Ohio University Press.
Villey, M. (1961) 'Abrégé du droit naturel classique', *Archives de philosophie du droit* 6: 27–72.
—— (1964) 'La genèse du droit subjectif chez Guillaume d'Occam', *Archives de philosophie de droit* 9: 97–127.
—— (1983) *Le droit et les droits de l'homme*, Paris: Presses universitaires de France.
Walzer, M. (1963–4) 'Puritanism as a revolutionary ideology', *History and Theory* 3: 59–90.
—— (1966) *The Revolution of the Saints. A Study in the Origins of Radical Politics*, London: Weidenfeld and Nicolson.
Ward, W.R. (1993) 'The eighteenth century Church; a European view', in J. Walsh, C. Haydon and S. Taylor (eds) *The Church of England c. 1689–c. 1833. From Toleration to Tractarianism*, Cambridge: Cambridge University Press.
Watson, A. (1988) *Failures of the Legal Imagination*, Philadelphia: University of Philadelphia Press.
—— (1991) *Legal Origins and Legal Change*, London: Hambledon Press.
Weber, M. (1930) *The Protestant Ethic and the Spirit of Capitalism*, London: Allen and Unwin.
——(1946) 'Politics as a vocation', in H.H. Gerth and C.W. Mill (eds) *From Max Weber*, London: Routledge.
—— (1968) *Economy and Society: An Outline of Interpretive Sociology*, New York: Bedminister Press.
—— (1989) 'Science as a vocation', in P. Lassman, I. Velody and H. Martins (eds) *Max Weber's 'Science as a Vocation'*, London: Unwin Hyman.
Weschler, H. (1959) 'Toward neutral principles of constitutional law', *Harvard Law Review* 73: 1–35.
Whaley, J. (1981) 'The Protestant Enlightenment in Germany', in R. Porter and M. Teich (eds) *The Enlightenment in National Context*, Cambridge: Cambridge University Press.
White, P. (1983) 'The rise of Arminianism reconsidered', *Past and Present* 101: 34–54.
Whitgift, J. (1968) *Works of John Whitgift*, New York: Johnson Reprint Corporation.
Yale, D.E.C. (ed.) (1957/1961) *Lord Nottingham's Chancery Cases*, vols 1 and 2, London: Selden Society.
—— (1972) 'Hobbes and Hale on law, legislation and the sovereign', *Cambridge Law Journal* 31, 1: 121–56.
Zakai, A. (1992) *Exile and Kingdom. History and Apocalypse in the Puritan Migration to America*, Cambridge: Cambridge University Press.

INDEX

Abel, R. 152
Absolutism ix–x, 3–4, 6, 8, 10, 13, 15–17, 35–6, 48–51, 72–4, 83, 85, 87, 89–90, 93, 101, 103–4, 110, 120; and religion 33, 73; *see also* Hobbes; *raison d'état*
abstraction 40, 42–3, 48, 54, 65, 102, 110, 125, 127, 129, 135, 137–40, 146; *see also* theory
adiaphora 58, 165
administrators x, 3, 15, 74, 77, 80, 86–7, 89–91, 94, 96, 143, 149, 153; ethical achievement of 14, 87, 97, 149
aesthetics 13, 102, 125–6, 138, 147; *see also* critique; dialectic
America x, 1, 16, 85, 88, 112–23, 133, 143
Anabaptists 26
Anglicanism, Anglicans ix, 11, 16, 18–19, 27, 33–4, 72, 112, 114–18, 120
anti-positivism 31, 100, 102, 143, 145
anti-statism x, 8–10, 16, 19, 85, 102, 121, 136, 143
antinomy 10–12, 48, 103, 105, 134–5; *see also* duality
apatheia 66
Aquinas 22
Aristotle, Aristotelianism 87, 97, 108, 132
asceticism 122
Aubrey, J. 33–4
Augsburg, Peace of 76, 83
autopoiesis 169

Bacon, Lord Francis 23, 33–4, 35
Baxter, R. 58
Bentham, J. 1, 54
Berlin, I. 62
Berman, H. 152
Bildung 88
Blackstone, Sir William 118
Bobbio, N. 48–9
Bodin, J. 3, 4, 73–6, 87, 89, 121; *De republica* 2–3, 74
Bonney, R. 73, 87
Book of Common Prayer 118
books, printed matter 78, 116, 117
Boyle, Sir Robert 65
Bracton, H. de 63
Brockliss, L.W.B. 77
bureaucracy 80–1, 84, 100, 143; *see also* cameralism; government
Burnet, G. 27, 59

Calvinism, Calvinists ix, 19–20, 31, 76, 79, 82–4, 94, 138
Cambridge, University of 70, 71
cameralism 91, 103
canon law 23, 30, 57, 118, 122, 145
Caplan, J. 143
Carrington, P.D. 133
Cartwright, T. 17
Castiglione, B. 68, 95
casuistry 19, 22–3, 24
Catholic League 76
Catholicism, Catholics ix, 2, 16, 19, 21, 57, 74, 76, 79, 82, 94, 138
Chancery, Court of 2, 23–7, 35, 39
Chartism 117
Christ 11, 117; second coming of 29
Christianisation 77–80, 84; *see also* discipline, social
church government 16–17, 58, 75, 113–14; *see also* visible church
circumstances, role of ix, 13–14, 17–18, 41, 43, 45–6, 50–3, 56, 58–9, 64–5, 82, 87, 96, 99, 104–5, 109–10, 121, 129, 131, 138, 144, 146, 150

citizen, as status 4–5, 8, 11, 15, 28, 70, 81, 85, 102
civil capacities 17, 65, 86–7, 91, 95–7
civil law, civil lawyers 24, 30–1, 62, 70, 77, 102, 106, 118, 145, 148
civil peace 3–4, 7, 16, 35, 56, 73, 75, 93
civil religion 120, 147
civil war ix, 4–5, 8, 10, 14, 15–16, 34, 35–6, 72, 73, 75–6, 79, 81, 83–7, 89, 94, 103, 114, 116, 142; in England 21, 49–51; in France 50–1, 72; in Germany 72
civility 65, 91, 95; *see also decorum*; manners
Clark, J.C.D. 56, 114–20, 123, 143
closure 45–6, 146
Coke, Sir Edward 18, 23, 34–5, 37–9, 56, 62, 63, 72, 104, 118
Cold War 4
Collins, J.B. 76
Comenius, J.A. 122
common law 1, 19, 23–4, 27, 32, 41, 42–7, 49–54, 57–8, 62–3, 70, 71, 118–19, 140, 144–8, 149–51
common lawyers 18, 30–9, 36–7, 49, 51, 70–1, 106
community viii–x, 8–9, 12, 19–20, 35, 37, 64, 76, 78, 81–2, 85, 88–9, 102, 108, 110, 116, 136, 146–8, 153; sectarian origins of 4, 18
conduct manuals 65, 68, 86, 95
conducts of life (*Lebensführungen*) 19, 26–7, 81, 94, 106, 122, 127, 138, 140–1, 146
confessional religion, as cause of war x, 4, 15, 72, 73, 75–6, 79, 81, 83–5, 94, 103, 114, 116, 142, 153
confessional State ix, 12, 15, 79–85
confessionalisation ix–x, 15, 29, 59, 72, 77–9, 81, 89, 111–12; and social discipline 78–9; and State formation 15, 81–2, 88; *see also* Christianisation; Counter-Reformation; Reformation
Conquest, the 60–1, 63
conscience viii, x, 5, 8, 10, 16, 19, 21–9, 50, 68, 89, 107, 121, 123, 145, 147; Age of 21–2, 27; as cause of war 4, 6, 102; Hobbes on 6; legal 2, 22–6, 29; as private opinion 5–7, 56, 58, 75, 90, 92; separation from law 88, 92, 143
conscience-formation 126
constitutions 3, 12, 35, 49, 56, 74, 102, 104, 138; English 16, 18, 53, 60–1, 63–4, 119
contingency 98, 108, 124, 130, 137, 144, 146, 148, 152
Conway, Lady Anne 28–9
Corradus, J.B. 22
cosmopolitanism 76, 70–1, 91
counter-politics 8–9, 32, 110, 137–9, 145–7, 148
Counter-Reformation 79, 112; *see also* confessionalisation
Court of Conscience *see* Chancery, Court of
court society 67–9, 71
courtly arts 66–8, 70, 91, 95
criminal law 22–3, 34, 35, 37, 56, 58, 60, 93, 96, 103; *see also* decriminalisation
crisis ix, 8, 13, 113, 125–6, 130–1, 133; and law school 1, 139–40; as metaphor 14
critical intellectuals viii, 8, 10, 16, 31–2, 46, 54, 105, 107, 123, 139, 142, 149, 153; as heirs of religion 8, 10, 13, 32, 85, 87, 111, 142, 153
critical legal studies viii–x, 32, 126, 132, 136, 139–40, 144, 146
critique x, 3–4, 8, 12–13, 32, 45–6, 72, 98–100, 102, 104–5, 130–1, 147–8, 153; as transcendental exercise 12–13, 31–2, 111; *see also* critical intellectuals
Cromartie, A. 26, 55–6, 58, 66
Cromwell, O. 50, 59–60
Cropsey, J. 33–5, 37
Cushman, R. 113
custom 18, 20, 41, 63–4

Davenport, J. 113
Davis, N.Z. 78
Decalogue 61
decorum 61, 65, 69–70, 92, 95–7, 153
decriminalisation 37, 59, 93–4
deism 28, 115, 119–20
Delumeau, J. 77–8, 80
denominations 58, 112, 114–15
depoliticisation 4–6, 10, 74, 90, 92–3
Descartes, R. 28
de-theologisation ix–x, 4, 7, 15, 72, 74, 85, 87, 99–100, 103, 128, 143, 147, 153
dialectic 13, 31, 102, 105, 127, 129–31, 135–40, 144–6, 152; *see also* aesthetics; critique; historicism
difference 99, 105
discipline 10, 19, 22, 87, 103–4; social ix, 15, 78, 80, 84, 102; spiritual viii, 7, 14–15, 17, 72, 81, 84

discretion 25–6, 43, 59, 145
Dissenters ix, 18, 20, 27, 31, 58, 114, 116, 119
doctrines 17–19, 22, 79–80, 84, 94–5, 116, 122, 128, 140
Domat, J. 76–7, 104, 119
Douzinas, C. 144–8
Dreitzel, H. 94
dress 26, 72
duality 15, 130, 143; *see also* antinomy
Dworkin, R. 121, 144–5, 150–1

ecclesiastical laws 18, 24, 55–8, 92–3
eclecticism 42
Edict of Nantes 21, 50, 77
Elias, N. 67–9, 71–2, 83, 95
emergency, politics of 35–6, 46–7
Endtime 29, 84, 148
England ix–x, 7, 15–16, 17–18, 23–4, 58–9, 67, 80, 104
Enlightenment ix, 4, 7, 10, 12, 14, 16, 67, 72, 87, 101–2, 104, 114–15, 119–20, 125, 147; and religion 29, 88
enthusiasm ix, 27, 85, 128; *see also* zealotry
equity 23, 25, 27, 37, 39; *see also* Chancery, Court of
Erasmus, D. 68, 87
estates 16, 18, 70, 80–1, 83
ethics x, 5, 13–14, 20, 20, 66, 86–8, 140, 145, 149; and comportment 13–14, 59, 67, 72, 85–6, 106, 108, 125, 135; political 5–6
ethos 16, 94, 97, 109, 116, 134, 137, 139; *see also* personae
eucharist 75

fanaticism 28, 31, 51, 55, 78, 86, 94–5, 110, 117, 143
formalism 102, 126, 128–9, 136–7, 145, 148
Fortescue, Sir John 70
Foucault, M. ix, 157; and genealogy 14, 103–4; on government 102–4
France x, 2–3, 22–3, 50–1, 68, 72, 73–8, 90, 95, 104
Francke, A.H. 91, 95–6
Frank, J. 128
Franklin, B. 120
Fraunce, A. 30–1
freedom 19–20, 24, 50, 82, 90, 98–9, 101, 103–4, 110, 119, 136–7
fundamentalism viii, 40, 56, 110, 128

genealogy 14, 103–4, 109, 131, 139
gentleman 55, 65, 70, 87, 91, 95
Germany x, 3, 15, 76, 80, 88, 95, 102, 104; comparison with England 7, 15, 17, 59, 70, 72, 93, 112
Gierke, O. von 121
Glanvill, Ranulf de 63, 149
Goodrich, P. 30–3, 144–8, 152
government viii, ix, 4, 18–19, 80, 99, 102–4; autonomy of 12, 73, 76, 87–8, 90–9; and expertise 3, 27, 81, 85, 103; *see also* bureaucracy; cameralism
Gracian, B. 95
Gray, C.M. 55, 60, 62, 66
Grotius, H. 86, 94, 97, 119
Gundling, N.H. 142, 153
Guy, J. 24–5

Haakonssen, K. 122–3
habitus 29, 31, 45, 54, 65, 68, 70, 106
Hachamovitch, Y. 144–8
Hadot, P. 105
Hale, Sir Matthew 26–7, 34–5, 40, 53, 55–66, 77, 87, 92–3, 134, 153; *History of the Common Law of England* 41, 45–6, 62, 64; 'Reflections on Mr Hobbes his Dialogue of the Lawe' 40, 41–7, 65
Halle, University of 90–2, 95–8
Haskell, T. 123
Hegel, G.W.F. 102
Helmont, F.M. van 28–9
Hennis, W. 106–8
heresy 35, 37, 75, 92–3, 145
hermeneutics 32, 107, 123–4, 131
Heward, E. 56, 58
Hexter, J. 44, 52–3, 62
Hinrichs, C. 96
historicism 12–13, 31, 55, 64, 67, 102, 108, 130–1, 147–8, 169
history, as providence 112–13
history of ideas 55, 66, 72
history of law 30–1, 44, 62–3, 118, 127–8, 146–7, 149–52; and moral philosophy x, 52–3, 150–1; and social theory 151–2
history, philosophical 12–14, 102, 131, 148–9; *see also* historicism
history, rewriting of xi, 9–10, 55, 101–2, 121
Hobbes, T. ix, 3–4, 6–8, 12, 16, 28, 32–3, 41–4, 46–7, 54, 59, 63–4, 74, 140; and common lawyers 32–40;

Hobbes, T. – *contd*
  Dialogue between a Philosopher and a Student of the Common Laws of England 33–40, 46, 51–2, 54, 65; as legal positivist 47–9; *Leviathan* 5, 7–8, 33, 46, 52, 103, 114; and natural law 47–9
Holmes, S. 73–6, 105
honestum 61, 65, 69, 72, 92, 94, 97, 142, 153; *see also* morality
Hooker, R. 11, 17, 113–14
Horwitz, M., *The Transformation of American Law, 1870–1960: The Crisis of Legal Orthodoxy* 124–31
Hotman, F. 22, 62, 104
Huguenots 74, 76, 90
humanities academy 9, 13–14, 16, 88, 123, 139, 143–4
humanity 8, 11–13, 32, 87, 100, 102, 142–3; fallen 55, 66, 96, 109, 153; rights of 9, 87, 121–3, 131
Hunter, I. 130

ideology 12, 18, 82, 85, 110, 116; ideology critique 37, 105
imperial law (Germany) 83
impersonality: as cultural achievement x, 23, 59, 102, 149; as target of critique 102
Inns of Court 30, 33, 36, 66–7, 69, 70–1, 91, 106
interiorisation 8–10, 17–18, 56, 67–8, 95, 107, 125
invisible church 16–17

Jansenism, Jansenists 77
Jefferson, T. 114, 120–2
judges, judging 21–3, 28, 35, 38, 43, 45, 59, 77, 104, 107, 115, 133–5, 145, 148
jurisdictions 2, 26, 31, 35, 39, 56–8, 93, 118–19
jurisprudence ix, 24, 30, 60, 76, 91–2, 96–8, 101, 125, 127–9, 140, 142, 144–5, 150–1, 152
Justi, J. von 3, 80
justice 59, 100–1, 144–5
justum 61, 65, 69, 72, 92, 94, 97, 142, 153; *see also* positive law

Kant, I. 4, 67, 69, 98–102, 107, 112, 125, 131, 142; *Conflict of the Faculties* 98–100
Kelley, D. 18
Kennedy, D. 135–6, 144
King, P. 73
Koenigsberger, H.K. 67, 79–80
Koselleck, R. viii–x, 3–16, 19, 29, 32–3, 40–1, 49, 73–4, 85, 88, 90, 102, 107, 110–11, 119, 126, 128–9, 131, 136, 142–3, 147–9, 153; *Critique and Crisis* ix, 3–10, 12–14, 140
Kriele, M. 49–51, 90
Kronman, A. 1–2, 14, 53–4, 126, 131–41, 149; *The Lost Lawyer: Failing Ideals of the Legal Profession* 1–2, 131–41

Langdell, C.C. 54, 132–3
Laud, Archbishop 56, 59
Law and Economics 128, 132
Law and Society 152
law schools 1, 54, 88, 91, 126, 132, 140, 144
legal education 1–2, 32, 44–5, 53, 70–1, 77, 94–5, 108, 132, 139–40, 144, 146, 149
Legal Realism 53, 126, 128, 129–31, 133, 148
legality 4–5, 58, 59–60, 101, 144–5
legislation 20, 94, 99, 101, 104–5, 110
liberalism, liberal government ix, 73–4, 89, 104–5, 121, 132, 137–8, 148
Lippe (Westphalia) 82–3
Lipsius, J. 86–7, 102; *De constantia* 86
Little, D. 19–20
Llewellyn, K. x, 133–5, 144
Locke, J. 16, 116, 119
Louis XIV 21, 50, 77, 90
Luther, M. 79
Lutheranism, Lutherans ix, 18, 76, 79, 82–4, 88, 138, 146

McClelland, C.E. 91–2, 95–6
Machiavelli, N. 68, 75, 87
Magna Carta 118
Maitland, F.W. 62, 152
manners 61, 65–9, 92, 95–6, 102, 153; *see also* civility; *decorum*
Marx, K., Marxism 12, 67, 102, 137
masons 9–10, 19, 107
maxims 35, 38, 74, 94, 99, 150
metaphysics 13, 28–9, 89, 97, 100–2, 108, 149
millenarianism, millenarians 21, 29, 34, 116, 158
Milsom, S.F.C. 46, 149
moderates 55–6, 58, 87
modernity 103–4, 106, 110, 129, 145

modes of knowledge 42, 52–3; historical 47, 53, 62, 101, 124–5; mathematical 52–3, 132; *see also* abstraction
moral anthropology 24, 33, 51, 109, 137
morality x, 3, 6, 8–9, 12, 14, 20, 40–1, 61, 63, 67, 71, 73, 85, 89, 94–5, 98–101, 107, 117, 121, 127, 131, 142, 145, 151, 153; and difference 28, 99; historicity of 10, 14; *see also honestum*
More, H. 28–9
mysticism 17, 28–9

natural law 12, 34, 61, 76, 93–5, 105, 115, 118–20, 121–2; minimalist version of 61, 94, 97
Nazism 4, 12, 143
necessity 6
neo-Kantianism 1, 31, 95, 97, 110, 126–8, 133–6, 157
neo-stoicism 66, 86–7, 95, 102
Netherlands Movement 86
neutrality x, 4–7, 6–7, 59, 93, 126; as ethical achievement 66, 102, 149; as moral failure x, 8, 12, 14, 126–8; *see also* impersonality
Newton, I. 29
normativity x, 31–2, 39–40, 41, 69, 82, 85, 109–10, 131, 137, 145–6
Norton, T. 66
Nottingham, Lord (Sir Heneage Finch) 2–3, 21, 23–4, 25, 27–9, 35, 69, 77
Novick, P. 129

Oestreich, G. 86–7
Oxford, University of 70–1

pacification ix, 4, 6–8, 16, 34, 36, 50, 73, 75, 83, 90, 92, 102
pastoral care 81–2
Paulsen, F. 90–1, 97
Pepys, S. 69
perfectionism 17, 31, 43–4, 64, 75, 113, 117, 153
personae 13, 17, 37, 65, 68, 72, 88, 95, 106–11, 131, 138–40; plurality of 28, 55, 66, 93, 102, 106–11
Peter of Aragon 22
philosophy 9, 28–9, 40, 43, 65, 67, 69, 85, 92, 96–101, 104, 106, 122–3, 131, 132, 136, 138, 140, 149–50
Pietism, Pietists 17–18, 88, 95–6
Plucknett, T.F.T. and Barton, J.L. 24
pluralism 13, 26–8, 55, 62, 72, 75, 79, 84, 89, 94, 102–3, 108, 120, 143, 154; ethical 97, 107; *see also* conducts of life; personae
Pocock, J.G.A. 18, 53
polemic 12, 24, 33, 114, 121
police 81, 89, 91, 103
political romanticism 125
political science 41, 52, 87
politics, autonomy of 5–6, 73, 92, 100; historical specificity of 15–18, 50, 58–9, 121
Politiques 2, 50–1, 73, 76
Popish plot 21
Popkin, R. 28–9, 122
positive law x, 5, 8, 19–20, 49, 90, 92–5, 102, 111, 118, 142, 147
positivity of law 22, 26–7, 105
Postema, G. 64
postmodernity 110, 125, 147
practical reason 1, 97, 132
Presbyterians 17, 28, 33
Prest, W. 17, 67, 70–1
private/public distinction 5, 35, 36–7, 73, 92, 124, 130
procedures 2, 25, 26–7, 43, 46, 55, 59, 64, 97; as ethical achievement 29
property 36, 37, 52, 54, 56, 59, 61, 98, 116
Protestantism, Protestants 21, 31, 78, 81, 83
prudentialism 1–2, 22, 53–4, 58, 64, 87, 101, 132, 136–40; *see also apatheia*
Prussia 18, 90, 143
psychoanalysis 32, 131, 147
public sphere ix–x, 17; expulsion of religion from 7, 17, 59, 90, 92–3
Pufendorf, S. von 119
Puritanism, Puritans 11, 16, 18–20, 25, 30, 32, 34, 55, 106, 112–14, 125, 155

Quakers 28–9

radicalism 31–2, 58, 129, 144–5
Radin, M. 22–3
raison d'état ix, 3, 6, 8, 14, 33, 73, 85, 89, 93, 97, 103; *see also* Absolutism; Hobbes
Ramism 30
rationality 71, 106, 139; bureaucratic 87; court 68–9; formal and substantive 126–7;
reason 7–8, 28, 36–7, 39, 40–2, 98–9, 102; religion of 8

reflexivity x, 14, 31, 68–9, 78, 107, 109–10, 123–4, 130, 133, 136–7, 149
reform of laws 64–5, 79
Reformation ix, 15, 33, 79–80, 112, 149–50; *see also* confessionalisation
Reid, J.P. 121
religious conformity 50, 56, 75–6
religious difference 6, 7, 22, 28, 76, 79–80, 83–4, 90, 94, 99–100, 117, 120–1
religious toleration x, 6, 8, 10, 50–1, 74–6, 90, 101–2, 105, 121, 160
repression 31–2, 102–4, 146–7
resistance 31–2, 82, 148
Reventlow, H. 8, 32–3, 40
Revolution: American 112, 114–20; French ix, 101, 104, 122, 143
rhetoric 30, 38, 53, 55, 61, 95, 130
rights x, 1, 9, 13, 39, 52, 60–1, 82, 87, 89–90, 94, 118, 120–3, 131, 138; and Enlightenment 13; origins of 73–4, 105, 118–19, 121–2
Ritterakademie 91–2
Romanticism 13, 125, 148
Rorty, A.O. 108–11, 143
Rousseau, J.J. 12
Royal Society 33, 65
Rüping, H. 142

St Augustine 11, 109
St Bartholomew's Day 2, 75
St German, C. 24–5, 33, 100
St Paul 11
salvation ix, 4, 8, 15, 29–30, 75, 80, 83–5, 89–90, 93, 107, 109, 117, 124, 149
scepticism 28, 99, 115, 120, 123
Schiller, F. 102, 125, 145
Schilling, H. viii–ix, 15, 79, 81–5, 112, 149
Schmitt, C. 3, 8, 13, 51, 73, 125, 142–3, 148–9
Scripture 17, 26, 28–9, 33, 39, 58, 75, 98, 124
Scudéry, Mme de 95
sectarianism 31, 75, 85, 100, 115–16, 120
secularisation 14, 17, 58, 66, 71, 74, 80, 84–5, 87, 90, 111, 115–17, 128, 147
security 6, 15, 34–6, 70
Selden, J. 25, 59–62
self 8, 13, 88, 125; techniques of 13, 56, 105–6
Shapin, S. 65–6
Shapiro, B. 69
Simpson, A.W.B. 150–1
Small, A. 85
society x, 8, 9–10, 14, 15, 19, 81, 85, 113–14, 148
sovereignty 5, 7, 12, 33–4, 36, 38–9, 46–8, 63, 74–5, 80, 103–4, 118
Spinoza, B. 28
spirit 15, 17, 24, 28–9, 31–2, 80, 87, 90, 96, 115, 147, 152; *see also* invisible church
Stafford, Lord 21
State ix–x, 4, 7–8, 14, 19, 22, 26, 73–6, 89, 94, 100, 102, 113, 121, 131, 141, 143, 149, 152–3; administrative (governmental) 8, 10, 15, 27, 80–1, 85, 103, 107; confessional 79–85, 89; formation of 68, 73, 80, 82–3, 96; management (*Staatswirthschaft*) 3, 81, 91; *see also raison d'état*
statutes 38, 69, 97, 100, 142; *see also* legislation
Stoicism 87; *see also* Lipsius; neo-stoicism
Stoner, J.R. 33, 36–7
Strauss, L. 123
Stromholm, S. 77
Stroup, J. 88

theocracy 109, 113–14, 127, 143
theologians, theology 17–19, 70–2, 77–80, 84, 87, 89, 91–2, 94, 96–9, 108, 116, 122, 128, 142–3, 149
theory 1, 30, 32, 43–5, 51–2, 54, 56, 103, 106–7, 110, 134–5, 150
Thirty Years War (1618–48) 15, 17, 83, 85, 113
Thomasius, C. 17–18, 37, 90–8, 100, 102, 120, 138, 142–3, 153
Tierney, B. 122
transformative exercises: individual 32, 68, 96, 102, 129, 135, 138; social 96, 109, 129, 136
Travers, W. 17
Tuck, R. 59–62, 94–5, 105

Unger, R. 135, 136–9, 143–4, 148
universities 32, 54, 70–2, 76–7, 79, 90, 96–9, 104, 106, 122–3, 132–3, 140
utopianism 1–2, 4, 12, 117, 155

Vaughan, Sir John 34, 59, 61
Villey, M. 121–2
visible church 16–17

Walzer, M. 18, 31, 55
Watson, A. 151–2
Weber, M. viii, 3, 70, 78, 106–9, 125, 140, 143
Weschler, H. 126–7
Whaley, J. 88
Whitgift, Archbishop 16–18
William of Ockham 122
Wilson, J. 119
Wiseman, Sir Robert 30–1
witches 58–9, 93–4
Witherspoon, J. 123
Wolff, C. 91, 96–7

Yale, D.E.C. 27, 28, 47, 60, 69

Zakai, A. 112–13
zealotry 1–2, 21, 78, 89–90, 93, 116, 138; *see also* enthusiasm

NOTES

NOTES

NOTES

NOTES

NOTES